Current Problems in Dermatology

Vol. 36

Series Editor

P. Itin Basel

Safety Assessment of Cosmetics in Europe

Volume Editors

Vera Rogiers Brussels
Marleen Pauwels Brussels

Authors

Vera Rogiers and Marleen Pauwels

17 figures and 47 tables, 2008

Basel · Freiburg · Paris · London · New York · Bangalore ·
Bangkok · Shanghai · Singapore · Tokyo · Sydney

Current Problems in Dermatology

Prof. Vera Rogiers
Head of the Department of Toxicology
Tel. +32 2 477 45 16
Fax +32 2 477 45 82
E-Mail vrogiers@vub.ac.be

Dr. Marleen Pauwels
Tel. +32 2 477 45 94
Fax +32 2 477 45 82
E-Mail mnpauwels@vub.ac.be

Vrije Universiteit Brussel
Department of Toxicology
Dermato-Cosmetology and Pharmacognosy
Laarbeeklaan 103
B–1090 Brussel

Prof. Vera Rogiers   **Dr. Marleen Pauwels**

Library of Congress Cataloging-in-Publication Data

Safety assessment of cosmetics in Europe / volume editors, Vera Rogiers,
Marleen Pauwels.
        p. ; cm. -- (Current problems in dermatology, ISSN 1421-5721 ; v.
36)
    Includes bibliographical references and index.
    ISBN 978-3-8055-8655-9 (hard cover : alk. paper)
  1.   Cosmetics--Safety measures--Europe. 2.   Cosmetics--Toxicology--Europe.
3.   Cosmetics--Analysis--Europe. 4.   Cosmetics--Law and legislation--Europe.
I. Rogiers, Vera. II. Pauwels, Marleen. III. Series.
    [DNLM: 1.   Cosmetics--standards. 2.   Consumer Product Safety--legislation
& jurisprudence. 3.   Consumer Product Safety--standards.   W1 CU804L v.36
2008 / WA 744 S128 2008]
    RA1270.C65S24 2008
    646.7'20289--dc22

                                                            2008033473

Bibliographic Indices. This publication is listed in bibliographic services, including Current Contents® PubMed/MEDLINE

Disclaimer. The statements, opinions and data contained in this publication are solely those of the individual authors and contributors and not of the publisher and the editor(s). The appearance of advertisements in the book is not a warranty, endorsement, or approval of the products or services advertised or of their effectiveness, quality or safety. The publisher and the editor(s) disclaim responsibility for any injury to persons or property resulting from any ideas, methods, instructions or products referred to in the content or advertisements.

Drug Dosage. The authors and the publisher have exerted every effort to ensure that drug selection and dosage set forth in this text are in accord with current recommendations and practice at the time of publication. However, in view of ongoing research, changes in government regulations, and the constant flow of information relating to drug therapy and drug reactions, the reader is urged to check the package insert for each drug for any change in indications and dosage and for added warnings and precautions. This is particularly important when the recommended agent is a new and/or infrequently employed drug.

© Copyright 2008 by S. Karger AG, P.O. Box, CH–4009 Basel (Switzerland)
www.karger.com
Printed in Switzerland on acid-free and non-aging paper (ISO 9706) by Reinhardt Druck, Basel
ISSN 1421–5721
ISBN 978–3–8055–8655–9

Contents

Chapter 2: Challenges Related to Cosmetic Safety Assessment in the EU 29

Chapter 3: Critical Analysis of the Safety Assessment of Cosmetic Ingredients Performed at the European Level 58

List of Abbreviations

3R	Refinement, reduction, replacement
3T3 NRU PT	3T3 Neutral Red Uptake Phototoxicity Test
A	Amount
ADI	Acceptable daily intake
AICS	Australian Inventory of Chemical Substances
Art.	Article
ASHP	American Society of Health-System Pharmacists
BCOP	Bovine corneal opacity and permeability
BMD	Benchmark dose
BMDL	BMD lower limit
bw	Body weight
C	Concentration
CAS nr	Chemical Abstracts Service registry number
CCRIS	Chemical Carcinogenesis Research Information System
CHRIS	Chemical Hazard Response Information System
CI	Colour index
CICAD	Concise International Chemical Assessment Document
CIR	Cosmetic ingredient review
CMR	Carcinogenic, mutagenic, toxic to reproduction
Colipa	European Cosmetic Toiletry and Perfumery Association
CoNTC	Concentration of no toxicological concern
CSNB	Chemical Safety NewsBase
CSTEE	Scientific Committee on Toxicity, Ecotoxicity and the Environment
CTFA	Cosmetic, Toiletry and Fragrance Association
CV	Curriculum vitae
DA	Dermal absorption

DA_a	Dermal Absorption reported as amount/cm^2
DA_p	Dermal Absorption expressed as a percentage
DART	Developmental and Reproductive Toxicology Database
DG ENTR	Directorate-General Enterprise
DG ENV	Directorate-General Environment
DG SANCO	Directorate-General Health and Consumer Protection
Dir.	Directive
DNA	Deoxyribonucleic acid
Doc.	Document
DSL	Domestic Substances List (Canada)
EC	European Community
ECB	European Chemicals Bureau
ECETOC	European Centre for Ecotoxicology and Toxicology of Chemicals
EChA	European Chemicals Agency
ECL	Existing Chemicals List (Korea)
ecopa	European Consensus Platform on 3R Alternatives
ECVAM	European Centre for the Validation of Alternative Methods
EDETOX	Evaluations and predictions of dermal absorption of toxic chemicals
EEC	European Economic Community
EEMCO	European expert group for Efficacy Measurements of Cosmetics and Other topical products
EFSA	European Food Safety Authority
EHC	Environmental Health Criteria
EINECS	European Inventory of Existing Commercial Chemical Substances
ELINCS	European List of Notified Chemical Substances
EMBASE	Excerpta Medica database
EMEA	European Agency for the Evaluation of Medicinal Products
ENCS	Existing and New Chemical Substances (Japan)
EPA	Environmental Protection Agency (USA)
epaa	European Partnership for Alternative Approaches
ESAC	ECVAM Scientific Advisory Committee
EST	Embryotoxic Stem Cell Test
EU	European Union
F	Frequency of application
FDA	Food and Drug Administration
FDIS	Final Draft International Standard (ISO)
GLP	Good Laboratory Practice
GMP	Good Manufacturing Practice
GPSD	General Product Safety Directive
HERA	Human and Environmental Risk Assessment
HET-CAM	Hen's Egg Test-Chorio Allantoic Membrane

(H)PV	(High) production volume
HPVIS	High Production Volume Information System (USA)
HSDB	Hazardous Substances Data Bank
IARC	International Agency for Research on Cancer
ICCG	Inter-Committee Coordination Group
ICCVAM	Interagency Coordinating Committee on the Validation of Alternative Methods
ICE	Isolated chicken eye
IFRA	International Fragrance Research Association
IFSCC	International Federation of the Societies of Cosmetic Chemists
ILSI	International Life Sciences Institute
INCI	International Nomenclature of Cosmetic Ingredients
INCOS	Intergovernmental Information Network for Cosmetic Products
INN	International Non-Proprietary Name
IPA	International Pharmaceutical Abstracts
IPCS	International Programme on Chemical Safety
IRE	Isolated rabbit eye
IRIS	Integrated Risk Information System
ISO	International Organization for Standardization
IUCLID	International Uniform Chemical Information Database
IUPAC	International Union of Pure and Applied Chemistry
JaCVAM	Japanese Center for the Validation of Alternative Methods
JRC	Joint research centre
LD_{50}	Lethal dose 50%
LED_{10}	Lower limit on effective dose-10
LLNA	Local lymph node assay
LO(A)EL	Lowest observed (adverse) effect level
LVET	Low Volume Eye Test
MD	Medical doctor
MEST	Mouse Ear Swelling Test
(MK)GPMT	(Magnusson Kligman) Guinea Pig Maximisation Test
MM	Micromass
MoS	Margin of safety
MR	Mitotic recombination
MSDS	Material Safety Data Sheet
MSN	Microsoft Network
MTT	3-(4,5)-dimethyl-2-thiazolyl-2,5-dimethyl-2H-tetrazolium bromide
NDSL	Non-Domestic Substances List (Canada)
NICNAS	National Industrial Chemicals Notification and Assessment Scheme (Australia)
NIOSH	National Institute for Occupational Safety and Health (USA)
NLM	National Library of Medicine

NLP	No longer polymer
NO(A)EL	No observed (adverse) effect level
NRU	Neutral red uptake
NTP	National Toxicology Program (USA)
OECD	Organisation for Economic Co-operation and Development
OHMTADS	Oil and Hazardous Material, Technical Assistance Data Systems
OHS	Occupational health and safety
OSHA	Occupational Safety and Health Administration (USA)
PBT	Persistent, bioaccumulative and toxic
Ph. Eur.	European Pharmacopoeia
PI(R)(F)	Product information (requirement)(file)
P_{ow}	n-Octanol/water partition coefficient
QSAR	Quantitative Structure-Activity Relationship
R	Retention factor
RAPEX	Rapid exchange of information
RBC	Red blood cell
REACH	Registration, Evaluation, Authorisation and Restriction of Chemicals
RIVM	RijksInstituut voor Volksgezondheid en Milieu
rLLNA	Reduced local lymph node assay
RTECS	Registry of Toxic Effects of Chemical Substances
SCCNFP	Scientific Committee on Cosmetic Products and Non-Food Products intended for consumers
SCCP	Scientific Committee on Consumer Products
SCE	Sister Chromatid Exchange
SCENIHR	Scientific Committee on Emerging and Newly Identified Health Risks
SCHER	Scientific Committee on Health and Environmental Risks
SD	Standard deviation
SED	Systemic exposure dosage
SHE	Syrian hamster embryo
SME	Small and medium-sized enterprise
SOP	Standard operating procedure
SPF	Sun protection factor
SSA	Skin surface area
STN	Scientific and Technical Network
TD_{50}	Tolerated dose 50%
TER	Transcutaneous electrical resistance
TIF	Technical Information File
TOXLINE	Toxicology Literature Online
TSCA	Toxic Substances Control Act (USA)
TTC	Threshold of toxicological concern
UDS	Unscheduled DNA synthesis
UV	Ultraviolet

VIS	Visible light
vPvB	Very persistent and very bioaccumulative
WoE	Weight of evidence
WEC	Whole embryo culture
WHO	World Health Organisation

Foreword

Many European citizens consider the European Commission in Brussels as very bureaucratic, making their lives with directives more complicated and putting national diversity in danger. They often do not realize that important initiatives for the consumer, safety and health have resulted from the work of European institutions. A paramount example is the field of cosmetics that is regulated by the Cosmetic Products Directive (76/768/EEC). This Directive defines what a cosmetic product is and what safety requirements have to be fulfilled to bring it onto the European market. The safety assessment of cosmetics as demanded by the Directive strives to protect the consumer on one side, while avoiding animal experiments on the other side. In this respect, stringent deadlines for animal testing have been implemented which will seriously affect the safety assessment process.

In putting the Directive into practice, the independent Scientific Committee on Consumer Products (SCCP) provides scientific advice to the Directorate-General of Health and Consumer Protection. This advice helps the Commission when preparing policy and proposals related to consumer safety and public health especially regarding cosmetics. In particular, the safety of cosmetic ingredients including UV filters, colorants, preservatives, and hair dyes are scientifically evaluated by the SCCP. This is a monumental review work of toxicological data performed by a group of scientists covering a wide field of experience and expertise and coming from several European countries. The work of the SCCP is documented in opinions that are freely accessible through the Internet. For many academics, regulatory bodies dealing with cosmetics and scientists from the cosmetics industry the EU regulatory framework and the process of the safety assessment of cosmetics are a great puzzle, difficult to put together. Therefore, a monograph explaining the 'mechanics' of the EU regulations in the field of cosmetics and their practical application was badly needed. The present book, written by Prof. Vera Rogiers and Dr. Marleen Pauwels from the Department of

Toxicology of the Vrije Universiteit Brussel fills this gap. Prof. Vera Rogiers has been an active member of the SCCP (previously called SCCNFP) for many years and is also leading a renowned research group on in vitro experimental toxicology intensively involved in the development of 3R-alternative methods. As such, she knows the EU activities on cosmetics and their ingredients from a close perspective. Together with Dr. Pauwels, she has been organizing in Brussels the course Safety Assessment of Cosmetics in the EU for more than a decade teaching cosmetic safety assessors from all over the world. Their extensive experience and knowledge are laid down in this book. It will be most useful to everyone interested in cosmetics and the protection of consumer health in Europe. Especially safety assessors will find the new information important for their daily work. I hope this excellent book will spread the message that high-quality work for consumer safety is done in Brussels from which so many people in Europe can benefit.

Peter Elsner, Jena

Preface

The cosmetic world is often perceived as the land of luxury, in which science fails to play any part. This is, however, not justified since several aspects of the development of cosmetic products require significant scientific input. Multiple research groups are involved in the formulation of innovative cosmetic products in the quest for new galenic forms on the macro- or nano-scale and/or in the objective assessment of the efficacy of cosmetic products. In addition and most importantly, cosmetic products are not allowed to be placed on the market unless their safety for the consumer has been scientifically proven. Whereas the safety standards for cosmetic products vary between different parts of the globe, it is generally agreed upon that Europe has put in place a relatively stringent regulatory framework to ensure cosmetic safety, in which the development of validated alternative methods plays a key role. It is a real challenge for industry, academia and regulatory bodies to maintain, under these conditions, the standards for cosmetic safety high. This book, therefore, solely focuses on the challenging subject of safety assessment of cosmetics in the current European regulatory framework and does not cover the interesting topics of cosmetic product development and claim substantiation.

Cosmetic safety evaluation appears to be a complex process, which in first instance requires knowledge of the extensive web of Directives, Regulations and Recommendations intended to ensure the free movement and safe use of these products. Of most relevance is the Cosmetic Products Directive (76/768/EEC), laying down the principal rules for marketing and labelling cosmetic products in the EU. One of its major provisions is that every cosmetic product on the EU market is considered to be safe for use. In order to substantiate this, a specific set of technical data must be assembled and made readily accessible to the competent authorities of the EU Member States. This data set is more commonly referred to as a cosmetic product's technical information file or TIF. Within the context of this TIF (sometimes called PIR or product information requirement), a document needs to be provided in which a qualified safety assessor declares the cosmetic product safe for use. The guidance on how to perform such a safety assessment is usually summarised as *'the manufacturer should take into consideration the general toxicological profile of the ingredients, their chemical structure and their level of exposure'*. As a positive answer to the need expressed by small and medium-sized enterprises for guidance on the compilation of cosmetic TIFs, a practical proposal for a structured standard format was developed in the year 2000 and refined over the years. The currently presented chapter on the subject is based upon 8 years of personal experience with constituting TIFs for cosmetic companies and upon interactions with competent authorities and industrial senior regulatory persons, expressing their views. To that respect, the yearly postgraduate courses of 'Safety Assessment of Cosmetics in the EU – Training Course', organised at the Vrije Universiteit Brussel by our Department under the wings of the Instituut voor Post-Academische vorming, were of high value.

The second and most debated feature of the EU cosmetic legislation is that since 1993, the European authorities have expressed their disapproval to the performance of animal experiments with cosmetic products and their ingredients. This resulted in the enforcement of a European animal testing ban on cosmetic ingredients from March 2009 on, accompanied by a gradual marketing ban for cosmetic ingredients tested on animals. As such, cosmetics are still considered to be inherently safe, but the tools that have enabled the scientific exercise of hazard and safety assessment of cosmetic ingredients to date, will be significantly restricted in the near future.

Indeed, animal tests have been used for more than 4 decades and most toxicologists have gained a certain level of confidence. However, urgent replacement by non-animal alternative methods is now legally required.

The positive side of this legislative evolution is that not only the efforts in scientific research and ethics, but also financial resources in the field of in vitro toxicology have significantly increased over the past couple of years. The inclusion of the development of alternatives in EU funding (5th, 6th and 7th Framework Programmes), the creation of the European Consensus Platform on 3R-Alternatives and the foundation of the European Partnership for Alternative Approaches, are only a couple of examples of collaboration between all parties involved.

A negative outcome of the cosmetic animal testing ban, however, is the initiation of a political movement which introduced drastic measures such as a complete abolition of animal testing, without taking into account the scientific feasibility of the timely development of alternatives to prove human safety.

Experience in the field of safety assessment of cosmetic ingredients has been built up, especially by safety assessors of finished cosmetic products all over Europe, and by the scientific experts of the Scientific Committee on Consumer Products or SCCP (formerly called Scientific Committee on Cosmetic products and Non-Food Products intended for consumers or SCCNFP). This European scientific committee assesses on a regular basis colourants, preservatives, UV filters, hair dyes and other specific ingredients for which suspicion of potential toxicity exists. Over time, the SCC(NF)P has studied dossiers for more than 250 substances and the detailed opinions can be freely downloaded from the European Commission's web pages.

With the existing uncertainty around the future safety assessment of cosmetics, the idea emerged to translate the multitude of knowledge on cosmetic ingredients gathered through the discussions of the SCC(NF)P, into a carefully tailored searchable database. With the help of this database, in first instance, the typical content of a toxicological data set considered complete by the SCC(NF)P, is determined. Subsequently, the quality of the individual types of tests is assessed and the mostly encountered hurdles in the safety assessment of cosmetic ingredients at EU level are identified. Finally, the database enables further in-depth analysis of these newly identified problem areas, resulting in some findings useful for the safety assessor.

It must be emphasised, however, that the data availability for a cosmetic ingredient discussed by the SCC(NF)P does not apply for all cosmetic ingredients as they appear on the EU market in finished cosmetic products. For ingredients not studied by the SCC(NF)P, the available toxicological data packages usually are much more restricted and, unless additional tests are performed on a voluntary basis or through extra-EU requirements, their data availability largely depends on the requirements of other EU Directives. Therefore, a separate section is dedicated to the question which toxicological data sets are expected to be available for those cosmetic ingredients not studied by the SCC(NF)P. Relevant data-generating EU legislations are summarised and personal practical experience on how to perform effective quality searches on toxicity data for cosmetic ingredients, is shared. Subsequently the process to come to a proposal for risk assessments of finished products is briefly discussed.

The database with the information on 185 substances studied by the SCC(NF)P between 2000 and 2006 is used to illustrate the specific problems related to the foreseen abolition of animal testing for cosmetic ingredients in the field of cosmetic safety assessment.

For each toxicological endpoint, the current status of the development of validated alternatives is discussed, together with figures and side information out of the database illustrating how safety assessment of cosmetic ingredients was performed over the past years. It allows evaluation of the number of animals involved, of the rate at which alternatives are currently being used and it helps to identify or confirm earlier identified problem areas.

In summary, the goal of this issue is to provide guidance and scientific background to the manifold challenges industrial/governmental/academic cosmetic safety assessors are faced with today and in the near future.

A practical proposal and guidance for constituting a European TIF is made, including the indication of relevant pieces of EU legislation and a procedure to effectively find toxicological data on cosmetic ingredients in public and commercial databases. Also the process of finished cosmetic product safety assessment is discussed.

Above all, this book aims at demonstrating the usefulness of a newly created database on SCC(NF)P-studied cosmetic ingredients. Therefore the database's content and search possibilities are used to identify and further analyze problem points in the safety assessment of cosmetic ingredients, and to estimate animal numbers and the extent to which 3R-alternative methods have found their way into European cosmetic ingredient dossiers.

Without having the ambition to overcome the deadlock of the concurrent animal testing ban and the 'safe for use' requirement in the cosmetic field, the results obtained through this database enable the formulation of a number of important conclusions with regard to the present and future safety assessment of cosmetic products and their ingredients in the EU.

Vera Rogiers, Marleen Pauwels
Brussels

Cosmetic Products and Their Current European Regulatory Framework

Rogiers V, Pauwels M (eds): Safety Assessment of Cosmetics in Europe.
Curr Probl Dermatol. Basel, Karger, 2008, vol 36, pp 1–28

1.1 Introduction

Although Dir. 76/768/EEC relating to cosmetic products [EU, 1976b] is a vertical legislation and every cosmetic product placed on the European market must fulfil its requirements, it would be very unrealistic to assume that this is a stand-alone piece of legislation that is not affected by other legal texts. In practice, Dir. 76/768/EEC forms part of a complex legislative process that was initiated more than 40 years ago to guarantee the free movement of goods within Europe while simultaneously ensuring the safety of the European citizens and their environment. The major milestones in this process are depicted in figure 1.

The current chapter provides an overview of the most relevant features of the Cosmetic Products Directive, which in fact forms the basis of this book. Thereafter, the milestones depicted in figure 1 are individually discussed in the light of their relevance to the cosmetic regulatory framework.

1.2 The Cosmetic Products Directive

1.2.1. Definition of a Cosmetic Product

According to the European Commission Dir. 93/35/EEC, Art. 1, a cosmetic product is defined as 'any substance or preparation intended to be placed in contact with the various parts of the human body (epidermis, hair system, nails, lips and external genital organs) or with the teeth and the mucous membranes of the oral cavity with a view exclusively or mainly to cleaning them, perfuming them, changing their appearance and/or correcting body odours and/or protecting them or keeping them in good condition' [EU, 1993a]. This definition gives an indication on the target site of application of a cosmetic product and on its allowed functions [Colipa, 2004]. Thus, products such as skin creams, lotions, perfumes, lipsticks, fingernail polishes, eye and facial make-up preparations, soap products, shampoos, permanent waves, hair colours, toothpastes, deodorants, … fall under the category of cosmetic products in the EU. More questionable product types such as suntanning preparations, antiperspirants and antidandruff shampoos are also considered cosmetics within Europe, whereas this may differ in other parts of the world [Pauwels and Rogiers, 2004].

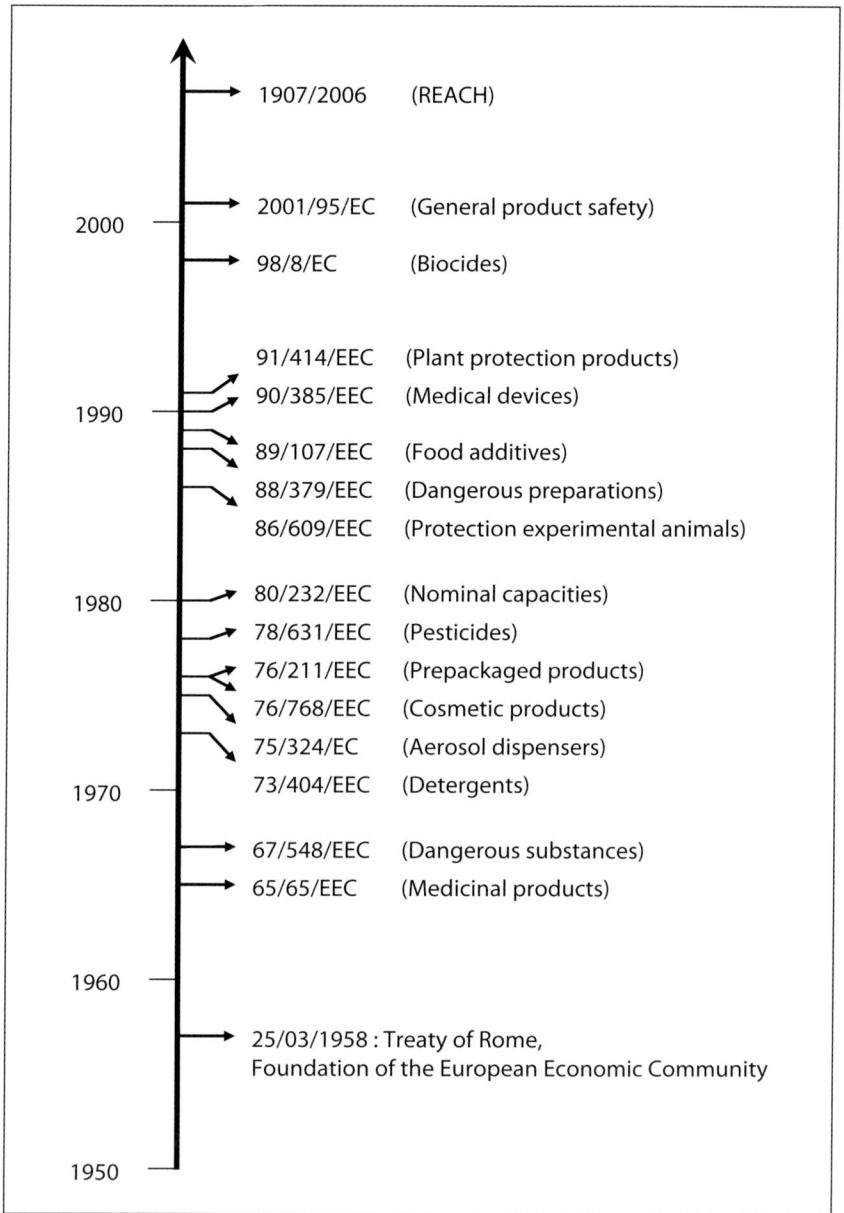

Fig. 1. Overview of the major milestones in the EU chemical-related legislative process.

1.2.2. The Safety Prerequisite and Responsibilities

The current EU legislation on cosmetics literally states that 'a cosmetic product put on the market within the Community must not cause damage to human health when applied under normal or reasonably foreseeable conditions of use, taking account, in particular, of the product's presentation, its labelling, any instructions for its use and disposal as well as any other indication or information provided by the manufacturer or his authorised agent or by any other person responsible for placing the product on the Community market' (Art. 2). The responsibility to ensure that cosmetic products are safe for consumer use is placed upon the manufacturer or his authorised agent or any other person responsible for placing the product on the Community market [EU, 1993a].

A qualified safety assessor, holding a specified diploma [EU, 1989b] in the field of pharmacy, toxicology, dermatology, medicine or a similar discipline, undersigns the safety assessment of the cosmetic product under consideration and thus takes responsibility for the safety of the product when applied under reasonably foreseeable conditions of use.

By means of a post-marketing surveillance system, the EU Member States are on their turn expected to take all necessary measures to ensure that only cosmetic products which conform to the provisions of Dir. 76/768/EEC and its Annexes may be placed on the European market (Art. 3) [EU, 1993a]. Nevertheless, the ultimate responsibility for the safety of a cosmetic product resides with industry.

1.2.3. The Public Information Prerequisite

In order to optimally inform the consumer, every cosmetic product sold in the EU must contain the following information on its label (Art. 6):
a name and address of manufacturer or responsible for placing on the market within the EU,
b nominal content of the finished product at the time of packaging (weight or volume),
c date of minimal durability (products with a minimum durability less than 30 months) or an indication of the period of time after opening for which the product can be used without any harm to the consumer,
d particular precautions to be observed in use, especially those indicated in the Annexes to Dir. 76/768/EEC,
e batch number, enabling identification of manufacturing,
f function of the product, unless evident,
g a list of ingredients in INCI in descending order of weight at the time they were added, unless they are present at a concentration below 1%, in which case they may be mentioned in any chosen order.

Moreover, the qualitative and quantitative composition of the cosmetic and the existing data on undesirable effects on human health resulting from use of the cosmetic product are enforced to be made easily accessible to the public by any appropriate means, including electronic means. Whereas the qualitative composition already features on the label (ingredient list mandatory), the quantitative composition is limited to 'dangerous substances' according to Dir. 67/548/EEC (see section 1.4.1).

1.2.4. The 'Technical Information File' Prerequisite

For cosmetic products, the EU legislation does not foresee an extensive pre-marketing notification/authorisation procedure involving a full toxicological dossier on the ingredients and the finished cosmetic product. Instead the EU Member States are charged with the installation of a post-marketing surveillance system to check industry's compliance with the provisions of the Cosmetic Products Directive.

To this respect, Art. 7a of the Cosmetic Products Directive imposes that the following information should be readily accessible to the Member States' Competent Authorities [EU, 1993a, 2003]:

a the qualitative and quantitative composition of the product,
b physicochemistry, microbiology and purity of the ingredients and the cosmetic product,
c the manufacturing method,
d safety assessment of the finished cosmetic product,
e name and address of the safety assessor,
f existing data on undesirable effects on human health,
g proof of the effects claimed,
h data on animal testing.

The compilation of points a–h is commonly referred to as a cosmetic's TIF or PIR.

1.2.5. The Annexes to the Cosmetic Products Directive and the SCC(NF)P

Like the majority of EU Directives, Dir. 76/768/EEC is composed of the classical set of articles (definitions, responsibilities of the EU Member States, safeguard clause, ...), followed by a number of technical annexes. Five of them consist of ingredient lists:

– Annex II: list of forbidden substances in cosmetic products.
– Annex III: list of substances which are not allowed to be used in cosmetic products outside the restrictions and conditions laid down.
– Annexes IV, VI and VII: lists of allowed colorants, preservatives and UV filters, respectively, accompanied by their maximum levels and/or conditions of use in cosmetic products.

The content of the Annexes is regularly updated through amendments or adaptations to technical progress of the Cosmetics Directive. The cosmetic legislation charges the EU Member States with the designation of a competent authority responsible for checking that every cosmetic product's composition complies with the provisions laid down in the above Annexes [Art. 4; EU, 1993a].

For the safety assessment of the ingredients appearing on the Annexes, the Commission is assisted by the SCCP, previously called the SCCNFP. The SCCP forms part of DG SANCO and owns the official mandate to provide opinions on questions concerning the safety of consumer products (non-food products intended for the consumer). It is composed of independent scientists in the field of medicine, toxicology, pharmacy, dermatology, biology, chemistry, and other disciplines, collectively covering a wide range of expertise for this multidisciplinary committee [SCCP, 2006]. Together with the SCHER and the SCENIHR, the SCCP provides the Commission with sound scientific advice needed when preparing policy and proposals relating to consumer safety, public health and the environment. In addition, the ICCG, consisting of the chairs and vice-chairs of SCCP, SCHER and SCENIHR, warrants harmonisation of risk assessment and deals with questions which are common to more than one Committee, diverging scientific opinions and exchange of information on the activities of the three Committees[1].

The SCCP specifically addresses questions in relation to the safety and allergenic properties of cosmetic products and ingredients with respect to their impact on consumer health, toys, textiles, clothing, personal care products, domestic products such as detergents, and consumer services such as tattooing [SCCP, 2006; EU, 2004a]. In this context, the committee also performs full risk assessments for candidate ingredients to be included in the Annexes to the Cosmetic Products Directive. The SCCP is not responsible for the safety assessment of cosmetic ingredients not taken up in the Annexes to the Cosmetic Products Directive [SCCP, 2006].

Since 1997, the opinions of the SCCP and SCCNFP are made publicly available through the Committees' websites[2].

1.2.6. The Animal Testing Ban for Cosmetics and Their Ingredients

Since the cosmetic field is often seen as a luxury area, posing no health benefits, being innocuous and not needing any innovation, it turned out to be a fruitful battlefield for animal protection organisations, politicians and Parliament lobbyists to introduce an animal testing ban. Although it was clear from the start that only a limited number of animals could be saved by banning animal tests for the safety of cosmetics and their ingredients [EU, 2007b], the 'cosmetics case' became a remarkable example of how to introduce alternative methods into legislation in a politically driven and not scientifically driven way. The Sixth Amendment to the Cosmetic Products Directive for the first time introduced the concept of an animal testing ban on cosmetics and their ingredients. More specifically, its Art. 4(1) stated that cosmetic products should not contain 'ingredients or combinations of ingredients tested on animals after 1 January 1998 in order to meet the requirements of this Directive'. This statement was

---

1 http://ec.europa.eu/health/ph_risk/committees/committees_en.htm (consulted November 2007).

2 http://ec.europa.eu/health/ph_risk/committees/sccp/sccp_opinions_en.htm, http://ec.europa.eu/health/ph_risk/committees/04_sccp/sccp_opinions_en.htm, and http://ec.europa.eu/health/ph_risk/committees/sccp/sccp_opinions_en.htm (consulted November 2007).

Rogiers · Pauwels

somewhat mitigated by the provision that 'if there has been insufficient progress in developing satisfactory methods to replace animal testing, …, the Commission shall, by 1 January 1997, submit draft measures to postpone the date of implementation of this provision, for a sufficient period, and in any case for no less than two years, …' [EU, 1993a]. The mentioned date of implementation was postponed twice [EU, 1997, 2000].

Nevertheless, as a result of the limited progress in alternative method development and with the clear aim of pursuing the abolishment of animal testing for cosmetic products, the 7th Amendment [EU, 2003] to Dir. 76/768/EEC introduced explicit marketing and testing ban provisions for cosmetic products and their ingredients. More specifically, from 11 September 2004 onwards, animal experiments with finished cosmetic products are subject to an absolute ban, whereas a testing ban on ingredients or combinations of ingredients applies step by step as soon as alternative methods are validated and adopted, but with a maximum cut-off date of 11 March 2009, irrespective of the availability of alternative non-animal tests.

In addition, a marketing ban applies step by step as soon as alternative methods are validated and adopted in EU legislation. This marketing ban will be introduced at the latest on 11 March 2009, for all human health effects with the exception of repeated-dose toxicity, reproductive toxicity and toxicokinetics. For these specific health effects, the deadline of 11 March 2013 is put forward, irrespective of the availability of alternative non-animal tests.

More details on the actual status of alternative methods and future prospects can be found in section 3.2.1 and chapter 6.

1.2.7. Safety Assessment of Cosmetic Ingredients under the Cosmetic Products Directive

According to the actual cosmetic legislation in the EU, two distinct channels are operative for the safety evaluation of cosmetic ingredients (fig. 2), namely:

(i) The safety evaluation of cosmetic ingredients of direct relevance to Council Directive 76/768/EEC, thus substances to be taken up in the Directive's Annexes IV, VI, VII, III or II being colourants, preservatives, UV filters, substances for which restrictions in application and/or concentration apply, or which end up forbidden, respectively. For these compounds, concern for human health has been expressed [Pauwels and Rogiers, 2004]. They are subject to an evaluation by the SCCP, previously by the SCCNFP. When the outcome is favourable, a substance can be taken up in its corresponding Annex to the Directive [EU, 1976b]. In case the opinion is unfavourable, industry usually is asked to provide additional information and/or argumentation. The final decision on the inclusion lies with the European Directorate General Enterprise. As stated earlier, full reports of SCC(NF)P evaluations, including data with respect to the performed physico-

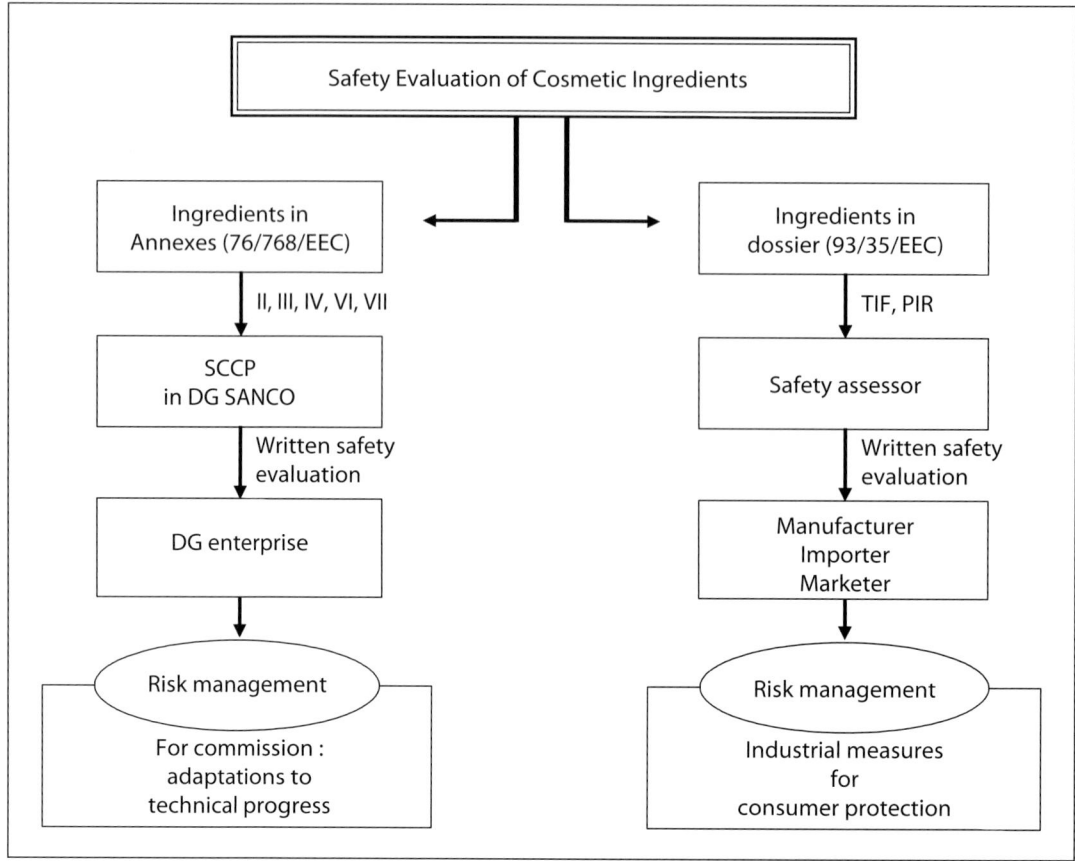

Fig. 2. Existing two ways in the safety evaluation of cosmetic ingredients in the EU [SCCP, 2006].

chemical and toxicological studies with their flaws and strengths, are publicly available through the Internet[3].

(ii) The safety evaluation of all ingredients present in finished cosmetic products. The latter constitutes relevant information for the toxicological data compilation of the cosmetic product under consideration (TIF or PIR). According to Art. 7.a.1.(e) of the 6th Amendment to the cosmetic legislation [EU, 1993a], the safety evaluation needs to be carried out by a qualified safety assessor, whereas the ultimate responsibility for the finished product lies with the manufacturer, importer or marketer. For substances not taken up in one of the Annexes to Dir. 76/768/ EEC [EU, 1976b], no specific additional data requirements apply. This means that, besides the results of the safety tests that are carried out on a voluntary basis for certain cosmetic ingredients, the availability of data depends on data requirements

---

3 http://ec.europa.eu/health/ph_risk/committees/04_sccp/sccp_opinions_en.htm and http://ec.europa.eu/health/ ph_risk/committees/sccp/sccp_opinions_en.htm (consulted July 2007).

and data accessibility measures laid down in the other legislation(s) with which these substances have to comply.

In the SCCP 'Notes of Guidance' [SCCP, 2006], a list of the data requirements applicable to the substances taken up in the Annexes of Directive 76/768/EEC [EU, 1976b] is present. It consists of acute toxicity, skin and eye irritation, skin sensitisation, repeated dose toxicity, mutagenicity, reproductive toxicity, carcinogenicity, dermal absorption, toxicokinetics, photo-induced toxicity and human data. Although not every ingredient taken up in a TIF/PIR will benefit of the presence of such a comprehensive toxicological data package, the main principles of hazard and risk assessment, as proposed by the SCCP still can be applied. They are in line with the European Technical Guidance Document on Risk Assessment of the European Chemicals Bureau [ECB, 2003], supplemented with the comments of the SCHER [SCHER, 2005]. The latter clearly highlight the importance of expert judgment in case the data packages are reduced and/or of poor quality.

The general safety assessment paradigm as employed in the cosmetic field will be discussed in section 2.2 and the specific risk assessment of cosmetic ingredients reappears in chapters 3 and 4.

1.2.8. Proposal for a Recast of the Cosmetic Products Directive

Quite recently, the European Commission published a proposal for a Regulation on cosmetic products [EU, 2008], the so-called recast of the 32-year-old Cosmetic Products Directive [EU, 1976b]. This recast is meant to bring together the original directive with all its amendments, simultaneously introducing some substantive changes to the individual texts when incorporated. Since the recast is at the Commission proposal stage, it requires extensive discussions between the Member States and within the European Parliament, implying that it will not remain unchanged. Nevertheless, it is useful to provide an overview of the major changes that are currently introduced. It should, however, be noted that the list below is not exhaustive and that it cannot be foreseen which of the provisions will actually be taken up in the final version of the regulation.

a) Moving from a Directive to a Regulation
One of the main goals for the recast being simplification of the administrative procedures related to the Cosmetic Products Directive, the text proposed aims at becoming a 'Regulation on cosmetics'. European regulations have the advantage that they are binding in their entirety and directly applicable in all Member States, whereas directives need to be transposed into the national legal frameworks of the individual Member States. To demonstrate the complexity of this process, the transposition of Dir. 76/768/EEC into Belgian law is worked out in appendix 1. With the 27 Member States Europe currently counts, regulations automatically represent a major administrative simplification for the Member States.

The articles of the original directive have been reorganised into chapters displayed in a logical order.

b) Introduction of a Set of Definitions
The recast aims at clarifying a number of issues for which legal uncertainty exists. Therefore, definitions for terms such as 'manufacturer', 'importer', 'placing on the market', 'making available on the market', 'harmonised standard', 'traces', 'preservatives', 'colourants', 'UV-filters', '(serious) undesirable effect', 'repeal' and 'withdrawal' are introduced in Art. 2 and some definitions of different cosmetic product types, such as 'rinse-off product', 'leave-on product', 'hair product', 'skin product', etc. are included in a preamble to Annexes II–VI. This preamble would replace the original Annex I to the Cosmetic Products Directive [EU, 1976b], which contains a non-exhaustive list of possible cosmetic product types.

c) One Single European Notification and a Strengthened Market Control
The proposed recast introduces a single centralised electronic notification of certain information concerning the product placed on the market. Instead of having to notify in every individual Member State and needing to comply with all the national provisions (e.g. communication to poison control centres), the recast now foresees one single notification and one single poison control communication at the European level.

The Member States are responsible for in-market control and in case of non-compliance, some specific possibilities for actions to be taken are mentioned in the recast (e.g. the introduction of penalties).

d) New Provisions for CMR Substances
Substances classified as CMR Category 1 or 2 according to the principles of Directive 67/548/EEC [EU, 1967], are actually prohibited for use in cosmetic products [EU, 2003]. The basic principle would remain unchanged, but the recast opens more possibilities in the sense that *there should be a possibility, in the exceptional case where these substances are legally used in food and no suitable alternative substances exist, to use such substances in cosmetic products if such use has been found safe by the SCCP.*

e) Introduction of Harmonised Standards
Throughout the text, reference is made to the use of 'harmonised standards'. This implies that the Commission considers further development of European standards for analytical methods, claim substantiation, etc., enabling insurance of product compliance in these fields.

f) Clarifications on the Safety Assessment of Cosmetic Products
The TIF or PI(F) would be called the 'Cosmetic Safety Report'. A newly created Annex I to the regulation would contain some guidance on the content of this report.

A responsible person ensuring that the cosmetic safety report is kept up to date is to be designated.

The qualifications of the safety assessor are specified within the text and allow safety assessors from outside Europe to sign the cosmetic product safety assessment.

g) 'INCI' Becomes 'Name of Common Ingredients Glossary'
The recast replaces the original INCI list by the so-called 'Common Ingredients glossary'. This glossary is described to contain the names of relevant cosmetic ingredients (approximately 10,000), but not to constitute a list of authorised cosmetic ingredients. This is the same definition as was given for the INCI list, meaning that only the name has changed.

Viewing the preliminary stage of this new 'Regulation on cosmetics', its detailed content is not further taken up in this chapter. The final regulation is not expected before 2009.

The only certainty seems to be that all statements related to the animal testing ban as mentioned in the current cosmetic legislation [EU, 2003] are precluded to be changed.

1.3 Relevant 'Vertical' EU Legislations

In parallel to the Cosmetic Products Directive, some other important legal milestones deal with the protection of human health against specific types of substances. These so-called 'vertical' legislations are depicted in figure 3.

Since the current European legal context prohibits testing of finished cosmetic products on experimental animals, the impact of the above-mentioned Directives will individually be discussed with special focus on toxicological data generation and data availability potentially relevant for the safety assessment of cosmetic ingredients.

When compiling all the knowledge on data generation and data availability through the different legislations, it is in certain cases possible to foresee the type and amount of toxicological data one can expect to find on a particular cosmetic ingredient.

1.3.1. Impact of the Dangerous Substances Directive and REACH

a) General Provisions
Over the past four decades, chemical substances have been regulated at the European level by Dir. 67/548/EEC [EU, 1967], its amendments and adaptations to technical progress. In first instance, this chemical legislation covered the listing and review of existing substances in the EU, together with the notification of new chemicals. Basically, a new chemical substance could only be produced within or imported into

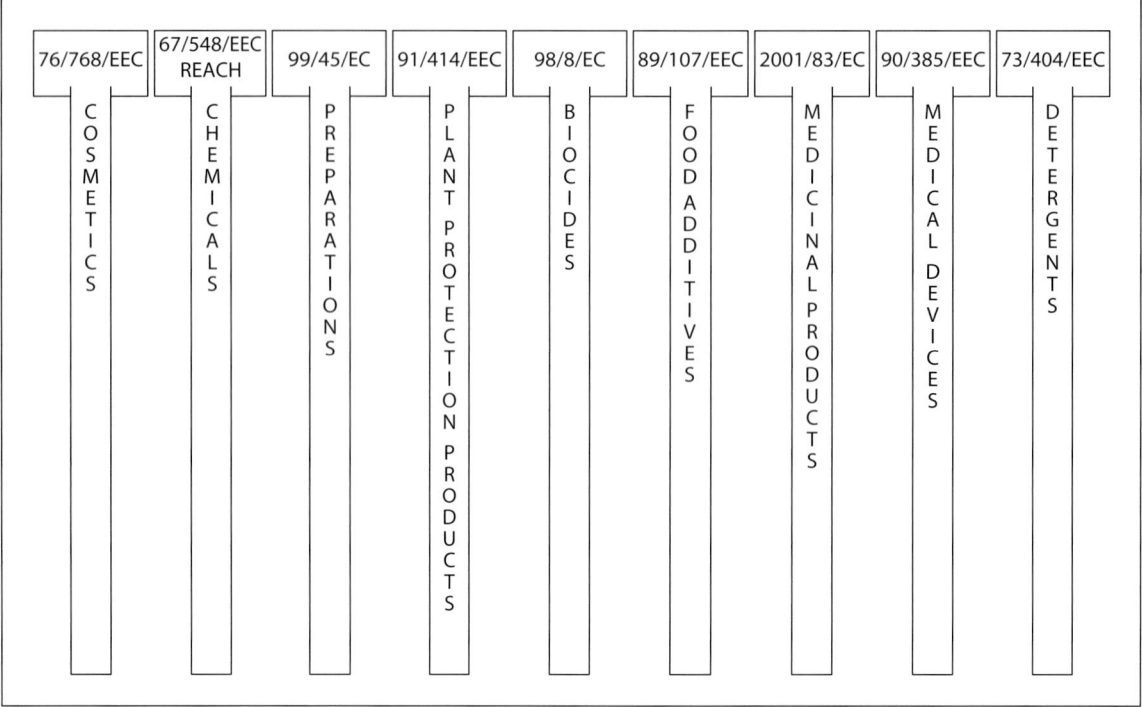

Fig. 3. Schematic presentation of 'vertical' cosmetic-related legislations in the EU.

the EU after having received a favourable judgment from the EU Member State's competent authority to which a full notification dossier has been addressed.

In a second stage, the Dangerous Substances Directive laid down the rules for classification and labelling of chemical substances in the EU. This means that not only test descriptions for physicochemical (Annex V, Part A), toxicological (Annex V, Part B) and ecotoxicological (Annex V, Part C) studies were provided, but also some explicit rules to translate the results from physicochemical and/or (eco)toxicological studies into a classification involving appropriate risk and safety phrases to be mentioned on the label (Annex VI). The classification and labelling principles of Directive 67/548/EEC are still referred to in many other EU legislative texts.

The recently published EU Regulation No. 1907/2006 [EU, 2006a] concerning the Registration, Evaluation, Authorisation and Restriction of Chemicals, commonly referred to as 'REACH', introduces some major changes in the EU regulatory framework for chemicals, among which:
- The reversal of the burden of proof: manufacturers and/or importers become fully responsible for proving and ensuring that their substances are safe to use, whereas previously the Member States' competent authorities equally expressed an approval for the safe use of the substance under consideration [Recitals 18, 25, 29, Art. 4; EU, 2006a].

- The creation of a European Chemicals Agency, established for the purposes of managing and in some cases carrying out the technical, scientific and administrative aspects of REACH and to ensure consistency at Community level in relation to these aspects [Art. 75; EU, 2006a].
- Protection of experimental animals: REACH intends to reduce testing on vertebrate animals as much as possible by imposing data sharing, by prohibiting duplication of animal testing, and by the promotion of $3R^4$-alternative methods [Recitals 1, 33, 37, 40, 47, 49, Art. 13(2),15, 25, 26(3), 27, Annex VI(1.4)]. Moreover, for the highest tonnage levels (>100 tonnes/year), testing proposals need to be officially approved before the animal experiments are initiated [Recital 64, Art. 22(1h), 40; EU, 2006a].
- 'PBT', 'vPvB', 'CMR' substances and the substitution principle: REACH describes specific procedures as well for environmentally PBT and vPvB substances, as for CMR substances [Art. 14(4), 40(1), 58(3)]. Moreover, every application for authorisation for such a substance must include an analysis of possible substitute substances or procedures as well as an analysis of their technical and economic feasibility [Recitals 12, 70, 72, Art. 55; EU, 2006a].
- Enforcement of restrictions: prohibitions on substances or restrictions on certain uses were previously imposed through Dir. 76/769/EEC [EU, 1976c], its amendments and numerous adaptations to technical progress. They will now be taken up by REACH through a faster and simplified procedure [Recitals 23, 80, 84, 85, Art. 68; EU, 2006a].
- The flow of information up and down the supply chain: suppliers of a substance or a preparation must provide to their customers a safety data sheet including as well information about any potential hazard as detailed exposure scenarios. In order to enable suppliers to draw up correct exposure scenarios, downstream users will need to ensure a good upstream communication on potential usage patterns [Recital 56, Art. 31, 32, 37, 38; EU, 2006a].

b) Relevance for Cosmetics

Although most cosmetic ingredients by definition are chemicals [EU, 1992], they are exempted from the classification, packaging and labelling provisions of the Dangerous Substances legislation and REACH. It remains, however, quite informative to consult it. For example, knowing whether the substance under consideration is taken up in one of the official chemical inventories (EINECS or ELINCS), already gives an indication on the amount of available data.

Indeed, EINECS lists and defines those chemical substances deemed to be on the European market between 1 January 1971 and 18 September 1981, the so-called 'existing' chemical substances. EINECS is a closed list containing about 100,000 substances, excluding polymers. For the majority of chemicals on EINECS, the amount of available information is limited.

---

4 Refinement, Reduction and Replacement.

Table 1. Summary of data requirements for notified chemical substances according to Dir. 92/32/EEC [EU, 1992]; exemptions, cumulative volume requirements or other exceptions are not mentioned

10–100 kg/year	100 kg to 1 tonne/year	1–10 tonnes/year 'Base set'	>10 tonnes/year
acute toxicity	acute toxicity	acute toxicity	acute toxicity
	skin irritation	skin irritation	skin irritation
	eye irritation	eye irritation	eye irritation
	skin sensitisation	skin sensitisation	skin sensitisation
	mutagenicity	mutagenicity	mutagenicity
		subacute toxicity (28 d)	subacute toxicity (28 d/90 d)
		toxicokinetics	toxicokinetics
		screening reproduction toxicity	screening reproduction toxicity
			reproduction toxicity
			carcinogenicity
			metabolism studies

ELINCS on the other hand, is an open list, containing per definition all substances not taken up in EINECS, unless they are polymers. As summarised in table 1, these so-called 'new' chemical substances are subject to data requirements triggered by the annual volumes in which they are produced within or imported into the EU [EU, 1992]. However, the repeated dose and reproductive toxicity data, as mentioned in the last column of the table (>10 tonnes/year), are only mandatory upon specific request by the competent authorities, based upon the outcome of previous testing.

All the study results and summaries are considered non-confidential [EU, 1992] and supplement the information figuring on the chemical's label and MSDS.

As stated earlier, the existing EU notification system for chemicals is in the process of being replaced by a set of new rules and procedures (including new sets of data requirements) through EU Regulation No. 1907/2006 [EU, 2006a], commonly referred to as 'REACH'.

REACH intends to bring the data requirements for existing and new chemical substances to the same level and therefore introduces tonnage-linked data requirements for existing substances.

Therefore, the latter are expected to display an overall increase in available toxicological data. As far as the new chemical substances are concerned, the data packages are reduced compared to the requirements defined in Dir. 92/32/EEC, e.g. the so-called 'Base Set' shifted from 1 to 10 tonnes [EU, 1992] to the >10 tonnes level [EU, 2006a].

The introduction of alternative approaches to animal testing under REACH is expected to significantly impact the type and amount of available toxicological data.

Nevertheless, the extent of this impact will depend on the policy followed by EChA and by the level of acceptance by the European competent authorities of those alternative approaches. Since REACH only recently entered into force (June 2007), the data collection under this new legislation is only in a preparatory phase.

Another important feature introduced by REACH consists of a number of duties of downstream users of chemicals, including the cosmetic industry. According to the Regulation [EU, 2006a], all supported existing chemicals need to be pre-registered between the 1st of June and the 1st of December 2008. Subsequently, the Commission will, by the 1st of January 2009, publish a list of those chemicals. Downstream users should carefully check this list to see whether all cosmetic ingredients in which they are particularly interested figure on it and are accompanied by the 'correct' use. Moreover, downstream users have the obligation to report information up the supply chain and, in some cases, compilation of own chemical safety reports is necessary. On their turn, the suppliers/manufacturers have the duty to communicate down the supply chain a minimal information package for those substances or preparations for which a safety data sheet is not required. This already applies from 1 June 2007 onwards. The MSDS itself is also reviewed and will provide more detailed toxicological information together with the inclusion of an annex on the identified uses and exposure scenarios of the substance/preparation under consideration [EU, 2006a].

1.3.2. Impact of the Dangerous Preparations Directive

a) General Provisions
As early as 1973 and 1977, solvents, paints, varnishes, printing inks, adhesives and similar products were identified as requiring special attention, and thus rules on these categories of preparations were laid down [EU, 1973a, 1977]. However, divergences in national legislations on the remaining types of preparations still constituted a significant barrier to trade within the EU and led to the publication of an overall Dangerous Preparations Directive [EU, 1988, 1999b].

b) Relevance for Cosmetics
Since 'preparations' are defined as *mixtures or solutions composed of one or more substances* [EU, 1999b], numerous cosmetic ingredients fall under this category.

Although cosmetics are exempted from its packaging, classification and labelling provisions, Dir. 99/45/EEC [EU, 1999b], replacing 88/379/EEC [EU, 1988], contains a number of features of interest for the data availability on cosmetic ingredients. When purchasing a preparation for use as a cosmetic ingredient, it is useful to know that a preparation containing one or more constituents classified in a danger class is not necessarily considered dangerous in its marketed form. The legislation leaves it up to the marketer to either subject the mixture to extensive toxicological and ecotoxicological testing, or to use the so-called 'conventional method'. The latter represents a conservative calculation combining the hazardous properties of the classified constituent with its final concentration in the preparation under study. For example, a simple aqueous formulation containing more than 20% of a compound classified as irritating to the skin, would automatically be classified as irritating to the skin without further testing. Viewing the ethical concerns in the EU with regard to animal testing, the conventional method is abundantly applied for the classification of dangerous preparations.

This means that in the majority of cases, no toxicological data on mixtures of chemicals were generated. In view of evaluating the safe use of a 'preparation' in a finished cosmetic product, having access to its quantitative composition is crucial. Dir. 99/45/EC [EU, 1999b], however, does not impose disclosure of all details. In several cases, it may be legal that the label and accompanying documents, including the MSDS, do not reveal the full composition of a (dangerous) preparation in the EU.

1.3.3. EU Legislation on Food Additives

a) General Provisions
Since food additives are intended to be ingested, this type of chemicals calls for a separate set of legal provisions and a risk assessment procedure. In Europe, food additives are regulated through a number of complementary Directives [EU, 1989a, 1994a, b, 1995], based upon the common principle that only those additives that are explicitly authorised and taken up in the official EU positive lists may be used and only subject to the specific restrictions laid down.

In 2002, after a number of serious food crises in Europe (bovine spongiform encephalopathy, dioxins, acrylamide), the general principles and requirements of food law were translated into a new Regulation [EU, 2002]. The EFSA was established to produce scientific opinions and advice for drawing European policies and legislation (inter alia the adaptations to the positive lists) and to support the European Commission, European Parliament and EU Member States in taking effective and timely risk management decisions with regard to food and food additives.

b) Relevance for Cosmetics
In general, an officially accepted food additive has been subject to a full risk assessment allowing calculation of the ADI by making use of the outcome of a full toxicological dossier consisting of acute and repeated dose toxicity studies. This exercise is currently performed by the EFSA Scientific Panel on food additives, flavourings, processing aids and materials in contact with food. The relevant opinions can be downloaded from the Internet[5].

---

5   http://www.efsa.europa.eu/en/science/afc/afc_opinions.html (consulted July 2007).

Rogiers · Pauwels

As a consequence, the cosmetic ingredients that are also accepted as food additives in the EU may have the benefit of a large data package of which the summary is freely available through the EFSA Website. Moreover, these ingredients are safe for daily ingestion up to a specific level, which often makes them ideal candidates to be used in cosmetic products at comparable exposure levels.

1.3.4. Impact of the Biocidal Products Directive

a) General Provisions
Since biocidal active substances are intended to kill living organisms, they need to be accurately classified, labelled and controlled in order to inform and protect the professional user and/or the general public. Therefore, the Biocidal Products Directive [EU, 1998] deals with data requirements and risk assessments of active substances and ready-to-use end products. Herein, the classification and labelling provisions of the Dangerous Chemicals and Preparations Directives are taken over.

b) Relevance for Cosmetics
Dir. 98/8/EC [EU, 1998] covers the placing on the market of 23 biocidal product types, currently existing in the EU. Active substances need to be approved and officially listed before they may be used. Not only their ecotoxicological and toxicological profiles need to be examined, but also their efficacy and avoidance of resistance of the organisms they are intended to counteract. The content of a typical toxicological dossier for a biocidal active substance consists of acute toxicity, skin and eye irritation, skin sensitisation, subacute and subchronic toxicity, mutagenicity and teratogenicity. Unless justification is given for not performing the tests, chronic toxicity, carcinogenicity and two-generation reproductive toxicity complete the data package. These data are not considered to be confidential information [EU, 1998].

The intersection between biocidal active substances and cosmetic ingredients mainly consists of preservatives used in cosmetics. These are substances taken up in Annex VI to the Cosmetic Products Directive [EU, 1976b]. The data packages generated under the Biocidal Products Directive may contain some additional useful data on these preservatives and therefore their summaries may be helpful to consult. Also data on the potential development of resistance may be of use.

1.3.5. Impact of the Medicinal Products Directive

a) General Provisions
The first version of a directive regulating the marketing of medicinal products in the EU was issued in 1965 [EU, 1965]. It has been repeatedly adapted and finally replaced by its current version in 2001 [EU, 2001a], significantly amended in 2004 [EU,

2004b]. The combination of the uncontested benefit and social value of medicines on the one hand and their potential side effects on the other hand, leads to the necessity of extensive regulatory requirements.

Full toxicological and clinical dossiers are presented to the Member States' competent authorities, and active medicinal substances are approved under the wings of the EMEA.

b) Relevance for Cosmetics

As the Medicinal Products Directive [EU, 1965, replaced by EU, 2001a] regulates chemicals intended to exert a pharmacological, immunological or metabolic action in the human body, the regulatory data requirements for their safety assessment are extensive. A new drug application consists of a comprehensive quality section, a non-clinical (in vitro tests and animal experiments) part and finally, an extensive clinical part, involving the use of groups of human volunteers and patients. The non-clinical test results include single and repeated dose toxicity, toxicokinetics, genotoxicity, carcinogenicity, reproductive and developmental toxicity and local tolerance [EMEA, 2006]. Knowledge on data accessibility for active medicinal substances involves insight in a complex web of data protection measures in order to safeguard the commercial property of the companies that have invested in such elaborated and costly quality, efficacy and safety dossiers [EU, 1993c]. Nevertheless, some data can be accessed when compounds come off patent protection and/or from the scientific press.

In the EU, the use of medicinal active substances in cosmetics is strongly discouraged. Many medicinal actives are taken up in Annex II to the Cosmetic Products Directive, meaning that their use in cosmetics is prohibited. A number of exceptions exist, but as a general rule, the intersection between active medicinal substances and ingredients allowed in cosmetics, is very restricted.

1.3.6. Impact of the EU Legislation on Detergents

a) General Provisions

Viewing their chemical nature (many are anionic surfactants), the primary objective of the EU regulator was to protect the environment by stipulating a minimal level of surfactant biodegradability [EU, 1973b]. Subsequently, the legislation on detergents has been amended on several occasions until it was published in its final form in 2004 [EU, 2004c]. Again, the focus was maintained on environmental aspects, although human local health effects were also taken into consideration.

b) Relevance for Cosmetics

Cleansing cosmetic products typically contain different kinds of surfactants which also form part of detergents. Human safety appearing to be of inferior importance in the assessment of these types of ingredients, only local health effects such as allergenicity and skin irritation, are addressed. Moreover, the only official data requirements

Rogiers · Pauwels

involve labelling of known allergens, thus usually no new data are generated. This strongly reduces the impact of the Detergents Directive on the safety data availability of cosmetic ingredients.

1.3.7. Impact of the Plant Protection Directive and the EU Legislations on Medical Devices

a) General Provisions

(i) As was the case for biocides, plant protection active substances kill living organisms, wherefore they need to be thoroughly assessed. Moreover, the actives may be found as residues on treated crops, implying that the available toxicological data should enable the calculation of an acceptable daily intake. Therefore, the EU Plant Protection Products Directive [EU, 1991a] deals with the extended data requirements and risk and efficacy assessments of active substances and ready-to-use end products.

(ii) In the medical field, not only medicinal products, but also a large number of instruments and high-tech devices are used for performing very specific examinations. The first regulation in this particular field dealt with active implantable medical devices [EU, 1990]. Three years later, the whole area was covered by a new Directive [EU, 1993b] which clearly defined all possible classes of medical devices together with their data requirements and further regulatory demands.

b) Relevance for Cosmetics

Although extensive toxicological data, of which the results are accessible, are generated through the Plant Protection Products Directive [EU, 1991a], only few to none of them are of relevance for cosmetic products.

The same applies to the data generated through the Medical Devices Directive [EU, 1993b], with the exception that the generated data are considered confidential and therefore not readily accessible [EU, 1993b].

1.3.8. Combined Impact of Relevant 'Vertical' EU Legislations on Data Availability for a Cosmetic Ingredient

In principle, any chemical substance legally marketed in the EU could be a cosmetic ingredient candidate, on the condition that all the restrictions and prohibitions imposed by the EU cosmetic legislation with respect to the different articles, annexes and animal testing, are taken into consideration. This implies that a cosmetic ingredient may have been tested through the requirements of diverging EU Directives, irrespective of its use in a finished cosmetic product. Out of the thousands of ingredients used in cosmetics, less than 400 are taken up in Annexes III to VII of Dir. 76/768/EEC

[SCCP, 2006]. Among these, the majority of preservatives (listed in Annex VI) were equally approved through the biocidal products (and/or plant protection products) legislation and therefore automatically benefited from of a large amount of physico-chemical, toxicological and ecotoxicological data.

A number of flavouring agents may equally be used as food additives, meaning that potentially the ADI and a full toxicological profile are available. Moreover, in the area of food contact materials a large number of substances have been evaluated[6] which could find a use in cosmetics. Several surfactants are applied in detergents, skin care and skin cleansing products and many skin care products contain constituents that are used as excipients in topical medicines.

Yet it is clear that the specific intersection between the pool of dangerous substances and that of cosmetic ingredients not taken up in any Annex will by far be the largest one. The chemicals in that intersection have solely been subject to the data requirements laid down by the Dangerous Substances Directive [EU, 1967]. This means that there are two possibilities with regard to their data availability:
- when listed on ELINCS, the amount of data depends on annual volumes on the market (table 1),
- when listed in EINECS, the expected data package cannot be predicted, but usually is rather limited.

Figure 4 summarises the information provided under the different EU legislations by giving an overview of data availability for different types of substances/preparations. It is a simplified representation since it contains neither non-EU regulatory requirements nor the numerous exceptions mentioned in the individual Directives.

The dermal absorption test does not occur separately in figure 4. Although of key relevance for cosmetic ingredients, dermal absorption data are not commonly generated for other types of substances, with the exception of plant protection products coming in contact with the skin. Consequently, in vitro dermal absorption studies, of basic importance for the cosmetic ingredients studied by the SCCP, will rarely if ever be found in data packages generated under legislative requirements outside the cosmetic field.

The current chapter clearly shows that it is quite important to understand the current chemical-related EU regulatory framework, not only to comply with the concerned pieces of legislation, but equally in order to retrieve a maximal amount of safety data on cosmetic ingredients, available through different sources. More specifically, it shows that, although cosmetics on the EU market are exempted from the legislations on dangerous substances, dangerous preparations, food additives, biocides, detergents, medicinal products, plant protection products and medical devices, a lot of useful safety information on cosmetic ingredients may have become available

---

6   http://ec.europa.eu/food/food/chemicalsafety/foodcontact/synoptic_doc_en.pdf (consulted July 2007).

Rogiers · Pauwels

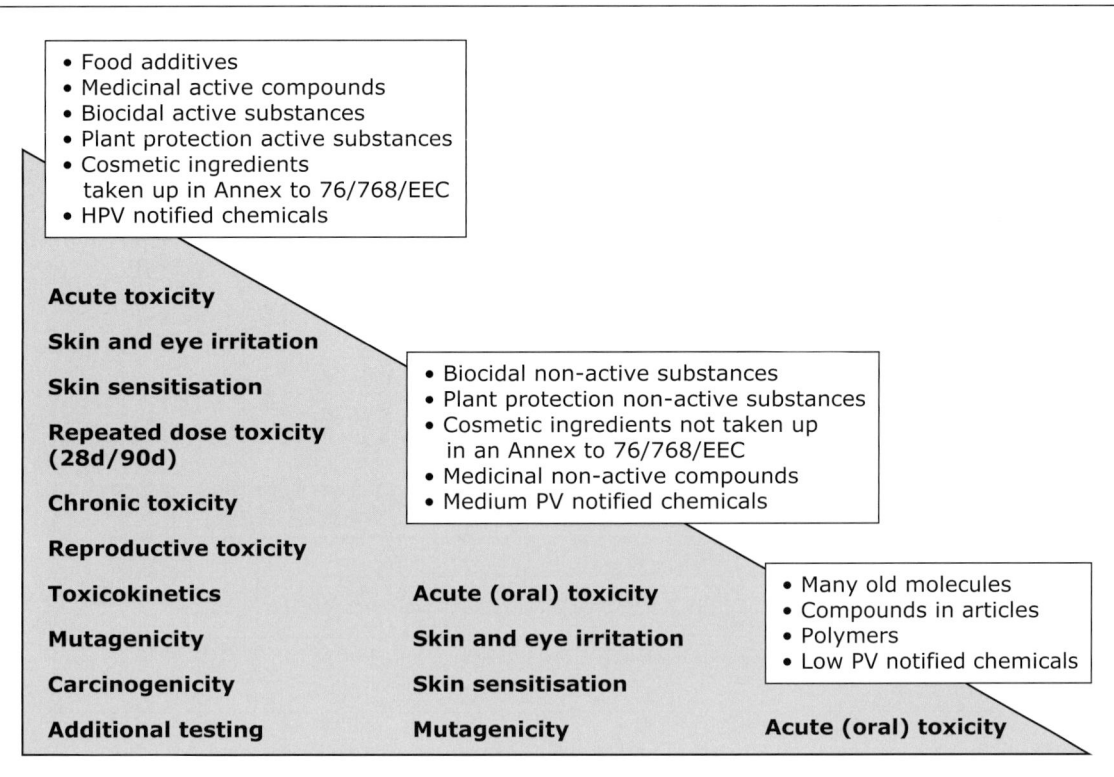

Fig. 4. Schematic representation of expected data availability for different types of substances as a result of current EU regulatory requirements.

through their provisions. Therefore, general knowledge of the chemical-related EU legislation has become indispensable and needs to be continuously updated.

A topic that merits continuing attention is the legislation on dangerous substances and more specifically the new road taken with REACH. Monitoring the implementation and practical realisation of REACH is crucial in maintaining a realistic view on safety data availability for a large number of cosmetic ingredients.

1.4 Relevant 'Horizontal' EU Legislations

Besides the above-mentioned 'vertical legislations' co-existing in the EU, some horizontal directives also affect the regulatory background for cosmetics (as visualised in figure 5). In most cases, they are complementary to the Cosmetic Products Directive, but sometimes their provisions overrule the cosmetic legislation, wherefore they certainly deserve to be mentioned.

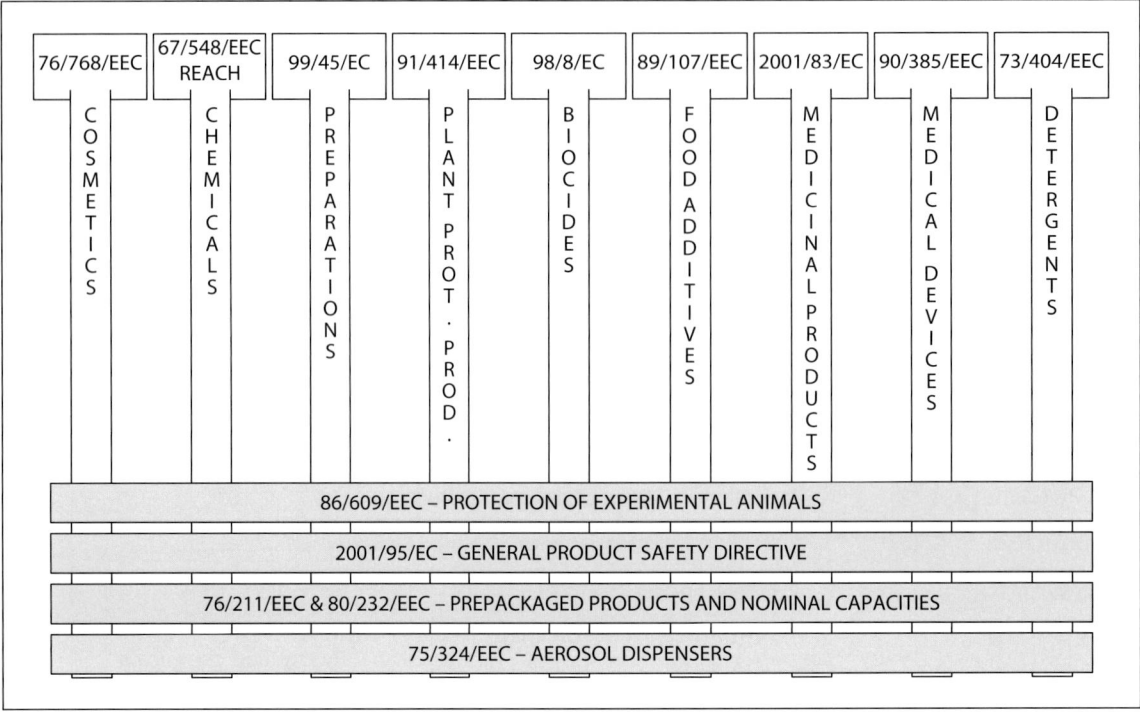

Fig. 5. Schematic presentation of 'vertical' and 'horizontal' cosmetic-related legislations in the EU.

1.4.1. Horizontal Provisions for the Protection of Animals

A Directive commonly referred to by other pieces of legislation is Dir. 86/609/EEC on the protection of animals used for experimental and other scientific purposes [EU, 1986]. Seeking to improve the controls on the use of laboratory animals in nearly all sectors, Dir. 86/609/EEC sets minimum standards for housing and care (Art. 5) and for the training of personnel handling animals and supervising the experiments [Art. 7(1), 14].

It also aims at reducing the numbers of animals used for experiments by requiring that an animal experiment should not be performed when an alternative method exists [Art. 7(2)], and by encouraging the development and validation of alternative methods to replace animal methods [Art. 23(1)]. The latter served as the basis for the Commission to set up the ECVAM [EU, 1991b]. Member States are imposed to collect statistical information on numbers and use of animals in experiments (Art. 13).

It should be emphasised, however, that the scope of Dir. 86/609/EEC is restricted to (1) animal use in the framework of the development, manufacture, quality, effectiveness and safety testing of drugs, foodstuffs and other substances or products, and (2) to the protection of the natural environment in the interest of the health or welfare of man or animal (Art. 3). Thus the fields of scientific research, education and training

Rogiers · Pauwels

and forensic research are not covered by this horizontal directive. Acknowledging this gap and in order to protect animals used in any procedure which may possibly cause pain, suffering, distress or lasting harm, the Council of Europe published Decision 1999/575/EC [EU, 1999a]. Herein, a number of conclusions of the 1986 European Convention for the protection of vertebrate animals used for experimental and other scientific purposes are officially approved. Basically, they defend the same principles as Dir. 86/609/EEC, but they additionally cover the neglected areas.

With the scientific progress made since 1986 and with the increasing political pressure on the development of alternative methods, a revision of Dir. 86/609/EEC was inevitable. Despite years of surveys and discussions on several aspects of the Directive such as scope, ethics, animal housing and care, statistical reporting, … allowing different parties to express their opinions and concerns, a generally revised version of the Directive is not yet available. The most recent developments can be obtained through the EU DG ENV website[7].

1.4.2. General Product Safety Directive

The aim of the GPSD [EU, 2001b] is to establish a coherent level of consumer protection for all consumer products on the internal market. Thus, it automatically covers many products which are simultaneously regulated by the provisions of the vertical legislations mentioned under 1.4. The legal provisions of Dir. 2001/95/EC are, however, intended to be fully complementary while conveniently taking up consumer products falling outside the scope of other community legislation (e.g. lighters) [DG SANCO, 2003].

Out of the numerous provisions of the GPSD, the following ones deserve special attention due to their relevance to the cosmetic field [DG SANCO, 2003]:
– The basic principle of the GPSD is that only 'safe' consumer products are allowed to be placed on the European market [Art. 3(1)]. A 'safe' product is defined as 'any product which, under normal or reasonably foreseeable conditions of use including duration and, where applicable, putting into service, installation and maintenance requirements, does not present any risk or only the minimum risks compatible with the product's use, considered to be acceptable and consistent with a high level of protection for the safety and health of persons' [Art. 2(B); EU, 2001b].

At first sight this completely corresponds with the provision of the Cosmetic Products Directive that a cosmetic product must not cause damage to human health [EU, 1976b]. Nevertheless, it should be noted that the GPSD goes further by also covering e.g. mechanical injuries caused by packaging of cosmetic products.

---

7   http://ec.europa.eu/environment/chemicals/lab_animals/revision_en.htm (consulted November 2007).

- The GPSD describes active post-marketing activities for producers as well as competent authorities. The producers are obliged to perform sample testing, to keep a register of complaints and to inform their distributors. They also need to alert the competent authorities. The latter are expected to take the appropriate steps to coordinate market surveillance and to report every consumer product health risk into the harmonised European RAPEX system. This allows other Member States to take necessary precautions with regard to similar products. The Cosmetic Products Directive includes a market follow-up requirement as part of the information that should be kept readily available to the Member States' competent authorities, but does not include any mandatory filing.
- The GPSD gives the Member States the authority to withdraw products from the market in case they are found unsafe. This provision is not taken up in the Cosmetic Products Directive, which means that for a withdrawal of a cosmetic product from the EU market, reference will be made to the GPSD.

1.4.3. EU Legislation on Prepackaged Products and Nominal Quantities

The term *prepackaged product* covers a wide range of consumer products, among which a large variety of foodstuffs, but also cosmetic products. As early as 1976, Dir. 76/211/EEC related to metrological requirements for prepackaged products introduced the concept of mentioning the EU-harmonised e-sign on the product label in case the metrological requirements specified in the Directive were respected (prepackages between 5 g and 10 kg) [EU, 1976a].

For example, the tolerated error between the actual content (measured weight/volume of product) and the nominal quantity (quantity indicated on the prepackage, i.e. the weight/volume the prepackage is deemed to contain) is not allowed to be exceeded, the nominal quantity needs to be preceded by the e-sign and displayed in correct metrological units and marked in figures of pre-defined sizes depending on the overall size of the package. It must be mentioned that this Directive is currently under revision[8].

In addition to the above-mentioned metrological requirements related to the use of the e-sign, Dir. 80/232/EEC imposes restrictions on the allowed nominal quantities for skin care and oral hygiene products, hair care and bathing products, alcohol-based cosmetics, deodorants and personal hygiene products and talcum powders [EU, 1980]. However, this was considered to hamper the freedom of producers to provide goods according to consumer tastes and to hinder competition as regards quality and price on the internal market, wherefore Dir. 80/323/EEC is repealed.

---

8 http://ec.europa.eu/enterprise/prepack/metrol_requir/inmetrolog_requir_en.htm (consulted November 2007).

From 11 April 2009 onwards, Member States may not, on grounds relating to the nominal quantities of the package, refuse, prohibit or restrict the placing on the market of prepackaged cosmetics [EU, 2007a].

1.4.4. EU Legislation on Aerosol Dispensers

In 1975, the Council of Europe drafted a Directive dealing with measures for the specific category of aerosol dispensers, independent of their content. The rationale was that, viewing the presence of a gas compressed, liquefied or dissolved under pressure, aerosol dispensers call for specific investigations. Capacities and volumes of individual powder, liquid or gas phases, flammability issues, coating of containers and valve sealing are examples of aspects that need to be addressed before the European ɜ-sign is allowed to be placed on the aerosol dispenser's label [EU, 1975]. Directive 75/324/EEC [EU, 1975] also covers deodorants and any other cosmetic spray.

However, it must be mentioned that this Directive is optional, meaning that Member States can, under their national law, allow the marketing of aerosol dispensers not complying to Dir. 75/324/EEC, provided they do not bear the ɜ-sign [DG ENTR, 2005].

In summary, it can be stated that the above-mentioned horizontal legislations may have an impact on the marketing of cosmetic products in the EU.

It is in particular worthwhile to follow up the usefulness and the evolution of the RAPEX system of the GPSD, since this may be of help to develop the so-called 'cosmetovigilance' approach, a harmonized market surveillance system for cosmetic products. The request for this approach was published at the end of 2006, in a resolution from the Council of Europe, recommending that every European Member State should implement in its national policies a cosmetovigilance system with involvement of all stakeholders (health professionals, consumers and manufacturers). The resolution was inter alia based upon pilot studies conducted in France, Austria and Norway. It provides clear definitions for 'undesirable effects' and 'serious undesirable effects', gives details on how to report these, and specifies the roles of the different stakeholders in the cosmetovigilance procedure. In addition, the need for an information exchange system between governments about serious undesirable effects caused by cosmetic products, is emphasized and leads to the official introduction of the INCOS, which is the cosmetic counterpart of RAPEX [EU, 2006b]. Mainly for the further elaboration of INCOS, which for the moment still is at an informal stage, experience with RAPEX can be of help. Although cosmetovigilance is another challenging aspect of the safety of cosmetics, this book focuses on the safety assessment process of cosmetics as such and therefore does not include detailed schemes of existing and potential innovative post-marketing surveillance procedures.

1.5 **References**

Colipa: Cosmetics Directive 76/768/EEC, Explanatory Brochure. The European Cosmetic Toiletry and Perfumery Association, January 2004.

DG ENTR: ENTR.H06/KS D(2004). Aerosol Dispensers Directive 75/324/EEC: Update to technical progress, Issue Paper. Brussels, European Commission Enterprise and Industry Directorate General, 28 January 2005, available through http://ec.europa.eu/enterprise/pressure_equipment/aerosol_sector/consultations/issue_paper.pdf (consulted Nov 2007).

DG SANCO: Guidance Document on the Relationship between the General Product Safety Directive (GPSD) and certain Sector Directives with Provisions on Product Safety. European Commission Directorate General Health and Consumer Protection (DGSANCO), November 2003, available through http://ec.europa.eu/consumers/cons_safe/prod_safe/gpsd/guidance_gpsd_en.pdf (consulted November 2007).

ECB: European Chemicals Bureau. Technical Guidance Document on Risk Assessment in support of Commission Directive 93/67/EEC on Risk Assessment for new notified substances, Commission Regulation (EC) No 1488/94 on Risk Assessment for existing substances and Directive 98/8/EC of the European Parliament and of the Council concerning the placing of biocidal products on the market. Doc. EUR 20418 EN/1, European Communities, 2003.

ECJ: European Court of Justice. Judgment of the Court (Fifth Chamber) of 16 April 1991. Upjohn Company and Upjohn NV v Farzoo Inc. and J. Kortmann. Reference for a preliminary ruling: Hoge Raad – Netherlands. Concepts of 'medicinal product' and 'cosmetic product'. Case C-112/89. European Court reports, 1991, p I-01703.

EMEA: Guidance Document on Non-clinical Day 80 Assessment Report. Revision 2, 2006. http://www.emea.europa.eu/pdfs/human/chmptemplates/CHMP-D80-AR-Guidance/D80AR-NonClinical-Guidance.pdf (consulted July 2007).

EU: Council Directive 65/65/EEC of 26 January 1965 on the approximation of provisions laid down by Law, Regulation or Administrative Action relating to proprietary medicinal products. Off J 1965;022:369–373.

EU: Council Directive 67/548/EEC of 27 June 1967 on the approximation of laws, regulations and administrative provisions relating to the classification, packaging and labelling of dangerous substances. Off J 1967;P196:1–98.

EU: Council Directive 73/173/EEC of 4 June 1973 on the approximation of Member States' laws, regulations and administrative provisions relating to the classification, packaging and labelling of dangerous preparations (solvents). Off J 1973a;L189:7–29.

EU: Council Directive 73/404/EEC of 22 November 1973 on the approximation of the laws of the Member States relating to detergents. Off J 1973b;L347:51–52.

EU: Council Directive 75/324/EEC of 20 May 1975 on the approximation of the laws of the Member States relating to aerosol dispensers. Off J 1975;L147:40–47.

EU: Council Directive 76/211/EEC of 20 January 1976 on the approximation of the laws of the Member States relating to the making-up by weight or by volume of certain prepackaged products. Off J 1976a;L046:1–11.

EU: Council Directive 76/768/EEC of 27 July 1976 on the approximation of the laws of the Member States relating to cosmetic products. Off J 1976b;L262:169–200.

EU: Council Directive 76/769/EEC of 27 July 1976 on the approximation of the laws, regulations and administrative provisions of the Member States relating to restrictions on the marketing and use of certain dangerous substances and preparations. Off J 1976c;L262:201–203.

EU: Council Directive 77/728/EEC of 7 November 1977 on the approximation of the laws, regulations and administrative provisions of the Member States relating to the classification, packaging and labelling of paints, varnishes, printing inks, adhesives and similar products. Off J 1977;L303:23–33.

EU: Council Directive 80/232/EEC of 15 January 1980 on the approximation of the laws of the Member States relating to the ranges of nominal quantities and nominal capacities permitted for certain prepackaged products. Off J 1980;L051:1–7.

EU: Council Directive 86/609/EEC of 24 November 1986 on the approximation of laws, regulations and administrative provisions of the Member States regarding the protection of animals used for experimental and other scientific purposes. Off J 1986;L358:1–28.

EU: Council Directive 88/379/EEC of 7 June 1988 on the approximation of the laws, regulations and administrative provisions of the Member States relating to the classification, packaging and labelling of dangerous preparations. Off J 1988;L187:14–30.

EU: Council Directive 89/107/EEC of 21 December 1988 on the approximation of the laws of the Member States concerning food additives authorised for use in foodstuffs intended for human consumption. Off J 1989a;L040:27–33.

EU: Council Recommendation 89/49/EEC of 21 December 1988 concerning nationals of Member States who hold a diploma conferred in a third State. Off J 1989b;L019:24.

EU: Council Directive 90/385/EEC of 20 June 1990 on the approximation of the laws of the Member States relating to active implantable medical devices. Off J 1990;L189:17–36.

EU: Council Directive 91/414/EEC of 15 July 1991 concerning the placing of plant protection products on the market. Off J 1991a;L230:1–32.

EU: SEC 91 1794 Final (1991b). Communication from the Commission to the Council and the Parliament: establishment of a European Centre for the Validation of Alternative Methods (CEVMA). Brussels, Commission of the European Communities, 29 October 1991, available through http://ecvam.jrc.it/index.htm (consulted Nov 2007).

EU: Council Directive 92/32/EEC of 30 April 1992 amending for the seventh time Directive 67/548/EEC on the approximation of the laws, Regulations and administrative provisions relating to the classification, packaging and labelling of dangerous substances. Off J 1992;L154:1–29.

EU: Council Directive 93/35/EEC of 14 June 1993 amending for the sixth time Directive 76/768/EEC on the approximation of the laws of the Member States relating to cosmetic products. Off J 1993a; L151:32–37.

EU: Council Directive 93/42/EEC of 14 June 1993 concerning medical devices. Off J 1993b;L169:1–43.

EU: Council Regulation (EEC) No 2309/93 of 22 July 1993 laying down Community procedures for the authorisation and supervision of medicinal products for human and veterinary use and establishing a European Agency for the Evaluation of Medicinal Products. Off J 1993c;L214:1–21.

EU: European Parliament and Council Directive 94/35/EC of 30 June 1994 on sweeteners for use in foodstuffs. Off J 1994a;L237:3–12.

EU: European Parliament and Council Directive 94/36/EC of 30 June 1994 on colours for use in foodstuffs. Off J 1994b;L237:13–29.

EU: European Parliament and Council Directive No 95/2/EC of 20 February 1995 on food additives other than colours and sweeteners. Off J 1995; L061:1–40.

EU: Commission Directive 97/18/EC of 17 April 1997 postponing the date after which animal tests are prohibited for ingredients or combinations of ingredients of cosmetic products. Off J 1997;L114:43–44.

EU: Directive 98/8/EC of the European Parliament and of the Council of 16 February 1998 concerning the placing of biocidal products on the market. Off J 1998;L123:1–63.

EU: Council Decision of 23 March 1998 concerning the conclusion by the Community of the European Convention for the protection of vertebrate animals used for experimental and other scientific purposes. Off J 1999a;L222:29–37.

EU: Directive 1999/45/EC of the European Parliament and of the Council of 31 May 1999 concerning the approximation of the laws, regulations and administrative provisions of the Member States relating to the classification, packaging and labelling of dangerous preparations. Off J 1999b;L200:1–68.

EU: Commission Directive 2000/41/EC of 19 June 2000 postponing for a second time the date after which animal tests are prohibited for ingredients or combinations of ingredients of cosmetic products. Off J 2000;L145:25–26.

EU: Directive 2001/83/EC of the European Parliament and of the Council of 6 November 2001 on the Community code relating to medicinal products for human use. Off J 2001a;L311:67–128.

EU: Directive 2001/95/EC of the European Parliament and of the Council of 3 December 2001 on general product safety. Off J 2001b;L011:4–17.

EU: Regulation (EC) No 178/2002 of the European Parliament and of the Council of 28 January 2002 laying down the general principles and requirements of food law, establishing the European Food Safety Authority and laying down procedures in matters of food safety. Off J 2002;L031:1–24.

EU: Directive 2003/15/EC of the European Parliament and of the Council of 27 February 2003 amending Council Directive 76/768/EEC on the approximation of the laws of the Member States relating to cosmetic products. Off J 2003;L066:26–35.

EU: Commission Decision 2004/210/EC of 3 March 2004 setting up Scientific Committees in the field of consumer safety, public health and the environment. Off J 2004a;L066:45–50.

EU: Directive 2004/27/EC of the European Parliament and of the Council of 31 March 2004 amending Directive 2001/83/EC on the Community code relating to medicinal products for human use. Off J 2004b;L136:34–57.

EU: Regulation (EC) No 648/2004 of the European Parliament and of the Council of 31 March 2004 on detergents. Off J 2004c;L104:1–35.

EU: Regulation (EC) No 1907/2006 of the European Parliament and of the Council of 18 December 2006 concerning the Registration, Evaluation, Authorisation and Restriction of Chemicals (REACH), establishing a European Chemicals Agency, amending Directive 1999/45/EC and repealing Council Regulation (EEC) No 793/93 and Commission Regulation (EC) No 1488/94 as well as Council Directive 76/769/EEC and Commission Directives 91/155/EEC, 93/67/EEC, 93/105/EC and 2000/21/EC. Off J 2006a;L396: 1–849. Corrigendum in Off J 2006a;L136:3–280.

EU (2006b): Resolution ResAP(2006)1 on a vigilance system for undesirable effects of cosmetic products ('cosmetovigilance') in Europe in order to protect public health. Adopted by the Committee of Ministers on 8 November 2006 at the 979th meeting of the Ministers' Deputies. Available through http://www.coe.int/ (consulted April 2008).

EU: Directive 2007/45/EC Of the European Parliament and of the Council of 5 September 2007 laying down rules on nominal quantities for prepacked products, repealing Council Directives 75/106/EEC and 80/232/EEC, and amending Council Directive 76/211/EEC. Off J 2007a;L247:17–20.

EU (2007b): Report from the Commission to the Council and the European Parliament. Fifth Report on the Statistics on the Number of Animals used for Experimental and other Scientific Purposes in the Member States of the European Union. {SEC(2007)1455}, Brussels, 5 November 2007, COM(2007) 675 final.

EU (2008): Commission of the European Communities proposal for a Regulation of the European Parliament and of the Council on cosmetic products (recast). {SEC(2008)117 & SEC(2008)118}, Brussels, 5 February 2008, COM(2008) 49 final, 2008/025 (COD).

Pauwels M, Rogiers V (2004): Considerations in the safety assessment of cosmetics; in: Business Briefing: Global Cosmetics Manufacturing 2004 (Ed. Touch Briefings, London, UK), accessible through http://www.touchbriefings.com/cdps/cditem.cfm?NID = 846 (consulted Dec 2006).

SCCP: SCCP/1005/06 (2006): The SCCP's Notes of Guidance for the Testing of Cosmetic Ingredients and their Safety Evaluation, adopted by the SCCP during the 10th plenary meeting of 19 December 2006.

Challenges Related to Cosmetic Safety Assessment in the EU

Rogiers V, Pauwels M (eds): Safety Assessment of Cosmetics in Europe.
Curr Probl Dermatol. Basel, Karger, 2008, vol 36, pp 29–57

2.1 Introduction

As explained in the previous chapter, two distinct channels can be identified with respect to the safety evaluation of cosmetic ingredients. One deals with colourants, preservatives, UV filters and/or cosmetic ingredients for which a health concern has been expressed. They will be subject to a full safety evaluation by the SCCP, after which they may or may not be taken up in the Annexes to Dir. 76/768/EEC. The other channel concerns all ingredients included in a finished cosmetic product and, as already mentioned, a qualified safety assessor needs to examine the ingredients' individual chemical structures, their toxicological profiles and their level of exposure in order to sign for their safe use in the finished cosmetic product under consideration.

According to the SCCP Notes of Guidance [SCCP, 2006b], the safety evaluation of a cosmetic ingredient is mainly based upon the same principles and practices of risk assessment as usually applied for other types of substances, namely constituents of medicinal products, food additives, plant protection products, … Therefore, the next chapter is dedicated to some features of the commonly applied EU risk assessment paradigm that are of relevance for cosmetic safety assessment.

2.2 Relevant Features of the General EU Risk Assessment Paradigm

2.2.1. Overview of the Classical Risk Assessment Process

The general principles and practices of the risk assessment process are presented in figure 1.

Manifold review articles, official guidelines and toxicology books cover this topic in detail [Beck et al., 1994; Dayan, 1999; IPCS, 1999; EU, 2000j; WHO, 2001; ECB, 2003; Renwick et al., 2003]. Therefore, this chapter will focus on features that are related to and useful in the safety assessment of cosmetic products and their ingredients. Only human health is considered here, not environmental risk assessment.

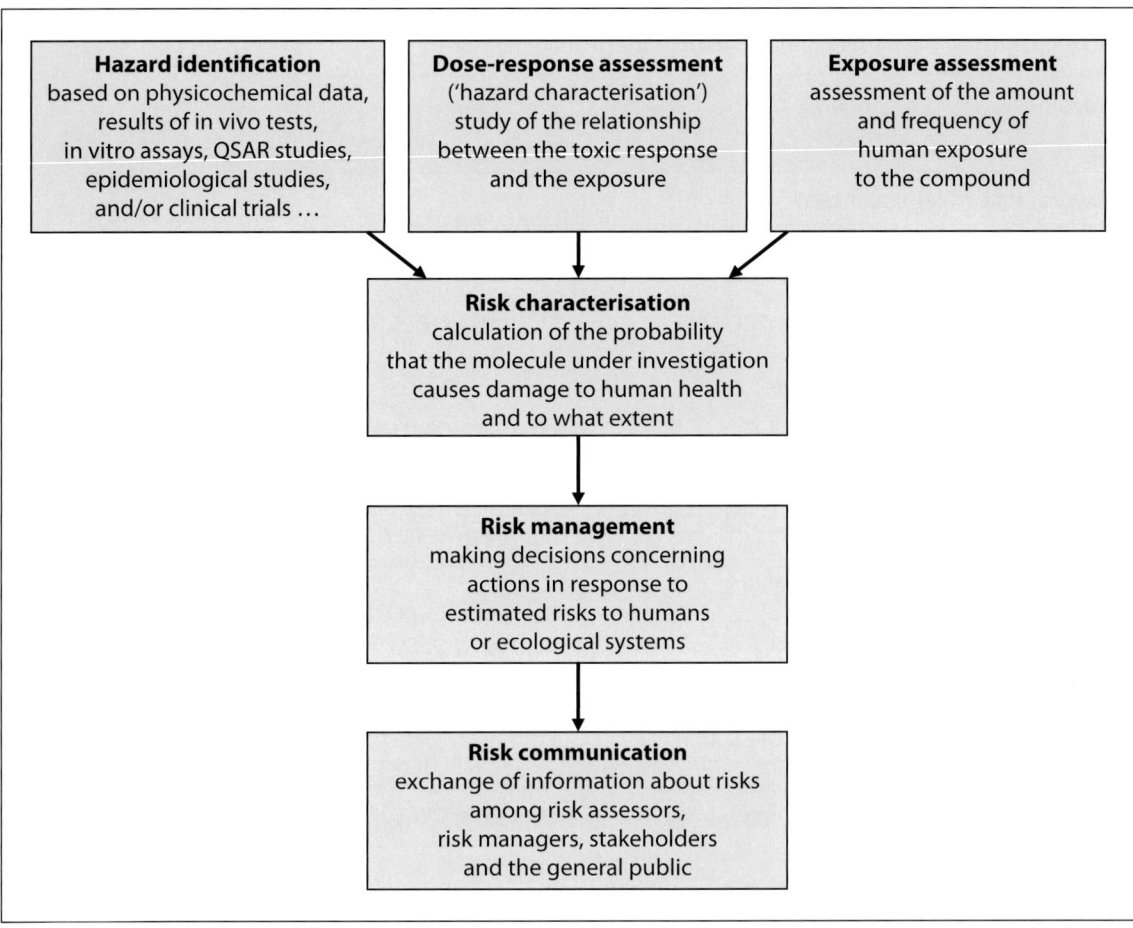

Fig. 1. The risk assessment process as internationally recognised. Based on SCCP [2006b] and WHO [2001].

2.2.2. Hazard Identification and Dose-Response Assessment

a) Determination of Physicochemical and Toxicological Properties
In the first step of hazard identification, the intrinsic physical, chemical and toxicological properties of the molecule under consideration are studied to identify whether the substance has the potential to damage human health. The subsequent dose-response assessment (sometimes referred to as 'hazard characterisation') studies the relationship between the toxic response and the exposure, and usually results in the determination of the dosage at which no adverse effects are observed (NOAEL) [SCCP, 2006b]. A large number of officially accepted guidelines for testing physicochemical and toxicological properties are available under the form of OECD

Table 1. Typical physicochemical data set for a cosmetic ingredient [SCCP, 2006b], accompanied by the most commonly used official testing methods

Physicochemical property (67/548/EEC Annex V Part A and OECD No.)	References
Physical state (solid, liquid, gas)	
Organoleptic properties (colour, odour, taste if relevant)	
Solubility (at …°C) in water (A.6, OECD 105) and relevant solvents, including receptor fluids of dermal absorption studies	EU, 1992e; OECD, 1995c
Partition coefficient (Log P_{ow}, at …°C) (A.8, OECD 107, 117, 122, 123)	EU, 1992f; OECD, 1995d; OECD, 2006b; OECD, 2000; OECD, 2004a
Flash point (A.9)	EU, 1992g
Specific physical properties for liquids: • Boiling point (A.2, OECD 103) • Density (at …°C) (A.3, OECD 109) • pK_a (at …°C) • Viscosity (at …°C) (OECD 114) • Vapour pressure (at …°C) (A.4, OECD 104)	EU, 1992b; OECD, 1995b EU, 1992c; OECD, 1995e OECD, 1981c EU, 1992d ; OECD, 2006a
Specific physical properties for solids: • General appearance (crystal, amorphous, …) • Melting point (A.1, OECD 102) • pK_a (…% in …, at …°C)	EU, 1992a; OECD, 1995a
Specific physical properties for gasses: • Density (at …°C) • Particle size (OECD 110) • Ignition point (A.15)	OECD, 1981b EU, 1992h
For UV light-absorbing ingredients: the UV light absorption spectrum (OECD 101)	OECD, 1981a

Technical Guidelines[1] and/or testing methods taken up in Annex V to Dir. 67/548/EEC [EU, 1967], Part A and Part B. The most relevant ones for the EU cosmetic hazard characterisation are displayed in tables 1 and 2.

It is important to notice that, with the exception of skin corrosion, dermal absorption, phototoxicity and the in vitro mutagenicity testing battery, all EU Annex V [EU, 1967] and OECD protocols mentioned in table 2 require the use of experimental animals. Their results are used to either directly classify the tested compound (e.g. irritation data, sensitisation data, LD_{50} values) or to be incorporated in further calculations.

---

1   OECD Chemicals Testing Guidelines, Section 1: Physical Chemical Properties, and Section 4: Health Effects.

Rogiers · Pauwels

Table 2. Toxicological endpoints to be addressed in dossiers submitted to the SCCP [SCCP, 2006b], accompanied by the most commonly used official testing methods

Toxicological endpoint and available testing methods (67/548/EEC Annex V Part B and OECD No.)	References
Acute oral toxicity (if available):	
• Fixed dose method (B.1 bis, OECD 420)	EU, 2004a; OECD, 2001c
• Acute toxic class method (B.1tris, OECD 423)	EU, 2004b; OECD, 2001d
• Up-and-down procedure (OECD 425)	OECD, 2001e
Irritation and corrosivity:	
• Skin irritation – Draize method (B.4, OECD 404)	EU, 2004c; OECD, 2002a
• Eye irritation – Draize method (B.5, OECD 405)	EU, 2004d; OECD, 2002b
• Skin corrosion (B.40, OECD 430, 431 and 435)	EU, 2000g; OECD, 2004c, OECD, 2004d; OECD, 2006c
Skin sensitisation:	
• Magnusson Kligman guinea pig maximisation test or	EU, 1996a; OECD, 2002c
Buehler guinea pig test (B.6, OECD 406)	EU, 1996a; OECD, 2002c
• LLNA (B.42, OECD 429)	EU, 2004g; OECD, 2002d
Dermal/percutaneous absorption:	
• In vitro skin absorption assay (OECD 428)	SCCP, 2006a; OECD, 2004b
Repeated dose toxicity:	
• 28-day oral toxicity study (B.7, OECD 407)	EU, 1996b; OECD, 1995f
• 28-day dermal toxicity study (B.9, OECD 410)	EU, 1992i; OECD, 1981d
• 90-day oral toxicity study in rodents (B.26, OECD 408)	EU, 2001; OECD, 1998
• 90-day dermal toxicity study in rodents (B.28, OECD 411)	EU, 1988c; OECD, 1981e
• Chronic (≥12 months) toxicity study (B.30, OECD 452)	EU, 1988d; OECD, 1981g
Mutagenicity/genotoxicity:	
• Bacterial reverse mutation test (B.13/14, OECD 471)	EU, 2000d; OECD, 1997a
• In vitro mammalian cell gene mutation test (B.17, OECD 476)	EU, 2000e; OECD, 1997e
• In vitro mammalian chromosome aberration test (B.10, OECD 473)	EU, 2000a; OECD, 1997b
• In vitro micronucleus test (OECD 487)	OECD, 2007
• In vitro unscheduled DNA synthesis assay (B.18, OECD 482)	EU, 1988a; OECD, 1986
• In vitro Syrian Hamster Embryo cell transformation assay (B.21)	EU, 1988b
• In vivo chromosomal aberration test (B.11, OECD 475)	EU, 2000b; OECD, 1997d
• In vivo micronucleus test (B.12, OECD 474)	EU, 2000c; OECD, 1997c
• In vivo unscheduled DNA synthesis assay (B.39, OECD 486)	EU, 2000f; OECD, 1997f
Carcinogenicity:	
• Carcinogenicity study (B.32, OECD 451)	EU, 1988e; OECD, 1981f
• Combined chronic toxicity/carcinogenicity (B.33, OECD 453)	EU, 1988f; OECD, 1981h
Reproductive toxicity:	
• Two-generation reproduction toxicity test (B.35, OECD 416)	EU, 2004f; OECD, 2001b
• Teratogenicity study (B.31, OECD 414)	EU, 2004e; OECD, 2001a

Table 2. (continued)

Toxicological endpoint and available testing methods (67/548/EEC Annex V Part B and OECD No.)	References
Toxicokinetics: • Toxicokinetic studies (B.36, OECD 417)	EU, 1988e; OECD, 1984
Photo-induced toxicity: • 3T3 neutral red uptake phototoxicity test (B.41, OECD 432)	EU, 2000h; OECD, 2004e

Nevertheless, the efforts in the development of alternative methods have also resulted in the following positive developments in the field of human toxicity testing:
(i)   a replacement alternative has been developed for the in vivo skin irritation test,
(ii)   a set of replacement tests is now available for eye irritation screening, allowing screening out of the most irritative compounds (not mildly and non-irritating substances) and reducing the number of animals to be tested via the in vivo eye irritation test,
(iii) the rLLNA method, which uses less animals than the original LLNA protocol, is available.

More detail on these methods and their exact status is given in chapter 6.

To conclude, it must be mentioned that with regard to human testing, the SCCNFP issued guidance on:
(i)   human volunteer compatibility studies [SCCNFP, 1999a, 1999b],
(ii)   human volunteer testing of potentially cutaneous irritant (mixtures of) cosmetic ingredients [SCCNFP, 1998],
(iii) human volunteer predictive testing of potentially cutaneous sensitising cosmetic (mixtures of) ingredients [SCCNFP, 2000].

b) The NOAEL Value and the BMD Approach
Risk assessors are interested in the NO(A)EL, which by definition represents the dosage (expressed as mg substance per kg body weight and per day) at which no (adverse) effects are observed in the experimental animal after repeated daily administration. This value will be used later in the risk characterisation phase for comparison with the reasonably foreseeable internal dosage to which a consumer or worker could be exposed.

Although the NOAEL approach is globally used, it has also been criticised. One of the comments is that in classical repeated dose toxicity studies [EU, 1996b, 1992i, 2001, 1988c, 1988d], animals are administered a test substance at three different dosage levels. The highest dosage is expected to elicit definite signs of toxicity without causing excessive lethality, whereas the lowest dosage should not produce any adverse effect. Generally a factor 2–4 separates the levels from each other (e.g. 100, 300 and 1,000 mg/kg bw/day). This means that, in case the derived NOAEL turns out to be 100 mg/kg/day, the actual NOAEL may be any value between 100 and 300 mg/kg/day.

Moreover, in some studies the lowest dosage level turns out to also produce adverse effects, which leads to the determination of a LOAEL instead of a NOAEL.

An alternative to this methodology is the use of the so-called benchmark dose. This approach is based on a mathematical model being fitted to the experimental data within the observable range and results in an estimate of the dose that causes a low but measurable response, typically chosen at a 5 or 10% incidence above the control. The BMDL refers to the corresponding lower limits of a one-sided 95% confidence interval on the BMD [SCCP, 2006b].

This means that the resulting starting point for risk assessment is not restricted to one of the experimentally selected dosage levels. Neither does the situation where the lowest level still produces adverse effects pose any problem for the determination of the BMDL. Drawbacks of this concept are that this methodology is less known than the well-established NOAEL approach, and that the commonly used three dosage levels in the animal studies are generally too few for the required statistical analysis, based on complex mathematical models. Calculation of a sound BMD value requires regrouping of the animals in more, but smaller dosage groups. Nevertheless, the BMD approach has grown since its first development and is considered a valuable complementary tool for the interpretation of some critical studies in a toxicological data package [Travis et al., 2005; Sand et al., 2008].

c) Non-Threshold Effects

In the case of genotoxic effects that have no threshold, extrapolation of dose-response data to very low exposure levels outside the range of the in vivo observations, may be necessary [EU, 2000j]. For non-threshold carcinogens, it is assumed that there is no level of exposure that does not pose a small, but finite, probability of inducing cancer [SCCP, 2006b].

Over the years, numerous mathematical models have been put forward and each regulatory body uses its own preferred descriptor. Some examples:
- The dose-descriptor T_{25} is defined as the chronic dose rate that will give 25% of the animal's tumours at a specific tissue site after correction for spontaneous incidence, within the standard life time of that species [Dybing et al., 1997; ECB, 1999; Sanner et al., 2001]. It is used by the SCCP to calculate the lifetime cancer risk of cosmetic ingredients [SCCP, 2004a, 2004b, 2005a].
- The 'LED$_{10}$ method' was proposed by the EPA [2005]. It mathematically extrapolates the dose associated with a 10% extra risk (the LED$_{10}$) from the lower 95% confidence limits of the available data [IPCS, 1999].
- The 'TD$_{50}$' is defined as the chronic dose rate (in mg/kg bw/day) which, for a given target site(s), would cause tumours in half of the animals within some standard experimental time – the 'standard lifespan' for the species. A TD$_{50}$ can be calculated either for a particular category of neoplastic lesions (e.g. malignant tumours only, liver tumours only) or for all tumours [EFSA, 2005].
- The aforementioned 'BMD' is the descriptor that is most commonly used by EFSA for assessing non-threshold effects, provided the available data are found adequate

for the determination of the 95% confidence interval. Otherwise EFSA advises the use of the T_{25} descriptor [EFSA, 2005].

2.2.3. Exposure Assessment

a) General Principles

Exposure assessment intends to characterise the nature and size of the human populations exposed to an emission source and the magnitude, frequency and duration of that exposure [EU, 2000j]. In this process, the potential routes of exposure (oral, dermal and/or inhalation) are determined.

A universal question to be answered in any exposure assessment is which 'type of exposure' requires quantitative assessment. Different possibilities exist (indicated with an asterisk in figure 2), including the externally applied dose, the absorbed/internal dose, the amount of substance in the blood circulation and the concentration in the target tissue or the fraction that may bind to critical receptors.

In the majority of cases, the absorbed/internal total dose is the one that needs to be obtained for later comparison with the aforementioned NOAEL, LOAEL or BMD values. Nearly every industry sector has its own paradigms, models and figures for exposure assessment. Mentioning them all would bring us far outside the scope of this issue. Here, for cosmetics, we focus on the so-called 'systemic exposure dosage' [SCCP, 2006b].

b) Exposure Levels per Cosmetic Product Type

As stated earlier, the safety evaluation of a finished cosmetic product is based upon the toxicological profile of the ingredients, their chemical structure *and their level of exposure*. Every specific exposure scenario will be linked to a certain amount of substance that may be ingested or absorbed through the skin or mucous membranes. Some external exposure levels and involved skin surface areas per specific cosmetic product type can be retrieved from the SCCP Notes of Guidance [SCCP, 2006b]. These figures have meanwhile been used for more than 15 years. Over the past decade, some studies/initiatives aimed a providing more faithful estimations of exposure to specific cosmetic product types. They include:

(i) A Dutch study on cosmetic exposure assessment performed by the RIVM, based upon an exposure assessment software model called ConsExpo[2]. It contains exposure data for 35 cosmetic product types, accompanied by their level of confidence [Bremmer, 2005].

(ii) Three comprehensive studies assessing consumer use practices of 360 female volunteers for 12 cosmetic product categories in total, namely face cream, lipstick,

---

2   More information through www.rivm.nl/consexpo (consulted February 2008).

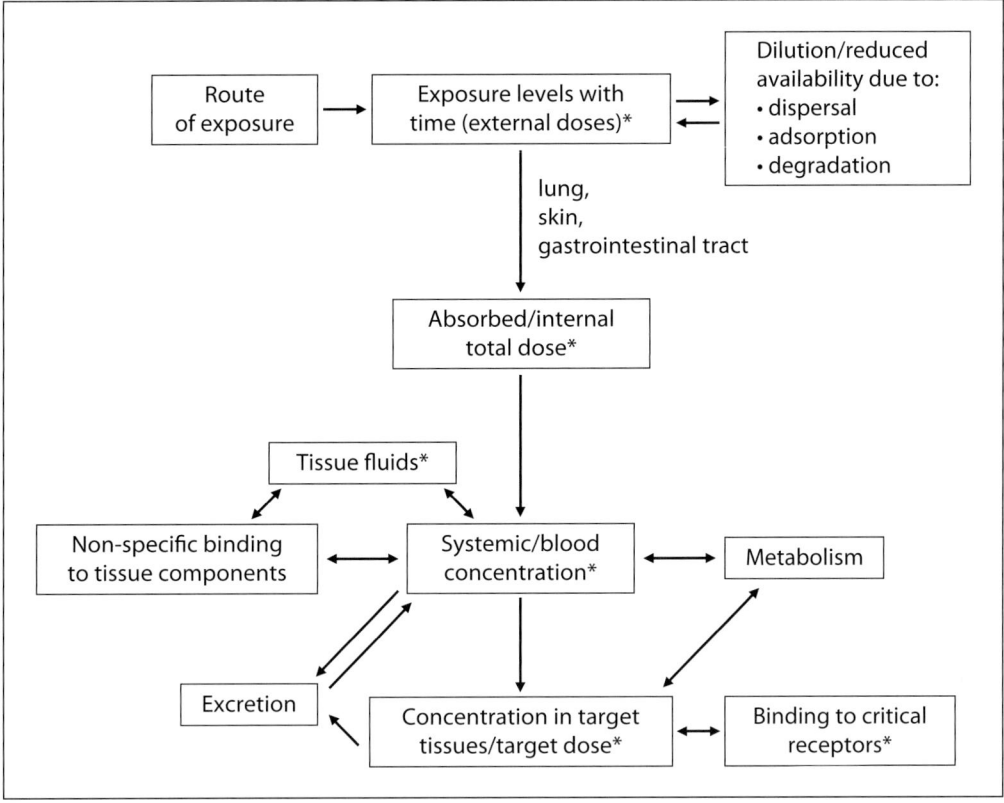

Fig. 2. Considerations in human exposure assessment: types of exposure [EU, 2000j].

body lotion, spray perfume, hairspray, liquid foundation, shampoo, body wash, solid antiperspirant, facial cleanser, hair conditioner and eye shadow [Loretz et al., 2005, 2006, 2008].

(iii) A large-scale study set up by European cosmetic manufacturers, acting within Colipa[3], and designed to provide recent and robust data for body lotion, deodorant, facial moisturiser, shampoo, lipstick and toothpaste [McNamara et al., 2007; Hall et al., 2007].

Four product types can be found as well in the Notes of Guidance [SCCP, 2006b] as in the three above-mentioned studies. Therefore, their results are placed next to each other for comparison (table 3).

As can be deduced from table 3, the estimated daily application levels slightly differ, but remain in the same order of magnitude.

---

3 European Cosmetic Toiletry and Perfumery Association.

Table 3. Estimated daily application levels (g/day) of body lotion, face cream, shampoo and lipstick, as estimated in separate documents/studies

Product type	SCCP [SCCP, 2006b]	RIVM [Bremmer et al., 2005]	Consumer study [Loretz et al., 2005, 2006]	Colipa [Hall et al., 2007]
Body lotion	8.0	8.0	8.7	7.8
Face cream	1.6	1.6	2.1	1.5
Shampoo[1]	8.0	20	12.8	11.0
Lipstick	0.040	0.040	0.024	0.057

[1]For the actual calculation of the daily exposure level of a shampoo, a retention factor of 0.01 is used to take into account rinsing off and dilution of the finished product by application on wet hair.

The Colipa figures are mentioned in the SCCP Notes of Guidance, though not officially taken up in the exposure table, since their format was different compared to the one that has been used by the SCC(NF)P over the years [SCCP, 2006b].

c) Calculation of the Cosmetic Systemic Exposure Dosage
In the next step, the external finished product values described above are transformed into an internal dosage or so-called systemic exposure dosage of the compound under consideration. Therefore the compound's concentration in the finished product and its dermal absorption value are taken into account. Since dermal absorption can be expressed in $\mu g/cm^2$ and/or in %, the SCCP offers two possible SED calculations [SCCP, 2006b]:

(i)   Dermal absorption of test substance reported in $\mu g/cm^2$:

$$SED = \frac{DA_a\ (\mu g/cm^2) \times 10^{-3}\,mg/\mu g \times SSA\ (cm^2) \times F\ (day^{-1}) \times R}{60\,kg}$$

where SED (mg/kg bw/day) = systemic exposure dosage; DA_a ($\mu g/cm^2$) = dermal absorption reported as amount/cm^2; SSA (cm^2) = skin surface area expected to be treated with the finished cosmetic product; F (day^{-1}) = frequency of application of the finished product; R = retention factor; 60 kg = default human body weight.

(ii)   Dermal absorption of test substance reported in %:

$$SED = \frac{A\ (g/day) \times 1{,}000\,mg/g \times C\ (\%)/100 \times DA_p\ (\%)/100}{60\,kg}$$

where SED (mg/kg bw/day) = systemic exposure dosage; A (g/day) = amount of the cosmetic product applied daily; C (%) = the concentration of the ingredient under study in the finished cosmetic product on the application site; DA_p (%) = dermal

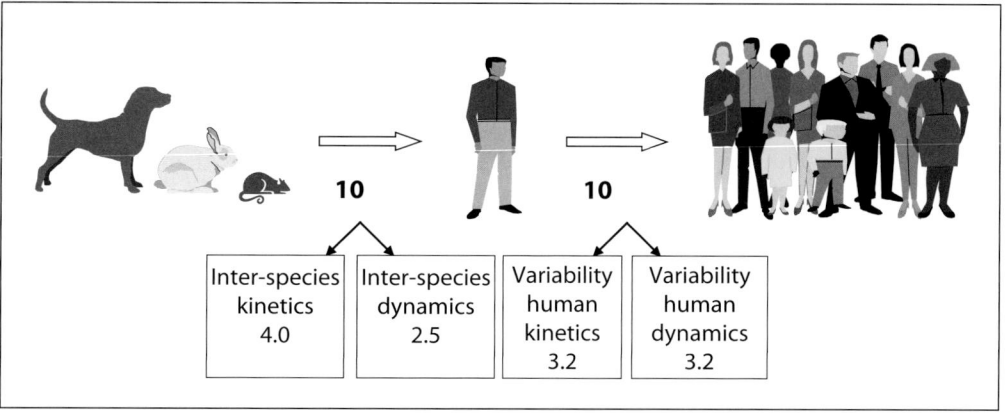

Fig. 3. Schematic representation of the extrapolation from animal to man, taking into account kinetic and dynamic inter- and intra-species extrapolation. Based on Renwick [1998] and IPCS [1994].

absorption expressed as a percentage of the test dose assumed to be applied in real-life conditions; 60 kg = default human body weight.

2.2.4. Risk Characterisation

The step of risk characterisation typically integrates information from exposure assessment and hazard characterisation into advice suitable for use in decision making or risk management [Renwick et al., 2003]. In the case of cosmetic 'safety assessment', as cosmetic risk characterisation is more commonly denominated, the probability for the molecule under investigation to cause damage to human health and the level of risk are calculated [SCCP, 2006b]. Use is made of the MoS, an uncertainty factor comparing the dosage at which no adverse effect is observed in the experimental animal with the dosage the consumer is expected to be exposed to.

a) Calculation of the Margin of Safety
The MoS of a cosmetic ingredient is calculated by dividing its lowest NO(A)EL value by its calculated SED [SCCP, 2006b].

$$\text{MoS} = \frac{\text{NO(A)EL}}{\text{SED}}$$

It is generally accepted that the MoS should at least be 100 to declare a substance safe for use [WHO, 1987]. As is also the case in many areas outside the cosmetic field, this value of 100 is used to extrapolate from a group of test animals to an average human being, and subsequently from average humans to sensitive subpopulations (fig. 3).

Whenever a NO(A)EL value is available, the above approach offers an easy to use calculation for attributing a 'safe' or 'unsafe' label to a test compound for a specific use.

However, the following needs to be considered:

- In the majority of MoS calculations for cosmetic ingredients, a dermal exposure figure (the SED) is compared to an oral NO(A)EL value. This means that the estimated actual systemic availability of the compound after dermal contact (taking into account the dermal absorption) is compared to an orally applied external dosage level. By doing this, it is assumed that the oral absorption value is 100%, which often is not the case. In the SCCP Notes of Guidance [SCCP, 2006b] this problem is acknowledged, and it is advised to include oral absorption data in the calculations whenever they are available. In addition, due to potential qualitative differences between hepatic and dermal biotransformation, the formed metabolites of the compound under study may be different after oral and dermal administration [Nohynek, 2005].
- It is often debated whether calculation of the MoS is scientifically relevant for cosmetic ingredients which are not used on a daily basis. Comparing the monthly usage level of a hair dye with a NO(A)EL value obtained after daily administration of the substance, is a clear overestimation of the risk [SCCP, 2006b].
- Although the choice of the NO(A)EL may be evident in some studies, there also may be discussions whether specific effects are relevant enough to be called 'adverse'. The observation of reduced body weight gain, for example, may be the result of an adverse effect but also a simple reflection of reduced food consumption due to low palatability of the test substance. Temporary disturbance of liver enzymes may be a first indicator of liver toxicity or nothing more than an adjustment effect to the test substance. Finally, in the specific field of cancer risk assessment the occurrence of rodent forestomach tumours is often considered non-relevant for human beings, given that a human counterpart for the rodent forestomach does not exist [Proctor et al., 2007].

b) Other Approaches Relevant to Cosmetic Safety Assessment

Lifetime Cancer Risk

In the case of non-threshold carcinogens, it is assumed that any level of exposure poses a small, but finite, probability of inducing cancer. As stated in section 2.2.2.c, several methods for quantitative risk characterisation have been used or proposed by regulatory authorities in Europe and the USA (T_{25}, LED_{10}, TD_{50}).

The SCCP has chosen to make use of the T_{25} as dose descriptor. For determination of the lifetime cancer risk of a compound, this animal dose descriptor is firstly converted to a human dose descriptor, after which the lifetime cancer risk is determined by linear extrapolation to the actual exposure dose [SCCP, 2006b].

The Threshold of Toxicological Concern

Firstly developed in the field of food and food additives, the TTC is a principle which refers to the establishment of a human exposure threshold value for all chemicals below which there would be no appreciable risk to human health [Kroes et al., 2000]. The human threshold approach has been promoted for more than 20 years and has significantly evolved over time. Whereas in the early years human thresholds were mainly based on LD_{50} values combined with carcinogenicity data and some results from repeated dose toxicity studies, the current concept of the TTC combines knowledge on carcinogenic potential, metabolism and accumulation, structural alerts, endocrine disrupting properties, neurotoxicity, teratogenicity, developmental toxicity, allergenicity and immunotoxicity on a large number of chemicals into a complex decision tree to establish appropriate TTC values [Kroes et al., 2004].

In the food sector, the general concept of a human threshold value has gained regulatory acceptance by the introduction of the threshold of regulation of 1.5 µg/person/day for indirect food additives [FDA, 1995].

Recently, a possible procedure to extend the use of the TTC approach to the safety evaluation of cosmetic ingredients was published [Kroes et al., 2007]. A number of important concerns when trying to use the approach in the proposed field were tackled:
– The (dis)similarity between cosmetic ingredients and the chemicals on which the original TTC approach was based.
– Moving from the oral (food sector) to the dermal (cosmetic) route: differences in metabolism and dermal absorption issues, differences in frequency of exposure: daily for food-related substances and potentially intermittently (e.g. oxidative hair dyes applied once per month) for the cosmetic sector.
– Total exposure to a cosmetic ingredient through the use of multiple cosmetic formulations containing the compound under study (aggregate exposure).
– Simultaneous exposure to different cosmetic ingredients.

The authors are convinced that it is scientifically justified to use the TTC approach and the database underlying the food TTC values for certain specific cases in the safety evaluation of cosmetic ingredients as far as systemic risks after dermal exposure are concerned [Kroes et al., 2007].

During the ICCG meeting of September 2007, a new mandate from DG Sanco was presented on the specific topic of the TTC and the assessment of its applicability in some specific fields [ICCG, 2007]. Meanwhile, the approach is not commonly used in the safety assessment of cosmetic ingredients.

In the field of risk assessment of airborne chemicals, it was recently proposed to introduce the concept of a concentration of no toxicological concern to form the inhalation counterpart of the TTC. More specifically, an ambient concentration of 0.03 µg/cm^3 is considered the CoNTC for an airborne chemical [Drew and Frangos, 2007].

2.2.5. Risk Management, Risk Communication and Risk Perception

Risk characterisation is ultimately followed by risk management and risk communication. Whereas risk assessment is commonly considered a scientific exercise, risk management deals with the choice of specific actions to be undertaken and is not necessarily performed by technical experts. The deliberations and decisions specific for risk management not only take into account the information on the potential adverse effects estimated by the risk assessment process, but also consider sociopolitical and economic implications of the envisaged decision and/or action [WHO, 2001]. Therefore, it is of key importance that the advice of the risk assessor to the risk manager clearly describes the nature of the available hazard identification, the rationale behind the use of any default value, details on any kind of extrapolation performed and an unambiguous description of the methods by which uncertainties have been taken into account [Renwick et al., 2003].

It is important to know that the risk manager has the authority to apply the so-called 'precautionary principle'. This principle typically applies in situations where relevant knowledge has an uncertain or imperfect character. Since dealing with uncertainty is an exercise that is highly open for interpretation and quite impossible to standardise, the precautionary principle allows decision makers to act in a constructive or restrictive way, based upon the (lack of) information they have at their disposal. In the chemical-related world, acting in a constructive way usually consists of replacing a substance by a less dangerous one, whereas the restrictive approach involves the ban, phasing out or stringent restriction of the substance without full risk assessment [Løkke, 2006].

The report of a regional European WHO meeting on the precautionary principle [WHO, 2006] provides the most recent definition for the concept: 'The precautionary principle provides justification for public policy actions in situations of scientific complexity, uncertainty and ignorance, where there may be a need to act in order to avoid, or reduce, potentially serious or irreversible threats to health or the environment, using an appropriate level of scientific evidence, and taking into account the likely pros and cons of action and inaction'. The approach considers complex scenarios for man and environment exposed to a multitude of chemicals potentially inducing cumulative effects. This aspect is nearly always neglected in the currently performed risk assessment procedures.

The workability of the precautionary principle approach in the future will inter alia depend on the ability to define at which point evidence is sufficient to take specific actions, to organise effective stakeholder consultations, and to perform cost-benefit analyses in a consistent and transparent way [WHO, 2006].

Finally, risk communication is an essential but difficult interactive process among risk assessors, risk managers, stakeholders, and other members of the public, in which information about risks is exchanged. In first instance, risk communication will be performed between risk assessors and risk managers, after which different stakeholders and the general public may be involved. The timing and extent of the latter communication depends on the investigated problem and its context [WHO, 2001].

Risk communication should not be taken lightly and needs to be considered in the light of what is known in the field of risk perception. Risk perception mainly deals with how much risk of what sort is perceived to be acceptable by the general public. It

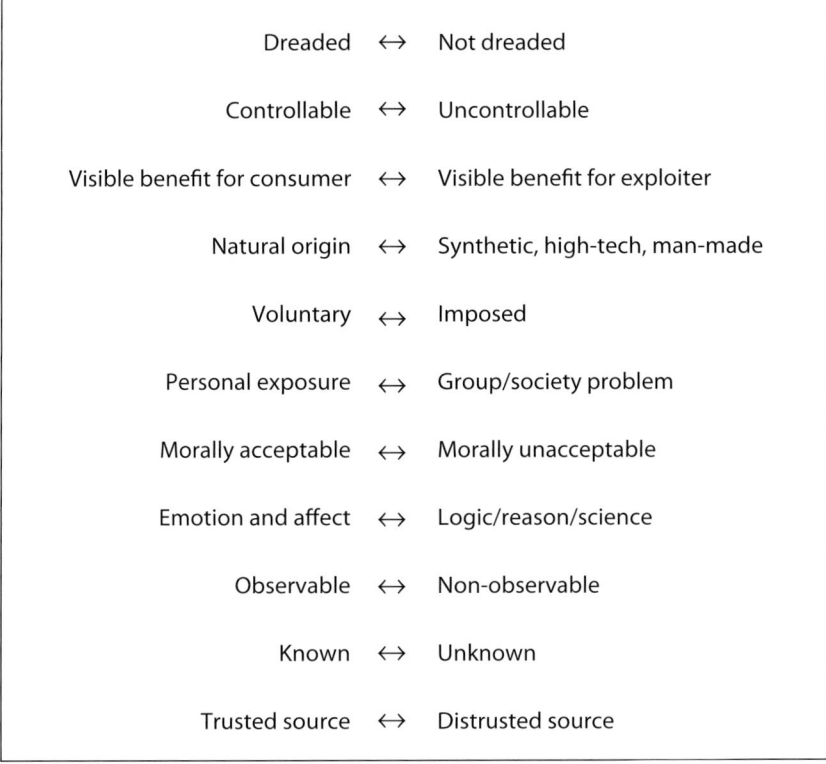

Fig. 4. Variables related to the nature of the anticipated effects that influence risk perception [Slovic, 1987, 1999, 2001; Blake, 1995; Slovic et al., 2004].

can be at the basis of media attention and political pressure, both potentially affecting regulations. The complex process of risk perception by the average consumer is influenced by many variables related to the nature of the anticipated effects (fig. 4) [Rogiers, 2007].

In addition, cultural and religious differences between and within populations co-determine individual perceptions of risks [Chuck-ling Lai and Tao, 2003] and will inevitably influence the weight of the variables mentioned in figure 4. Race, gender and socioeconomical factors still play the most important roles [Flynn et al., 1994].

It has also been shown that consumers express different levels of distrust towards several sources of information. University scientists, medical doctors and consumer organisations appear to be easily trusted, whereas industries, members of the Parliament and government ministries are faced with an atmosphere of distrust [Frewer et al., 1996]. Therefore companies and official bodies must take special care when conveying messages to the general public and the media. Although risk perception has been subject to intensive study, the affective mechanisms by which judgments are made and the interplay between affect and cognition in reasoning are not yet fully understood [Finucane et al., 2000; Slovic et al., 2004].

2.3 Actual Challenges for the European Cosmetic Safety Assessor

2.3.1. Moving Away from Animal Testing

Through the publication of subsequent directives, the European legislator has made it very clear that in the cosmetic sector the safety for human health needs to be guaranteed without the use of experimental animals [EU, 1993, 1997, 2000i, 2003]. Europe is currently faced with a legal prohibition to test finished cosmetic products on animals, whereas from 11 March 2009 on, also animal tests on cosmetic ingredients or combinations of ingredients will be prohibited [EU, 2003]. These strong provisions imply that in order to assess the safety of a new cosmetic ingredient after 2009, validated alternative methods must be used for a considerable battery of animal toxicity tests. A number of these tests are currently not available, not validated and still they should guarantee the same level of consumer protection. Only replacement methods are allowed, thereby ignoring refining and reduction methods as effective and realistic alternatives. It is clear that this constitutes a huge challenge for scientists and the cosmetic industry.

Validation of alternative methods is coordinated at the EU level in Ispra, Italy, at the ECVAM [Hartung, 2004]. Scientific advice on this validation process is subsequently provided by a group of experts from all Member States, called ESAC. An alternative method must pass ESAC and get its approval, before it can be taken up in the actual EU legislation (Annex V to Dir. 67/548/EEC). The SCCP advises on its use/suitability for cosmetic ingredients. On a global scale, not only ECVAM, but also its US and Japanese counterparts ICCVAM[4] and JaCVAM, are involved in the development of alternative methods.

In table 4, a summary is given of the actual status of validated alternative methodologies for safety testing of cosmetic ingredients.

As far as eye irritation is concerned, there are a number of so-called 'valid' alternative methods as used by major cosmetic companies for screening of finished products. A valid alternative method is defined as a technique that has not necessarily gone through the complete validation process, but for which a sufficient amount of scientific data exist proving its relevance and reliability [SCCP, 2006b]. Examples relevant for cosmetic testing are the HET-CAM test, the BCOP test, the ICE test, the IRE test, the RBC test and the NRU test. Unfortunately, these methods cannot be considered as validated alternative methods for eye irritation, though solely as screening tools for hazard identification (not risk assessment) to eliminate severe eye irritants [SCCP, 2007a]. More details on the exact status of these and other promising alternatives will be presented per toxicological endpoint in chapter 6.

---

4   More information through http://iccvam.niehs.nih.gov/about/about_ICCVAM.htm (consulted February 2008).

Table 4. Actual status on validated alternative methods at the EU level (based on SCCP [2007a])

Acute toxicity:	fixed dose method[1] acute toxic class method[1] up-and-down procedure[1]
Skin corrosivity:	Transcutaneous Electrical Resistance test, EPISKIN™, EPIDERM®, CORROSITEX®[1]
Skin irritation:	EPISKIN™
Skin sensitisation:	(reduced) LLNA[1]
Phototoxicity (photoirritation):	3T3 Neutral Red Uptake – Phototoxicity Test
Dermal absorption:	in vitro dermal absorption study with human/pig skin[1]
Mutagenicity/genotoxicity:	bacterial reverse mutation test, in vitro mammalian cell gene mutation test, in vitro micronucleus test, in vitro mammalian chromosome aberration test, in vitro unscheduled DNA synthesis, Syrian hamster embryo test, …[1]
Embryotoxicity:	WEC, MM test and EST[2]

[1]Not officially validated by ECVAM, but accepted by ESAC and SCC(NF)P.
[2]Officially validated by ECVAM, but not yet accepted by SCC(NF)P.

Important to notice is that for the endpoints that enable determination of a NOAEL requested for the calculation of the MoS, no alternatives are available. This problem has been addressed by many concerned parties in the cosmetic and other sectors [CSTEE, 2004; SCCNFP, 2004c; ICCG, 2006; Greim et al., 2006; Greim, 2007; ECVAM, 2007] and constitutes the most important challenge for the European cosmetic safety assessor.

2.3.2. Urgent Need for Appropriate Exposure Data

As explained in section 2.2.3.b, some recent exposure data have become available. Although these additional studies provide useful information, they still fail to cover all product types not dealt with by the SCCP in its Notes of Guidance [SCCP, 2006]. They merely confirm, refine or contradict the existing figures. Therefore, the safety assessor will regularly need to work with a combination of extrapolations from existing figures and a set of assumptions (e.g. for bath oils, baby changing creams, etc.).

Subsequently, it can be stated that harmonised exposure levels for individual cosmetic product types, especially for those not mentioned in the SCCP Notes of Guidance [SCCP, 2006b], remain highly needed.

2.3.3. New Role of Raw Material Suppliers

The 6th Amendment [EU, 1993] to the Cosmetic Products Directive and its requirement to keep a TIF ready for inspection for the competent authorities has some serious indirect implications on cosmetic raw material suppliers.

More specifically, since the safety evaluation of a cosmetic product needs to be based on the structure, toxicological pattern and exposure of the ingredients, the availability, substantivity and completeness of high quality toxicological data of raw materials and new ingredients become of key importance. Moreover, the 7th Amendment [EU, 2003] to the Cosmetic Products Directive prohibits the use of substances classified as CMR Category 1 or 2 in cosmetic products. Simultaneously, it includes the provision that the quantitative composition of a finished cosmetic product, restricted to those substances considered as dangerous by Dir. 67/548/EEC, must be easily accessible to the public [EU, 2003]. This means that raw material suppliers not only need to provide detailed information on the official classification of any substance included in their ingredient, but equally on potential self-classification of constituents. This implies that they will need to disclose their compositions to a certain extent.

In addition, some specific categories of substances need special attention:

Mineral, Animal, Botanical and Biotechnological Ingredients
As pointed out in the SCCP Notes of Guidance [SCCP, 2006b], this category of complex ingredients forms a problem with regard to characterisation. Exact origin, preparation processes, extraction conditions, impurity profiles, microbiological contamination, etc. form major hurdles in identification. As far as the use of botanicals in food and food supplements is concerned, some useful guidance on their identification and risk assessment is published under the responsibility of the ILSI [Schilter et al., 2003].

Oxidative Hair Dyes
These particular cosmetic ingredients typically consist of a two-component system, containing so-called 'precursors' and 'couplers', intended to result in a chemical reaction [SCCP, 2005b]. This means that precursor(s), coupler(s), intermediate(s) and end products require adequate characterisation and potentially toxicological evaluation.

Fragrance Components
Whereas any chemical substance or preparation of synthetic or natural origin used in the composition of cosmetic products is considered a cosmetic ingredient, perfume and aromatic compositions of fragrances are not [Art. 5a; EU, 1976]. Moreover, materials used in strictly necessary quantities as solvents or as carriers for perfume and aromatic compositions, are not considered as cosmetic ingredients either [Art. 6g; EU, 1976]. Thus, the identification requirements for the complex fragrance mixtures are restricted to those substances taken up in the Annexes to Dir. 76/768/EEC and to

those classified as CMR Category 1 or 2 in Annex I to the Dangerous Substances Directive [EU, 1967].

Nanoparticles

The relatively new technological development of nanoparticles[5] and nanomaterials[6] has gained the attention of the SCENIHR and the SCCP [SCENIHR, 2005; SCCP, 2007b]. Recently, the SCCP expressed the opinion that in first instance a clear distinction needs to be made between soluble/biodegradable nanoparticles (liposomes, nanoemulsions, …) which disintegrate upon application to the skin, and insoluble nanoparticles (TiO_2, ZnO, …), for which health concerns related to possible uptake arise.

For the soluble/biodegradable group, it is assumed that the conventional risk assessment methodologies based on mass metrics are adequate, but for the insoluble nanoparticles other metrics such as the number of particles, their surface area and their distribution, constitute important additional information. Overall, nanomaterials are considered to require special attention with regard to the validation of testing methods or optimisation of existing in vivo/in vitro validated methods. Their safety assessment will be performed on a case by case basis [SCCP, 2007b].

Ideally, the above matters are discussed with the raw material supplier before the ingredient under consideration is incorporated in any finished cosmetic product.

Finally, in order to enable their customers to comply with all the cosmetics-related legislative requirements [Art. 1.7; EU, 2003], the raw material suppliers must disclose all animal tests performed on the ingredients under consideration.

2.3.4. The Need for Appropriate Training

All parties involved in the preparation of cosmetics, import in the EU, supply of raw materials, safety evaluation, development or application of alternative methods, regulation, etc. need appropriate training in safety evaluation of cosmetics, in particular with special attention to the changes in cosmetic legislation that took place over the past 10 years.

Several European universities foresee a Master degree in toxicology and/or risk assessment. Some examples are Surrey and Birmingham (UK), Wageningen and Utrecht (The Netherlands), Milan (Italy), Telemark (Sweden), Vienna (Austria), etc. This list is certainly not exhaustive, but shows that academic training in the field of toxicology and risk assessment exists. Additional 1-day to 1-week programmes can regularly be encountered on the World Wide Web.

---

5   Nanoparticle: a particle with one or more dimensions at the nanoscale (at least one dimension <100 nm).

6   Nanomaterial: a material with one or more external dimensions, or an internal structure, on the nanoscale.

Specific training in the field of safety assessment of cosmetics is given at the national level by the Deutsche Gesellschaft für Wissenschaftliche und Angewandte Kosmetik in Germany and at the European level through a 6-day academic course with a legal course certificate at the Vrije Universiteit Brussel, Department of Toxicology, in Belgium.

2.3.5. Ethical Constraints in Human Testing

By eliminating animal testing, the need for human testing is increased, especially since not every alternative method has a sufficient predictive value for human exposure.

Confirmatory safety tests are sometimes necessary and in certain cases can be carried out in man. Ethical concerns, however, should be considered. In one of its opinions on testing on human volunteers, the SCCNFP came to the conclusion that compatibility tests on humans can only be considered when the toxicological profiles of all ingredients and of the finished cosmetic product, based on animal and/or alternative methods, are available and have all been found favourable [SCCNFP, 1998].

Human tests should not be preferred to animal tests and cannot be considered as an alternative to the use of animals. The SCCNFP published guidelines for human volunteer testing of potential cutaneous irritant ingredients, finished products and potentially cutaneous sensitising cosmetic ingredients [SCCNFP, 1998, 1999a, 2000].

2.3.6. Special Problems for Small and Medium-Sized Enterprises

The full responsibility for the safety of cosmetics for human health is placed on the manufacturer, first importer in the EU or marketer. On several occasions, this has shown to be a heavy task for SMEs that are not really equipped to take such a high responsibility and to deal with the high costs resulting from the implementation of the 6th and 7th Amendments to the Cosmetic Products Directive [EU, 1993, 2003].

Safety evaluation of cosmetics and the application of in vitro methodologies require specialised personnel, which often is not available in SMEs. This means that extra resources are needed for advice by competent consultants, for in vitro testing by contract laboratories and for appropriate training.

2.3.7. Consumer Concerns

Awareness of the consumer is a key issue, which should be taken seriously. A first way of informing the consumer is through adequate labelling of cosmetics. Art. 6 of the cosmetics legislation foresees the indications that need to appear on the package and/or recipient of cosmetic products (see 1.2.3). These labelling obligations were introduced to provide useful information to the consumer. In particular, the appearance of a complete ingredients list on the finished product was asked by the medical profession in order to offer the possibility to sensitised or contact allergy-sensitive patients to avoid contact with certain cosmetic ingredients. Individual perfume/aroma components, however, are allowed to be replaced by the wording 'parfum' or 'aroma', unless they (1) belong to the list of 26 allergens recently taken up in Annex III to Dir. 76/768/EEC [EU, 2003] and (2) their concentration exceeds 0.01% in rinse-off or 0.001% in leave-on products.

Certain ingredients can be omitted through a confidentiality provision [EU, 1995], but experience has learned that this is only seldomly done.

Colourants are given as CI numbers and may be listed randomly at the end of the ingredients list. More colourants than present in the product may be indicated by the sentence 'may contain' or '+/−', giving the opportunity of using only one type of packaging for a number of differently coloured products of the same series.

In addition to the existing labelling requirements, the 7th Amendment introduced the question for additional consumer information by making the quantitative composition of every finished cosmetic product publicly available (at least for those ingredients that are officially classified in one of the danger classes through the chemicals' legislation), as well as the undesirable effects on human health. The mandatory mention of the period after opening for cosmetics that are stable for more than 30 months is also considered to be a useful piece of information for the consumer, but the practical framework for it is still missing.

Finally, the 7th Amendment to the Cosmetic Products Directive offers cosmetic companies the possibility to advertise on the label that no animal tests have been performed on the product or its ingredients [EU, 2003]. The application of this provision is explained in a guidance document issued by the Commission in 2006 [EU, 2006]. Unfortunately, the allowance criteria are so complex that the advertisement is extremely difficult to be put into practice.

2.4 References

Beck BD, Rudel R, Calabrese EJ: The use of toxicology in the regulatory process; in Hayes AW (ed): Principles and Methods of Toxicology, ed 3. New York, Raven Press, 1994, pp 19–58.

Blake ER: Understanding outrage: how scientists can help bridge the risk perception gap. Environ Health Perspect 1995;103(suppl 6):123–125.

Bremmer HJ, Prud'Homme de Lodder LCH, van Engelen JGM: Cosmetics fact sheet to assess the risks for the consumer, updated version for ConsExpo4. RIVM Rep 320104 001/2005.

Chuck-ling Lai J, Tao J: Perception of environmental hazards in Hong Kong Chinese. Risk Anal 2003;23: 669–684.

CSTEE: Opinion of the Scientific Committee on Toxicity, Ecotoxicity and the Environment (CSTEE) on the BUAV-ECEAE report on 'The way forward – action to end animal toxicity testing'. Doc. C7/VR/csteeop/anat/08014 D(04), European Commission, 2004.

Dayan AD: Risk assessment and risk communication; in Weiner HL, Kotkoskie LA (eds): Excipient Toxicity and Safety. New York, Marcel Dekker, 1999, pp 305–320.

Drew R, Frangos J: The concentration of no toxicological concern (CoNTC): a risk assessment screening tool for air toxics. J Toxicol Environ Health 2007;70;1584–1593.

Dybing E, Sanner T, Roelfzema H, Kroese D, Tennant RW: T25: a simplified carcinogenic potency index: description of the system and study of correlations between carcinogenic potency and species/site specificity and mutagenicity. Pharmacol Toxicol 1997;80:272–279.

ECB: Guidelines for setting specific concentration limits for carcinogens in Annex I of directive 67/548/EEC. Inclusion of potency considerations. Commission Working Group on the Classification and Labelling of Dangerous Substances. Brussels, 1999. Available through http://ecb.jrc.it/documents/classification-labelling/guidance_documents/guidelines_for_carcinogens.pdf (consulted November 2007).

ECVAM: Report from the Commission to the Council and the European Parliament – report on the development, validation and legal acceptance of alternative methods to animal tests in the field of cosmetics (2005). Cosmetics technical report drafted by ECVAM in 2005/2006 in support of the preparation of the above report. Brussels, 2007. Available through http://ec.europa.eu/enterprise/cosmetics/doc/antest_ecvam_2005v2.pdf (Consulted July 2007).

EFSA: Opinion of the Scientific Committee on a request from EFSA related to a harmonised approach for risk assessment of substances which are both genotoxic and carcinogenic (Request No EFSA-Q-2004-020), adopted on 18 October 2005. EFSA J 2005;282:1–31.

EPA: Guidelines for Carcinogen Risk Assessment (EPA/630/P-03/001F). Risk Assessment Forum. Washington, US Environmental Protection Agency, 2005.

EU: Council Directive 67/548/EEC of 27 June 1967 on the approximation of laws, regulations and administrative provisions relating to the classification, packaging and labelling of dangerous substances. Off J 1967;P196:1–98.

EU: Council Directive 76/768/EEC of 27 July 1976 on the approximation of the laws of the Member States relating to cosmetic products. Off J 1976;L262:169–200.

EU: B.18. DNA damage and repair – unscheduled DNA synthesis – mammalian cells in vitro. Commission Directive 88/302/EEC of 18 November 1987 adapting to technical progress for the ninth time Council Directive 67/548/EEC on the approximation of laws, regulations and administrative provisions relating to the classification, packaging and labelling of dangerous substances. Off J 1988a;L133:64–67.

EU: B.21. In vitro mammalian cell transformation tests. Commission Directive 88/302/EEC of 18 November 1987 adapting to technical progress for the ninth time Council Directive 67/548/EEC on the approximation of laws, regulations and administrative provisions relating to the classification, packaging and labelling of dangerous substances. Off J 1988b;L133:73–75.

EU: B.28. Sub-chronic inhalation toxicity study: 90-day repeated dermal dose study using rodent species. Commission Directive 88/302/EEC of 18 November 1987 adapting to technical progress for the ninth time Council Directive 67/548/EEC on the approximation of laws, regulations and administrative provisions relating to the classification, packaging and labelling of dangerous substances. Off J 1988c;L133:8–11.

EU: B.30. Chronic toxicity test. Commission Directive 88/302/EEC of 18 November 1987 adapting to technical progress for the ninth time Council Directive 67/548/EEC on the approximation of laws, regulations and administrative provisions relating to the classification, packaging and labelling of dangerous substances. Off J 1988d;L133:27–31.

EU: B.32. Carcinogenicity test. Commission Directive 88/302/EEC of 18 November 1987 adapting to technical progress for the ninth time Council Directive 67/548/EEC on the approximation of laws, regulations and administrative provisions relating to the classification, packaging and labelling of dangerous substances. Off J 1988e;L133:32–36.

EU: B.33. Combined chronic toxicity/carcinogenicity test. Commission Directive 88/302/EEC of 18 November 1987 adapting to technical progress for the ninth time Council Directive 67/548/EEC on the approximation of laws, regulations and administrative provisions relating to the classification, packaging and labelling of dangerous substances. Off J 1988f;L133:37–42.

EU: B.36. Toxicokinetics. Commission Directive 88/302/EEC of 18 November 1987 adapting to technical progress for the ninth time Council Directive 67/548/EEC on the approximation of laws, regulations and administrative provisions relating to the classification, packaging and labelling of dangerous substances. Off J 1988e;L133:51–54.

EU: A.1. Melting/freezing temperature. Commission Directive 92/69/EEC of 31 July 1992 adapting to technical progress for the seventeenth time Council Directive 67/548/EEC on the approximation of laws, regulations and administrative provisions relating to the classification, packaging and labelling of dangerous substances. Off J 1992a;L383A:5–14.

EU: A.2. Boiling temperature. Commission Directive 92/69/EEC of 31 July 1992 adapting to technical progress for the seventeenth time Council Directive 67/548/EEC on the approximation of laws, regulations and administrative provisions relating to the classification, packaging and labelling of dangerous substances. Off J 1992b;L383A:15–20.

EU: A.3. Relative density. Commission Directive 92/69/EEC of 31 July 1992 adapting to technical progress for the seventeenth time Council Directive 67/548/EEC on the approximation of laws, regulations and administrative provisions relating to the classification, packaging and labelling of dangerous substances. Off J 1992c;L383A:21–25.

EU: A.4. Vapour pressure. Commission Directive 92/69/EEC of 31 July 1992 adapting to technical progress for the seventeenth time Council Directive 67/548/EEC on the approximation of laws, regulations and administrative provisions relating to the classification, packaging and labelling of dangerous substances. Off J 1992d;L383A:26–47.

EU: A.6. Water solubility. Commission Directive 92/69/EEC of 31 July 1992 adapting to technical progress for the seventeenth time Council Directive 67/548/EEC on the approximation of laws, regulations and administrative provisions relating to the classification, packaging and labelling of dangerous substances. Off J 1992e;L383A:54–62.

EU: A.8. Partition coefficient. Commission Directive 92/69/EEC of 31 July 1992 adapting to technical progress for the seventeenth time Council Directive 67/548/EEC on the approximation of laws, regulations and administrative provisions relating to the classification, packaging and labelling of dangerous substances. Off J 1992f;L383A:63–73.

EU: A.9. Flash-point. Commission Directive 92/69/EEC of 31 July 1992 adapting to technical progress for the seventeenth time Council Directive 67/548/EEC on the approximation of laws, regulations and administrative provisions relating to the classification, packaging and labelling of dangerous substances. Off J 1992g;L383A:74–75.

EU: A.15. Auto-ignition temperature (liquids and gases). Commission Directive 92/69/EEC of 31 July 1992 adapting to technical progress for the seventeenth time Council Directive 67/548/EEC on the approximation of laws, regulations and administrative provisions relating to the classification, packaging and labelling of dangerous substances. Off J 1992h;L383A:98–99.

EU: B.9. Repeated dose (28 days) toxicity (dermal). Commission Directive 92/69/EEC of 31 July 1992 adapting to technical progress for the seventeenth time Council Directive 67/548/EEC on the approximation of laws, regulations and administrative provisions relating to the classification, packaging and labelling of dangerous substances. Off J 1992i;L383A:144–147.

EU: Council Directive 93/35/EEC of 14 June 1993 amending for the sixth time Directive 76/768/EEC on the approximation of the laws of the Member States relating to cosmetic products. Off J 1993; L151:32–37.

EU: Commission Directive 95/17/EC of 19 June 1995 laying down detailed rules for the application of Council Directive 76/768/EEC as regards the non-inclusion of one or more ingredients on the list used for the labelling of cosmetic products. Off J 1995; L140:26–29.

EU: B.6. Skin sensitisation. Commission Directive 96/54/EC of 30 July 1996 adapting to technical progress for the twenty-second time Council Directive 67/548/EEC on the approximation of the laws, regulations and administrative provisions relating to the classification, packaging and labelling of dangerous substances. Off J 1996a;L248:1–9, Annex IVC.

EU: B.7. Repeated dose (28 days) toxicity (oral). Commission Directive 96/54/EC of 30 July 1996 adapting to technical progress for the twenty-second time Council Directive 67/548/EEC on the approximation of the laws, regulations and administrative provisions relating to the classification, packaging and labelling of dangerous substances. Off J 1996b;L248: 1–5, Annex IVD.

EU: Commission Directive 97/18/EC of 17 April 1997 postponing the date after which animal tests are prohibited for ingredients or combinations of ingredients of cosmetic products. Off J 1997;L114:43–44.

EU: B.10. Mutagenicity – in vitro mammalian chromosome aberration test. Commission Directive 2000/32/EC of 19 May 2000 adapting to technical progress for the 26th time Council Directive 67/548/EEC on the approximation of the laws, regulations and administrative provisions relating to the classification, packaging and labelling of dangerous substances. Off J 2000a;L136:35–42.

EU: B.11. Mutagenicity – in vivo mammalian bone marrow chromosome aberration test. Commission Directive 2000/32/EC of 19 May 2000 adapting to technical progress for the 26th time Council Directive 67/548/EEC on the approximation of the laws, regulations and administrative provisions relating to the classification, packaging and labelling of dangerous substances. Off J 2000b;L136:43–49.

EU: B.12. Mutagenicity – in vivo mammalian erythrocyte micronucleus test. Commission Directive 2000/32/EC of 19 May 2000 adapting to technical progress for the 26th time Council Directive 67/548/EEC on the approximation of the laws, regulations and administrative provisions relating to the classification, packaging and labelling of dangerous substances. Off J 2000c;L136:50–56.

EU: B.13/14. Mutagenicity – reverse mutation test bacteria. Commission Directive 2000/32/EC of 19 May 2000 adapting to technical progress for the 26th time Council Directive 67/548/EEC on the approximation of the laws, regulations and administrative provisions relating to the classification, packaging and labelling of dangerous substances. Off J 2000d;L136:57–64.

EU: B.17. Mutagenicity – in vitro mammalian cell gene mutation test. Commission Directive 2000/32/EC of 19 May 2000 adapting to technical progress for the 26th time Council Directive 67/548/EEC on the approximation of the laws, regulations and administrative provisions relating to the classification, packaging and labelling of dangerous substances. Off J 2000e;L136:65–72.

EU: B.39. Mutagenicity – Unscheduled DNA synthesis (UDS) test with mammalian liver cells in vivo. Commission Directive 2000/32/EC of 19 May 2000 adapting to technical progress for the 26th time Council Directive 67/548/EEC on the approximation of the laws, regulations and administrative provisions relating to the classification, packaging and labelling of dangerous substances. Off J 2000f;L136:80–85.

EU: B.40. Skin corrosion (rat skin transcutaneous electrical resistance assay and human skin model assay). Commission Directive 2000/33/EC of 25 April 2000 adapting to technical progress for the 27th time Council Directive 67/548/EEC on the approximation of laws, regulations and administrative provisions relating to the classification, packaging and labelling of dangerous substances. Off J 2000g;L136:91–97.

EU: B.41. Phototoxicity – in vitro 3T3 NRU phototoxicity test. Commission Directive 2000/33/EC of 25 April 2000 adapting to technical progress for the 27th time Council Directive 67/548/EEC on the approximation of laws, regulations and administrative provisions relating to the classification, packaging and labelling of dangerous substances. Off J 2000h;L136:98–107.

EU: Commission Directive 2000/41/EC of 19 June 2000 postponing for a second time the date after which animal tests are prohibited for ingredients or combinations of ingredients of cosmetic products. Off J 2000i;L145:25–26.

EU (2000j): European Commission, DG Health and Consumer Protection. First Report on the Harmonisation of Risk Assessment Procedures, Part 1 · The Report of the Scientific Steering Committee's Working Group on Harmonisation of Risk Assessment Procedures in the Scientific Committees advising the European Commission in the area of human and environmental health, published on the Internet 20.12.2000:http://ec.europa.eu/food/fs/sc/ssc/out83_en.pdf (consulted Dec 2007).

EU: B.26. Sub-chronic oral toxicity test: repeated dose 90-day oral toxicity study in rodents. Commission Directive 2001/59/EC of 6 August 2001 adapting to technical progress for the 28th time Council Directive 67/548/EEC on the approximation of the laws, regulations and administrative provisions relating to the classification, packaging and labelling of dangerous substances. Off J 2001;L225:150–156.

EU: Directive 2003/15/EC of the European Parliament and of the Council of 27 February 2003 amending Council Directive 76/768/EEC on the approximation of the laws of the Member States relating to cosmetic products. Off J 2003;L066:26–35.

EU: B.1.bis. Acute toxicity (oral) – Fixed Dose Method. Commission Directive 2004/73/EC of 29 April 2004 adapting to technical progress for the 29th time Council Directive 67/548/EEC on the approximation of the laws, regulations and administrative provisions relating to the classification, packaging and labelling of dangerous substances. Off J 2004a; L152:156–168 & Corrigendum: Off J 2004a;L216: 177–189.

EU: B.1.tris. Acute toxicity (oral) – Acute toxic class method. Commission Directive 2004/73/EC of 29 April 2004 adapting to technical progress for the 29th time Council Directive 67/548/EEC on the approximation of the laws, regulations and administrative provisions relating to the classification, packaging and labelling of dangerous substances. Off J 2004b;L152:170–186 & Corrigendum: Off J 2004b;L216:190–205.

EU: B.4. Acute toxicity – Dermal irritation/skin corrosion. Commission Directive 2004/73/EC of 29 April 2004 adapting to technical progress for the 29th time Council Directive 67/548/EEC on the approximation of the laws, regulations and administrative provisions relating to the classification, packaging and labelling of dangerous substances. Off J 2004c;L152: 188–199 & Corrigendum: Off J 2004c;L216:206–215.

EU: B.5. Acute toxicity (eye irritation). Commission Directive 2004/73/EC of 29 April 2004 adapting to technical progress for the 29th time Council Directive 67/548/EEC on the approximation of the laws, regulations and administrative provisions relating to the classification, packaging and labelling of dangerous substances. Off J 2004d;L152:201–212 & Corrigendum: Off J 2004d;L216:216–226.

EU: B.31. Teratogenicity study – rodent and non-rodent. Commission Directive 2004/73/EC of 29 April 2004 adapting to technical progress for the 29th time Council Directive 67/548/EEC on the approximation of the laws, regulations and administrative provisions relating to the classification, packaging and labelling of dangerous substances. Off J 2004e;L152:214–225 & Corrigendum: Off J 2004e;L216:227–235.

EU: B.35. Two-generation reproduction toxicity test. Commission Directive 2004/73/EC of 29 April 2004 adapting to technical progress for the 29th time Council Directive 67/548/EEC on the approximation of the laws, regulations and administrative provisions relating to the classification, packaging and labelling of dangerous substances. Off J 2004f; L152:227–241 & Corrigendum: Off J 2004f;L216: 236–246.

EU: B.42. Skin sensitisation: Local Lymph Node Assay. Commission Directive 2004/73/EC of 29 April 2004 adapting to technical progress for the 29th time Council Directive 67/548/EEC on the approximation of the laws, regulations and administrative provisions relating to the classification, packaging and labelling of dangerous substances. Off J 2004g;L152:243–248 & Corrigendum: Off J 2004g;L216:247–252.

EU: Commission Recommendation 2006/406/EC of 7 June 2006 establishing guidelines on the use of claims referring to the absence of tests on animals pursuant to Council Directive 76/768/EEC. Off J 2006;L158:18–19.

FDA: Food additives, threshold of regulation for substances used in food-contact articles. Final rule. Fed Regist 1995;60:36582–36594.

Finucane ML, Alhakami A, Slovic P, Johnson SM: The affect heuristic in judgments of risks and benefits. J Behav Decis Making 2000;13:1–17.

Flynn J, Slovic P, Mertz CK: Gender, race and perception of environmental health risks. Risk Anal 1994;14: 1101–1108.

Frewer LJ, Howard C, Hedderley D, Shepherd R: What determines trust in information about food-related risks? Underlying psychological constructs. Risk Anal 1996;16:473–486.

Greim H, Arand M, Autrup H, Bolt HM, Bridges J, Dybing E, Glomot R, Foa V, Schulte-Hermann R: Toxicological comments to the discussion about REACH. Arch Toxicol 2006;80:121–124.

Greim H: Toxicological comments to the discussion about REACH (Greim H, Arand M, Autrup H, Bolt HM, Bridges J, Dybing E, Glomot R, Foa V, Schulte-Hermann R, Arch Toxicol 2006;80:121–124). Reply to the letter to the editor: the need for a new toxicity testing and risk analysis paradigm to implement REACH or any other large scale testing initiative, by Blaauboer BJ, Andersen ME (Arch Toxicol 2007; 81:385–387). Arch Toxicol 2007;81:895–896.

Hall B, Tozer S, Safford B, Coroama M, Steiling W, Leneveu-Duchemin MC, McNamara C, Gibney M: European consumer exposure to cosmetic products, a framework for conducting population exposure assessments. Food Chem Toxicol 2007;45:2097–2108.

Hartung T, Bremer S, Casati S, Coecke S, Corvi R, Fortaner S, Gribaldo L, Halder M, Hoffmann S, Janusch Roi A, Prieto P, Sabbioni E, Scott L, Worth A, Zuang V: A modular approach to the ECVAM principles on test validity. Altern Lab Anim 2004;32:467–472.

ICCG: ICCG/1/06 (2006): Inter Committee Coordination Group of Scientific Committees (ICCG) Position Statement 'Alternatives to animal tests'. Adopted by the ICCG during the ICCG meeting of 3 July 2006 after consultation of each of the non-food Scientific Committees.

ICCG (2007): Minutes of the 17th Meeting of the Inter Committee Coordination Group of Scientific Committees (ICCG) of 26 September 2007. Electronically available through http://ec.europa. eu/health/ph_risk/committees/coordination/docs/ coor_mi_017.pdf (consulted Feb 2008).

IPCS (1994): International Programme on Chemical Safety, Environmental Health Criteria 170: Assessing human health risks of chemicals: derivation of guidance values for health-based exposure limits. WHO, Geneva, 1994, available through http://www.inchem.org/documents/ehc/ehc/ehc170. htm (consulted Dec 2007).

IPCS (1999): International Programme on Chemical Safety, Environmental Health Criteria 210: Principles for the assessment of risks to human health from the exposure to chemicals. WHO, Geneva, 1999, available through http://www. inchem.org/documents/ehc/ehc/ehc210.htm (consulted Dec 2007).

Kroes R, Galli C, Munro I, Schilter B, Tran L, Walker R, Wurtzen G: Threshold of toxicological concern for chemical substances present in the diet: a practical tool for assessing the need for toxicity testing. Food Chem Toxicol 2000;38:255–312.

Kroes R, Renwick AG, Cheeseman M, Kleiner J, Mangelsdorf I, Piersma A, Schilter B, Schlatter J, van Schothorst F, Vos JG, Würtzen G: Structure-based thresholds of toxicological concern (TTC): guidance for application to substances present at low levels in the diet. Food Chem Toxicol 2004;42: 65–83.

Kroes R, Renwick AG, Feron V, Galli CL, Gibney M, Greim H, Guy RH, Lhuguenot JC, van de Sandt JJ: Application of the threshold of toxicological concern (TTC) to the safety evaluation of cosmetic ingredients. Food Chem Toxicol 2007;45:2533–2562.

Løkke S: The precautionary principle and chemicals regulation: past achievements and future possibilities. Environ Sci Pollut Res Int 2007;13:342–349.

Loretz LJ, Api AM, Barraj LM, Burdick J, Dressler WE, Gettings SD, Han Hsu H, Pan YH, Re TA, Renskers KJ, Rothenstein A, Scrafford CG, Sewall C: Exposure data for cosmetic products: lipstick, body lotion, and face cream. Food Chem Toxicol 2005;43:279–291.

Loretz LJ, Api AM, Barraj L, Burdick J, Davis de A, Dressler W, Gilberti E, Jarrett G, Mann S, Laurie Pan YH, Re T, Renskers K, Scrafford C, Vater S: Exposure data for personal care products: hairspray, spray perfume, liquid foundation, shampoo, body wash, and solid antiperspirant. Food Chem Toxicol 2006;44:2008–2018.

Loretz LJ, Api AM, Babcock L, Barraj LM, Burdick J, Cater KC, Jarrett G, Mann S, Pan YH, Re TA, Renskers KJ, Scrafford CG: Exposure data for cosmetic products: Facial cleanser, hair conditioner, and eye shadow. Food Chem Toxicol 2008;46: 1516–1524.

McNamara C, Rohan D, Golden D, Gibney M, Hall B, Tozer S, Safford B, Coroama M, Leneveu-Duchemin MC, Steiling W: Probabilistic modelling of European consumer exposure to cosmetic products. Food Chem Toxicol 2007;45:2086–2096.

OECD: OECD Guideline for testing of chemicals – Guideline 101 (1981a): UV-VIS Absorption Spectra. Organization for Economic Cooperation and Development, Paris, adopted 12 May 1981.

OECD: OECD Guideline for testing of chemicals – Guideline 110 (1981b): Particle Size Distribution/ Fibre Length and Diameter Distributions Organization for Economic Cooperation and Development, Paris, adopted 12 May 1981.

OECD: OECD Guideline for testing of chemicals – Guideline 114 (1981c): Viscosity of Liquids. Organization for Economic Cooperation and Development, Paris, adopted 12 May 1981.

OECD: OECD Guideline for testing of chemicals – Guideline 410 (1981d): Repeated Dose Dermal Toxicity: 21/28-Day Study. Organization for Economic Cooperation and Development, Paris, adopted 12 May 1981.

OECD: OECD Guideline for testing of chemicals – Guideline 411 (1981e): Subchronic Dermal Toxicity: 90-Day Study. Organization for Economic Cooperation and Development, Paris, adopted 12 May 1981.

OECD: OECD Guideline for testing of chemicals – Guideline 451 (1981f): Carcinogenicity Studies. Organization for Economic Cooperation and Development, Paris, adopted 12 May 1981.

OECD: OECD Guideline for testing of chemicals – Guideline 452 (1981g): Chronic Toxicity Studies. Organization for Economic Cooperation and Development, Paris, adopted 12 May 1981.

OECD: OECD Guideline for testing of chemicals – Guideline 453 (1981h): Combined Chronic Toxicity/ Carcinogenicity Studies. Organization for Economic Cooperation and Development, Paris, adopted 12 May 1981.

OECD: OECD Guideline for testing of chemicals – Guideline 417 (1984): Toxicokinetics. Organization for Economic Cooperation and Development, Paris, adopted 4 April 1984.

OECD: OECD Guideline for testing of chemicals – Guideline 482 (1986): Genetic Toxicology: DNA Damage and Repair, Unscheduled DNA Synthesis in Mammalian Cells in vitro. Organization for Economic Cooperation and Development, Paris, original guideline adopted 23 October 1986.

OECD: OECD Guideline for testing of chemicals – Guideline 102 (1995a): Melting Point/Melting Range. Organization for Economic Cooperation and Development, Paris, updated guideline adopted 27 July 1995.

OECD: OECD Guideline for testing of chemicals – Guideline 103 (1995b): Boiling Point. Organization for Economic Cooperation and Development, Paris, updated guideline adopted 27 July 1995.

OECD: OECD Guideline for testing of chemicals – Guideline 105 (1995c): Water Solubility. Organization for Economic Cooperation and Development, Paris, updated guideline adopted 27 July 1995.

OECD: OECD Guideline for testing of chemicals – Guideline 107 (1995d): Partition Coefficient (n-octanol/water): Shake Flask Method. Organization for Economic Cooperation and Development, Paris, updated guideline adopted 27 July 1995.

OECD: OECD Guideline for testing of chemicals – Guideline 109 (1995e): Density of Liquids and Solids. Organization for Economic Cooperation and Development, Paris, updated guideline adopted 27 July 1995.

OECD: OECD Guideline for testing of chemicals – Guideline 407 (1995f): Repeated Dose 28-Day Oral Toxicity Study in Rodents. Organization for Economic Cooperation and Development, Paris, adopted 12 May 1981, last updated 27 July 1995.

OECD: OECD Guideline for testing of chemicals – Guideline 471 (1997a): Bacterial Reverse Mutation Test. Organization for Economic Cooperation and Development, Paris, adopted 26 May 1983, last updated 21 July 1997.

OECD: OECD Guideline for testing of chemicals – Guideline 473 (1997b): In vitro Mammalian Chromosomal Aberration Test. Organization for Economic Cooperation and Development, Paris, updated 21 July 1997.

OECD: OECD Guideline for testing of chemicals – Guideline 474 (1997c): Mammalian Erythrocyte Micronucleus Test. Organization for Economic Cooperation and Development, Paris, adopted 21 July 1997.

OECD: OECD Guideline for testing of chemicals – Guideline 475 (1997d): Mammalian Bone Marrow Chromosomal Aberration Test. Organization for Economic Cooperation and Development, Paris, adopted 21 July 1997.

OECD: OECD Guideline for testing of chemicals – Guideline 476 (1997e): In vitro Mammalian Cell Gene Mutation Test. Organization for Economic Cooperation and Development, Paris, adopted 4 April 1984, last updated 21 July 1997.

OECD: OECD Guideline for testing of chemicals – Guideline 486 (1997f): Unscheduled DNA Synthesis (UDS) Test with Mammalian Liver Cells in vivo. Organization for Economic Cooperation and Development, Paris, adopted 21 July 1997.

OECD: OECD Guideline for testing of chemicals – Guideline 408 (1998): Repeated Dose 90-Day Oral Toxicity Study in Rodents. Organization for Economic Cooperation and Development, Paris, adopted 12 May 1981, last updated 21 September 1998.

OECD: OECD Guideline for testing of chemicals – Guideline 122 (2000): Partition Coefficient (n-Octanol/Water) pH-Metric Method for Ionisable Substances. Organization for Economic Cooperation and Development, Paris, draft guideline approved November 2000.

OECD: OECD Guideline for testing of chemicals – Guideline 414 (2001a): Prenatal Developmental Toxicity Study. Organization for Economic Cooperation and Development, Paris, adopted 12 May 1981, last updated 22 January 2001.

OECD: OECD Guideline for testing of chemicals – Guideline 416 (2001b): Two-Generation Reproduction Toxicity Study. Organization for Economic Cooperation and Development, Paris, adopted 26 May 1983, last updated 22 January 2001.

OECD: OECD Guideline for testing of chemicals – Guideline 420 (2001c): Acute Oral Toxicity – Fixed Dose Method. Organization for Economic Cooperation and Development, Paris, adopted 17 July 1992, last updated 17 December 2001.

OECD: OECD Guideline for testing of chemicals – Guideline 423 (2001d): Acute Oral toxicity – Acute Toxic Class Method. Organization for Economic Cooperation and Development, Paris, adopted 22 March 1996, last updated 17 December 2001.

OECD: OECD Guideline for testing of chemicals – Guideline 425 (2001e): Acute Oral Toxicity: Up-and-Down Procedure. Organization for Economic Cooperation and Development, Paris, adopted 21 September 1998, last updated 17 December 2001.

OECD: OECD Guideline for testing of chemicals – Guideline 404 (2002a): Acute Dermal Irritation/Corrosion. Organization for Economic Cooperation and Development, Paris, adopted 12 May 1981, last updated 24 April 2002.

OECD: OECD Guideline for testing of chemicals – Guideline 405 (2002b): Acute Eye Irritation/Corrosion. Organization for Economic Cooperation and Development, Paris, adopted 12 May 1981, last updated 24 April 2002.

OECD: OECD Guideline for testing of chemicals – Guideline 406 (2002c): Skin Sensitisation. Organization for Economic Cooperation and Development, Paris, adopted 12 May 1981, last updated 17 July 2002.

OECD: OECD Guideline for testing of chemicals – Guideline 429 (2002d): Skin Sensitisation: Local Lymph Node Assay. Organization for Economic Cooperation and Development, Paris, adopted 24 April 2002.

OECD: OECD Guideline for testing of chemicals – Guideline 117 (2004a): Partition Coefficient (n-octanol/water), HPLC Method. Organization for Economic Cooperation and Development, Paris, updated guideline adopted 13 April 2004.

OECD: OECD Guideline for testing of chemicals – Guideline 428 (2004b): Skin absorption: In vitro method. Organization for Economic Cooperation and Development, Paris, adopted 13 April 2004.

OECD: OECD Guideline for testing of chemicals – Guideline 430 (2004c): In vitro Skin Corrosion: Transcutaneous Electrical Resistance Test (TER). Organization for Economic Cooperation and Development, Paris, adopted 13 April 2004.

OECD: OECD Guideline for testing of chemicals – Guideline 431 (2004d): In vitro Skin Corrosion: Human Skin Model Test. Organization for Economic Cooperation and Development, Paris, adopted 13 April 2004.

OECD: OECD Guideline for testing of chemicals – Guideline 432 (2004e): In vitro 3T3 NRU phototoxicity test. Organization for Economic Cooperation and Development, Paris, adopted 13 April 2004.

OECD: OECD Guideline for testing of chemicals – Guideline 104 (2006a): Vapour Pressure. Organization for Economic Cooperation and Development, Paris, updated guideline adopted 23 March 2006.

OECD: OECD Guideline for testing of chemicals – Guideline 123 (2006b): Partition Co-efficient (1-Octanol/Water): Slow-Stirring method. Organization for Economic Cooperation and Development, Paris, adopted 23 March 2006.

OECD: OECD Guideline for testing of chemicals – Guideline 435 (2006c): In vitro Membrane Barrier Test Method for Skin Corrosion. Organization for Economic Cooperation and Development, Paris, adopted 19 July 2006.

OECD: OECD Guideline for testing of chemicals – Draft Guideline 487 (2007): In Vitro Mammalian Cell Micronucleus Test (MNvit). Organization for Economic Cooperation and Development, Paris, draft (3rd version) approved 13 December 2007.

Proctor DM, Gatto NM, Hong SJ, Allamneni KP: Mode-of-action framework for evaluating the relevance of rodent forestomach tumors in cancer risk assessment. Toxicol Sci 2007;98:313–326.

Renwick AG: Toxicokinetics in infants and children in relation to the ADI and TDI. Food Addit Contam 1998;15(suppl):17–35.

Renwick AG, Barlow SM, Hertz-Picciotto I, Boobis AR, Dybing E, Edler L, Eisenbrand G, Greig JB, Kleiner J, Lambe J, Müller DJG, Smith MR, Tritscher A, Tuijtelaars S, van den Brandt PA, Walker R, Kroes R: Risk characterization of chemicals in food and diet. Food Chem Toxicol 2003;41:1211–1271.

Rogiers V: Hazard, risk, risk assessment and risk perception: key factors in the safety evaluation of cosmetics; in Rogiers V, Pauwels M (eds): Proceedings of Safety Assessment of Cosmetics in the EU – Training Course, 16 April 2007. Brussels, Belgium, Book 1, pp 39–56.

Sand S, Victorin K, Filipsson AF: The current state of knowledge on the use of the benchmark dose concept in risk assessment. J Appl Toxicol 2008;28:405–421.

Sanner T, Dybing E, Willems MI, Kroese ED: A simple method for quantitative risk assessment of non-threshold carcinogens based on the dose descriptor T_{25}. Pharmacol Toxicol 2001;88:331–341.

SCCNFP: SCCNFP/0003/98 (1998): Guidelines on the use of human volunteers in the testing of potentially cutaneous irritant cosmetic ingredients or mixtures of ingredients, adopted by the plenary session of the SCCNFP of 25 November 1998.

SCCNFP: SCCNFP/0068/98 (1999a): Guidelines on the use of human volunteers in compatibility testing of finished cosmetic products, adopted by the SCC-NFP during the plenary session of 23 June 1999.

SCCNFP: SCCNFP/0245/99 (1999b): Opinion concerning basic criteria of the protocols for the skin compatibility testing of potentially cutaneous irritant cosmetic ingredients or mixtures of ingredients on human volunteers, adopted by the SCCNFP during the plenary session of 8 December 1999.

SCCNFP: SCCNFP/0120/99 (2000): Opinion concerning the predictive testing of potentially cutaneous sensitising cosmetic ingredients or mixtures of ingredients, adopted by the SCCNFP during the 11th plenary session of 17 February 2000.

SCCNFP: SCCNFP/0821/04 (2004a): Opinion concerning Acetaldehyde, adopted by the SCCNFP during the 28th plenary meeting of 25 May 2004.

SCCNFP: SCCNFP/0822/04 (2004b): Opinion concerning Furfural, adopted by the SCCNFP during the 28th plenary meeting of 25 May 2004.

SCCNFP: SCCNFP/0834/04 (2004c): Opinion concerning 'Report for establishing the timetable for phasing out animal testing for the purpose of the cosmetics directive' issued by ECVAM (30/04/2004), adopted by the SCCNFP on 1 July 2004 by means of the written procedure.

SCCP: SCCP/0902/05 (2005a): Opinion on the use of CI 26100 (CI Solvent Red 23) as a colorant in cosmetic products, adopted by the SCCP during the 4th plenary meeting of 21 June 2005.

SCCP: SCCP/0941/05 (2005b): Opinion on exposure to reactants and reaction products of oxidative hair dye formulations, adopted by the SCCP during the 6th plenary meeting of 13 December 2005.

SCCP: SCCP/0970/06 (2006a): Opinion on basic criteria for the in vitro assessment of dermal absorption of cosmetic ingredients – updated February 2006, adopted by the SCCP during the 7th plenary meeting of 28 March 2006.

SCCP: SCCP/1005/06 (2006b): The SCCP's Notes of Guidance for the Testing of Cosmetic Ingredients and their Safety Evaluation, adopted by the SCCP during the 10th plenary meeting of 19 December 2006.

SCCP: SCCP/1111/07 (2007a): Memorandum on the actual status of alternative methods on the use of experimental animals in the safety assessment of cosmetic ingredients in the European Union, adopted by the SCCP during the 12th plenary meeting of 19 June 2007.

SCCP (2007b): SCCP Opinion on the safety of nanomaterials in cosmetic products, adopted by the SCCP after the public consultation on the 14th plenary meeting of 18 December 2007.

SCENIHR: SCENIHR/002/05 (2005): Modified opinion (after public consultation) on the appropriateness of existing methodologies to assess the potential risks associated with engineered and adventitious products of nanotechnologies, adopted by the SCENIHR during the 10th plenary meeting of 10 March 2006.

Schilter B, Andersson C, Anton R, Constable A, Kleiner J, O'Brien J, Renwick AG, Korver O, Smit F, Walker R, Natural Toxin Task Force of the European Branch of the International Life Sciences Institute: Guidance for the safety assessment of botanicals and botanical preparations for use in food and food supplements. Food Chem Toxicol 2003;41:1625–1649.

Slovic P: Perception of risk. Science 1987;236:280–285.

Slovic P: Trust, emotion, sex, politics and science: surveying the risk-assessment battlefield. Risk Anal 1999;19:689–701.

Slovic P: The risk game. J Hazard Mater 2001;86:17–24.

Slovic P, Finucane ML, Peters E, MacGregor DG: Risk as analysis and risk as feelings: some thoughts about affect, reason, risk, and rationality. Risk Anal 2004; 24:311–322.

Travis KZ, Pate I, Welsh ZK: The role of the benchmark dose in a regulatory context. Regul Toxicol Pharmacol 2005;43:280–291.

WHO: Principles for the Safety Assessment of Food Additives and Contaminants in Food. IPCS Environmental Health Criteria 70, WHO, Geneva, 1987.

WHO: WHO/UNEP/ILO (2001). Approaches to Integrated Risk Assessment, Doc. WHO/IPCS/IRA/01/12 of December 2001.

WHO (2006): Dealing with uncertainty: setting the agenda for the 5th Ministerial Conference on environment and health, 2009, Copenhagen, Denmark, 15–16 December 2005, available through http://www.euro.who.int/Document/HMS/uncertainty_mtgrep.pdf (consulted Dec 2007).

2

3 **Critical Analysis of the Safety
Assessment of Cosmetic Ingredients
Performed at the European Level**

3. **Critical Analysis of the Safety Assessment of Cosmetic Ingredients Performed at the European Level**

Rogiers V, Pauwels M (eds): Safety Assessment of Cosmetics in Europe.
Curr Probl Dermatol. Basel, Karger, 2008, vol 36, pp 58–93

3.1 **Introduction**

According to the European cosmetic legislation, colourants, preservatives and UV filters are allowed in finished cosmetic products provided (a) they figure in Annex IV, VI or VII to the Cosmetic Products Directive [EU, 1976], respectively, and (b) they comply with the imposed restrictions and conditions. Substances taken up in Annex III are forbidden to be used outside the restrictions in concentrations and applications provided.

As stated in section 1.2.7, the procedure for inclusion of a cosmetic ingredient in the above-mentioned Annexes to the cosmetic legislation involves a full risk assessment by the SCCP. This independent scientific committee gives in particular advice to DG Enterprise and Industry that is ultimately responsible for risk management issues related to cosmetics, including the implementation of the EU cosmetic legislation. SCCNFP opinions can be downloaded from the Internet[1–3] and can be subdivided in two types:

(i) General opinions, providing state of the art information on particular problem areas in cosmetic safety assessment. They are mainly based on scientific literature and legislative texts. Examples are the SCC(NF)P's Notes of Guidance for the Testing of Cosmetic Ingredients and their Safety Evaluation [SCCNFP, 2000b, 2003b; SCCP, 2006g], DA issues [SCCNFP, 1999, 2003f; SCCP, 2006c], ethical considerations with regard to human testing [SCCP, 2005i], the use of alternative methods [SCCNFP, 2002b, 2004d], restrictions on CMR substances [SCCNFP, 2001c, 2004c; SCCP 2005g, 2005h], the safety assessment of hair dyes [SCCNFP, 2001d, 2002a, 2002d, 2003a, 2003c, 2004b], fragrance allergy in consumers [SCCNFP, 2000a, 2001a, 2001b, 2002e, 2003c, 2003h, 2003i; SCCP 2006h] and the safety of cosmetics for infants and children [SCCNFP, 2002c; SCCP, 2005e].

(ii) Ad hoc opinions, dealing with the safety assessment of specific substances already present or to be considered for inclusion in one of the Annexes to the Cosmetic Products Directive. They typically consist of an extended summary and a positive or negative evaluation of the combined physicochemical/toxicological dossiers submitted by industry. Negative evaluations often contain a request for additional data.

---

1 http://ec.europa.eu/health/ph_risk/committees/sccp/sccp_opinions_en.htm (consulted December 2007).

2 http://ec.europa.eu/health/ph_risk/committees/04_sccp/sccp_opinions_en.htm (consulted December 2007).

3 http://ec.europa.eu/health/ph_risk/committees/04_sccp/sccp_statements_en.htm (consulted December 2007).

This chapter focuses on the publicly available information of the SCC(NF)P ad hoc opinions issued between 2000 and 2006.

The distribution over the different cosmetic ingredient types (colourants, preservatives, UV filters, hair dyes, etc.) together with the outcome of the submissions (percentage of 'successful' industry submissions, resulting in a positive opinion) are studied as a function of time. The general content of the studied dossiers is discussed, together with the perceived quality of the individual studies and the type of additional data that are mostly requested. This information in light of the ensuing approval or rejection by the SCC(NF)P, helps to identify the main problem areas in the past and current EU safety assessments of cosmetic ingredients. As it appears indispensable to obtain some basic information on the internal organisation of the cosmetic industry, submitting dossiers, and the SCC(NF)P, evaluating them, the SCCP secretariat and the European cosmetic trade association Colipa were asked for some feedback. Colipa compiled a significant number of the submissions studied here.

Subsequently, a more in-depth analysis into the major identified problem area completes the chapter, together with a number of conclusions and recommendations.

3.2 General Analysis of Published SCC(NF)P Opinions (2000–2006)

3.2.1. Methodology

It is necessary to clarify a number of terms that will commonly be used throughout the current chapter.

SCC(NF)P Report Resulting in a Positive Opinion. Report concluding that the compound under study can be safely used in finished cosmetic products under the conditions laid down.

SCC(NF)P Report Resulting in a Negative Opinion. Report concluding that the compound under study cannot be declared as safe for use as a cosmetic ingredient and/or that additional data are required before a final statement can be made.

Full ad hoc Report. Report dealing with the general/complete toxicological profile of the compound(s) under investigation.

Partial ad hoc Report. Report dealing with specific toxicological aspects of the studied compound, e.g. its sensitizing [SCCNFP, 2004b, c; SCCP, 2005a, c, d, f, 2006a, e, f] or phototoxic potential [SCCNFP, 2003e, g; SCCP 2005b, 2006i].

Data Set. Information package on one single substance, either extracted from one SCC(NF)P report or representing a compilation of the data from multiple reports on the same substance.

Data Availability. Indication of the presence of a specific piece of information, irrespective of its level of detail or scientific validity.

Data Acceptance. Indication whether the presented piece of information was considered scientifically acceptable by the SCC(NF)P.

Overall, the study material consists of 109 SCCNFP and 76 SCCP opinions (full list in appendix 2a) issued between 17 February 2000 and 19 December 2006, dealing with 175 substances in total. No confidential data were used as all information came from opinions downloaded from the Committees' respective websites[4, 5]. Their content was translated into the pre-defined fields of a Microsoft Access database present at the Vrije Universiteit Brussel, Department of Toxicology. The initial aim was to create one entry per opinion, but the following cases necessitated a more complex structure, namely:

(i)   opinions dealing with multiple substances (full list in Appendix 2B): the concerned database entries were systematically split up so that the individual data sets per substance could be completed;

(ii) substances discussed in multiple opinions (full list in Appendix 2C): an additional database entry, compiling the information gathered over the years, was created for each individual substance.

Depending on the question raised, the appropriate combination of data sets was isolated and analyzed. Pivot tables and relevant graphs were obtained through Microsoft Excel.

When studying the influence of data availability and data acceptance on the positive/negative outcome of the opinion, both normal probability plots [Box et al., 1978] and the algorithm of Dong [Dong, 1993] were used to visually and statistically identify significant effects, respectively.

3.2.2. Number of Opinions

Between 2000 and 2006, the SCC(NF)P published more than 200 documents dealing with toxicological aspects of cosmetic ingredients[4, 5]. Out of these, 121 full ad hoc opinions were detailed enough (indication of individual tests performed, testing dates, guidelines followed, etc.) to allow extracting the required data sets. Their distribution over the years is displayed in table 1.

It is notable that only 3 data sets appear for the years 2000 and 2001, whereas the SCCNFP published 17 ad hoc reports over that period[6]. Although the full reports are available on a CD-ROM for internal use by the Commission services, the corresponding publicly available documents mainly consist of a brief summary. This low

---

4   http://ec.europa.eu/health/ph_risk/committees/sccp/sccp_opinions_en.htm (consulted December 2007).

5   http://ec.europa.eu/health/ph_risk/committees/04_sccp/sccp_opinions_en.htm (consulted December 2007).

6   http://ec.europa.eu/health/ph_risk/committees/sccp/sccp_opinions_en.htm (consulted December 2007).

Table 1. Number of data sets extracted from the SCC(NF)P full ad hoc reports

Year	Data sets
2000	1
2001	2
2002	11
2003	34
2004	25
2005	13
2006	35
Total	121

Table 2. Number (%) of data sets extracted out of 121 SCC(NF)P full ad hoc reports, displayed per cosmetic product type

Year	Hair dyes	Preservatives	UV filters	Colourants	Other functions[1]	Total per year
2000	0 (0)	0 (0)	1 (100)	0 (0)	0 (0)	1
2001	2 (100)	0 (0)	0 (0)	0 (0)	0 (0)	2
2002	4 (36)	1 (9)	0 (0)	0 (0)	6 (55)	11
2003	29 (85)	1 (3)	2 (6)	0 (0)	2 (6)	34
2004	18 (72)	1 (4)	2 (8)	0 (0)	4 (16)	25
2005	7 (54)	1 (8)	0 (0)	1 (7)	4 (31)	13
2006	26 (74)	0 (0)	4 (11)	0 (0)	5 (14)	35
Total	86 (71)	4 (3)	9 (7)	1 (1)	21 (17)	

[1]Bleaching, anti-dandruff and skin or hair conditioning agents, fragrance components, solvents, etc.

level of detail hampered in-depth analysis of the presented results explaining the low number of 3 data sets for 2000–2001.

In contrast, the years 2003 and 2006 display the highest numbers with 34 and 35 extractable data sets, respectively.

3.2.3. Ingredient Types

As displayed in table 2, more than 70% of the 121 full ad hoc SCC(NF)P opinions, issued between 2000 and 2006, deal with oxidative and/or non-oxidative hair dyes or hair dye components.

Undoubtedly, the dominant occurrence of hair dye products is a reflection of the fact that since 2001, the SCC(NF)P has on several occasions expressed its concern with regard to a potential link between the use of oxidative hair dyes and the development of leukemia and bladder cancer [SCCNFP, 2001d, 2004b; SCCP, 2005j]. The European Commission, the Member States and industry agreed upon a step-wise safety strategy[7] to regulate all hair dyes listed as ingredients in cosmetic products. Industry committed to submit by certain deadlines safety dossiers for a large number of hair dye components and possible mixtures [SCCP, 2006g], thus explaining the plenitude of hair dye-related opinions.

Since hair dye components dominate the scene, the question can be raised whether any further analysis beyond hair dyes of the 2000–2006 data sets reveals relevant information for cosmetic ingredients in general.

Therefore, it is necessary to emphasise that the only significant difference in data requirement between a hair dye and any other cosmetic ingredient resides in the type of data requested for mutagenicity/genotoxicity [SCCNFP, 2002d, 2003c; SCCP, 2006d]. The remaining part of a typical ingredient safety dossier for consideration by the SCC(NF)P covers the classical risk assessment process as applied for any other compound.

3.2.4. Success Rate

When plotted as a function of time, the number of positive SCC(NF)P before 2002 were ignored since they are based on a too low number of data sets to be meaningful. From 2003, where a minimum of only 6% success is seen, the success rate increases with a (provisional) maximum of 69% in 2006 (fig. 1). Therefore, a comparison between the data sets related to the 2003 negative opinions and those related to the 2006 positive opinions is expected to reveal a number of factors that may have contributed to the interesting shift.

For completeness, it must be mentioned that the adoption year of an SCC(NF)P report seldomly coincides with industry's submission year. Administrative and practical constraints have often led to delays of more than a year before the submitted dossiers were completely dealt with by the SCC(NF)P. Table 3 gives an overview of the time span between industry's submission and issue of a final report. It is based upon all opinions for which submission dates could be obtained (Colipa and SCCP secretariat), thus it covers more than the full ad hoc opinions under study in this paper.

From table 3, it appears that during the last years, from 2003 onwards, a tendency is noticed to reduce long delays. In particular, the maximum delays have dropped. As expected, table 3 also confirms that figure 1 does not represent the percentages of 'successful' industrial submissions over time, but solely the yearly SCC(NF)P acceptance rates.

---

7   All details available through http://europa.eu.int/comm/enterprise/cosmetics/html/cosm_ongoing_init.htm (consulted December 2007).

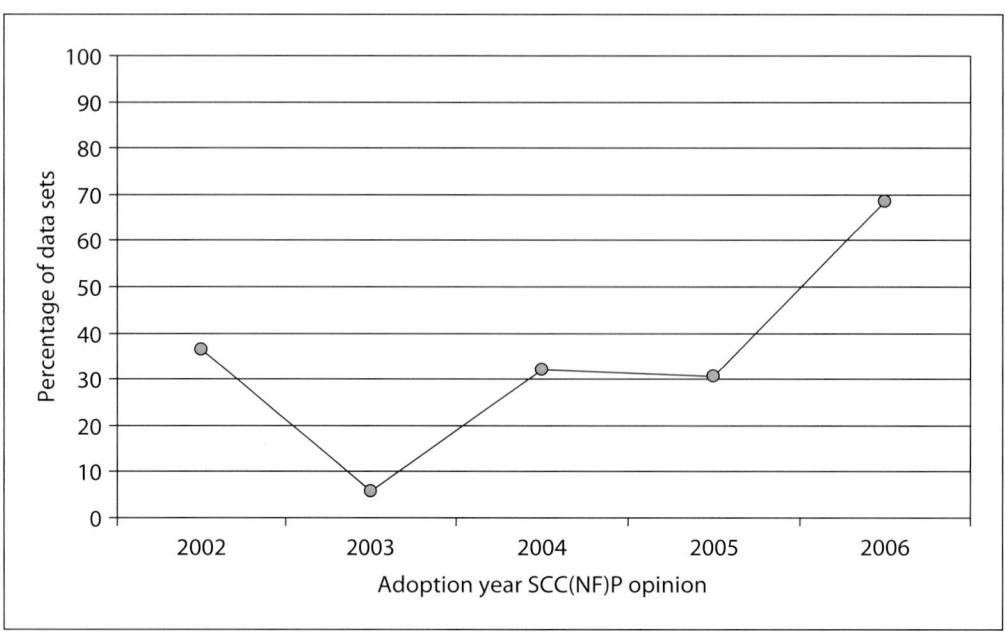

Fig. 1. Percentages of data sets from full ad hoc SCC(NF)P reports resulting in a positive opinion (plotted as a function of the reports' adoption years).

Table 3. Mean, minimum and maximum delays between industry's submission and issue of the final SCC(NF)P report

Year	Dossiers	Mean delay, years	Minimum, years	Maximum, years
2000	12	3.53	0.38	7.84
2001	3	3.63	1.24	4.95
2002	19	1.06	0.13	2.41
2003	45	1.88	0.19	8.48
2004	34	1.00	0.08	3.35
2005	21	1.32	0.45	3.71
2006	42	1.12	0.38	2.13

3.2.5. Content Comparison of Submissions Discussed in 2003 and 2006

In order to understand the observed shift from 6 to 69% of positive opinions between the years 2003 and 2006, the content of the SCC(NF)P documents was analyzed paying special attention to:

– data availability: the presence of specific individual studies,

Rogiers · Pauwels

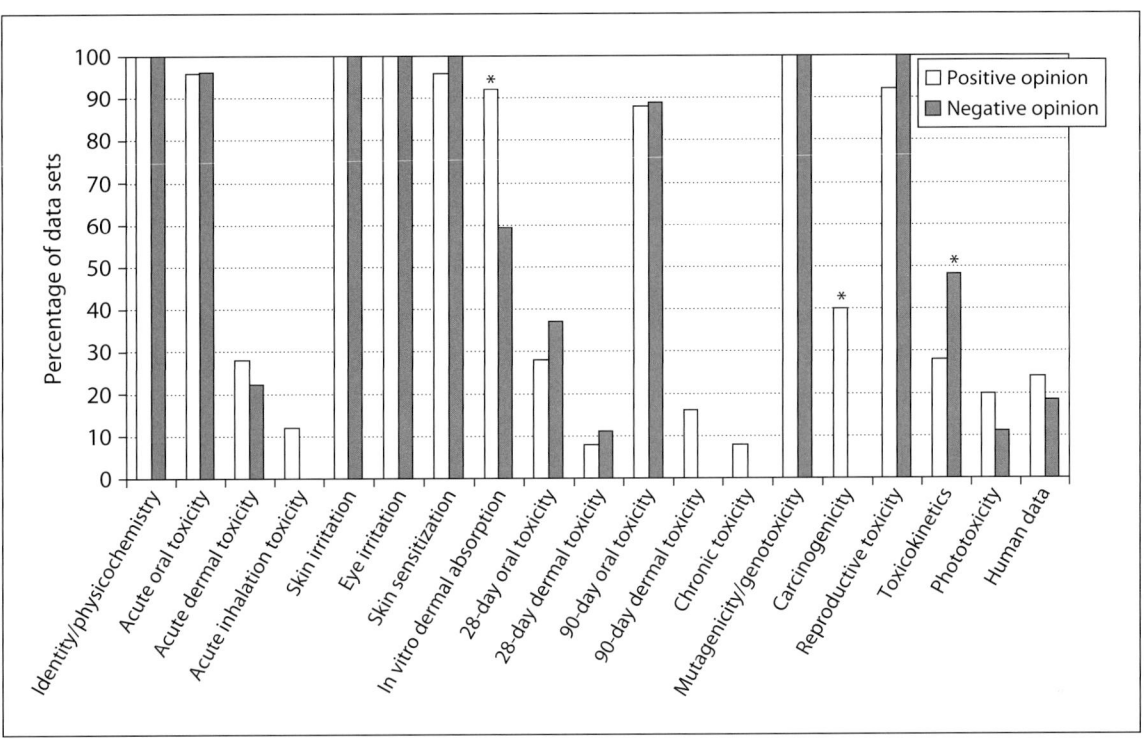

Fig. 2. Data availability (in percentage of number of data sets available) for substances declared as safe for use in 2006 (25 data sets) and for those that failed to do so in 2003 (27 data sets). Asterisk indicates statistically significant differences concerning data availability between negative and positive opinions according to Dong [1993].

– data acceptance: the perceived quality of those individual studies,
– required additional data: mostly required additional data as stated in the opinions.

a) Data Availability

The following studies are found to form part of more than 85% of the data sets leading to a positive opinion (fig. 2): (a) characterisation and physicochemical properties, (b) acute oral toxicity, (c) skin/eye irritation, (d) skin sensitisation, (e) in vitro DA, (f) 90-day oral toxicity, (g) mutagenicity/genotoxicity, (h) reproductive toxicity.

When comparing data sets leading to a positive opinion with those that failed to do so, significantly higher data availability is found for in vitro DA and carcinogenicity studies [Dong, 1993]. Toxicokinetic data display a significantly higher availability in submissions leading to a negative opinion (fig. 2).

This means that, with the exception of in vitro DA, data availability for studies a–h was similar, or in one isolated case even higher, for submissions leading to negative opinions. This indicates that data availability is not really an appropriate predictor of a positive outcome.

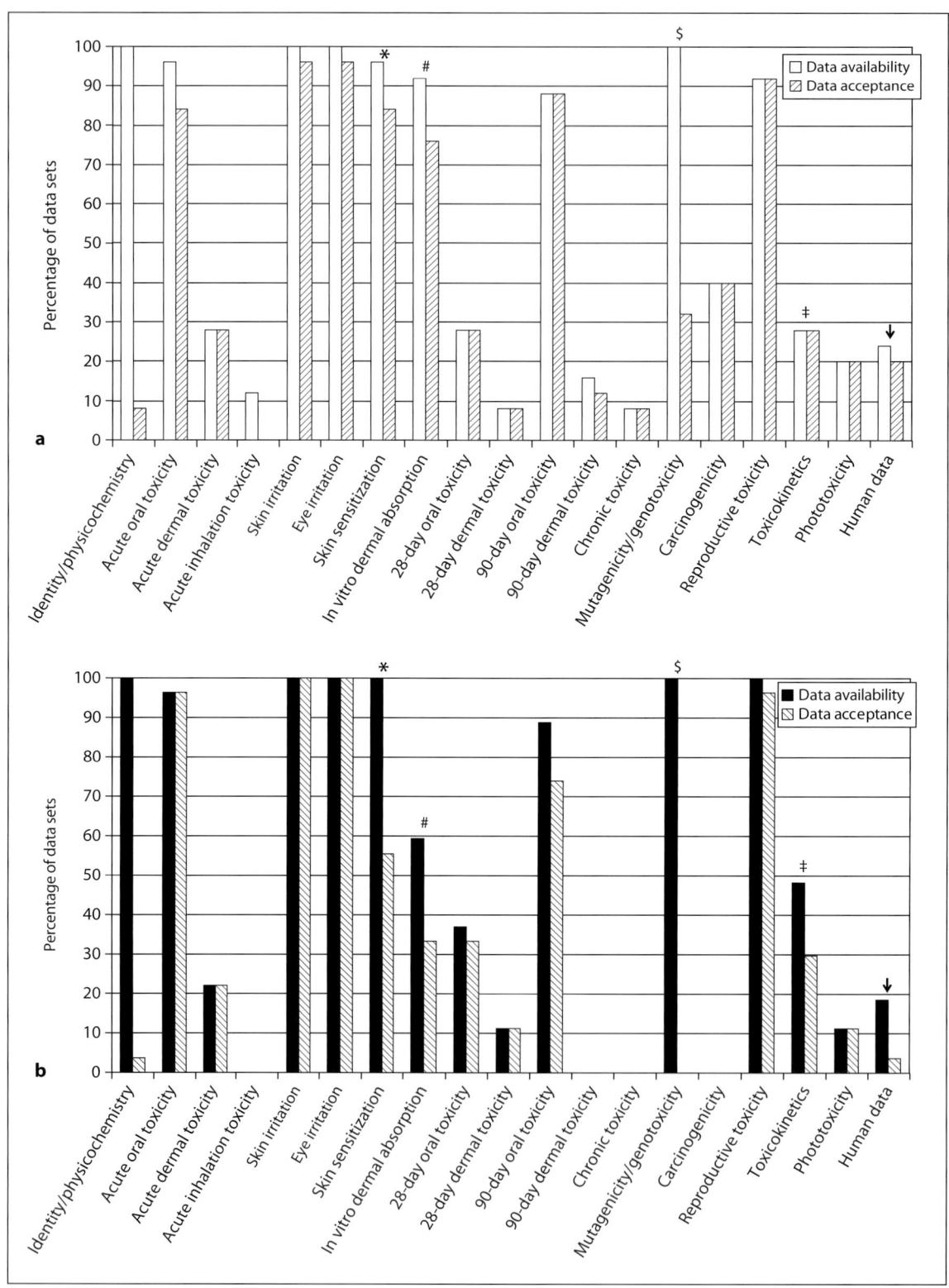

Rogiers · Pauwels

b) Data Acceptance

In figure 3, SCC(NF)P acceptance of each test is displayed next to the data availability percentages of figure 2. Please note that at this stage no in-depth investigation of specific flaws in the individual studies was performed.

A key observation is that data such as physicochemical characterisation and mutagenicity/genotoxicity, which occur in nearly every opinion, display very low acceptance levels. Even in submissions leading to a positive opinion, only 8% of the identity/physicochemistry and 32% of the mutagenicity/genotoxicity data sets were scientifically accepted. However, since they figure in nearly every industrial submission, one expects them to represent key information for the safety assessment of a cosmetic ingredient.

Statistical analysis reveals significant differences between data availability and data acceptance for positive and negative opinions in the areas of skin sensitisation, in vitro DA, mutagenicity/genotoxicity data, toxicokinetics and human data [Dong, 1993]. As the in vitro DA study is again identified as problematic, this area certainly requires further consideration.

c) Requested Additional Data

Since negative opinions are often linked to a request for additional data by the SCC(NF)P, it appears useful to extract the mostly required additional studies from the database for the years 2003 and 2006 (fig. 4).

A first finding is that in 2003 no extra data were requested for compounds declared safe for use, whereas in 2006 several ingredients were provisionally allowed awaiting additional data.

For substances not declared safe for use in 2003 and 2006, the mostly requested items show to be again identity/physicochemistry, in vitro DA and mutagenicity/genotoxicity data packages (fig. 4). Mutagenicity/genotoxicity dossiers were even claimed for a number of compounds that received a positive opinion in 2006.

d) Combining Data Availability, Data Acceptance and Additionally Requested Data

As mentioned earlier, dossiers of compounds resulting in a negative opinion did not systematically lack certain data, except for a significantly lower number of in vitro DA and carcinogenicity studies (fig. 3). Whereas DA tests are frequently additionally requested, this is not the case for carcinogenicity studies. Moreover, carcinogenicity studies only form part of 40% of the submissions leading to a positive opinion. A partial explanation for not requesting carcinogenicity studies may be the fact that other studies, such as 28-day or 90-day repeated toxicity studies provide a certain amount of secondary information which sufficiently answers the arising questions. Another

Fig. 3. Availability and acceptance of data sets leading to a positive opinion (2006; **a**) or a negative opinion (2003; **b**). *, #, $, ‡, ✦ indicate statistically significant differences between data availability and acceptance for negative and positive opinions according to Dong [1993].

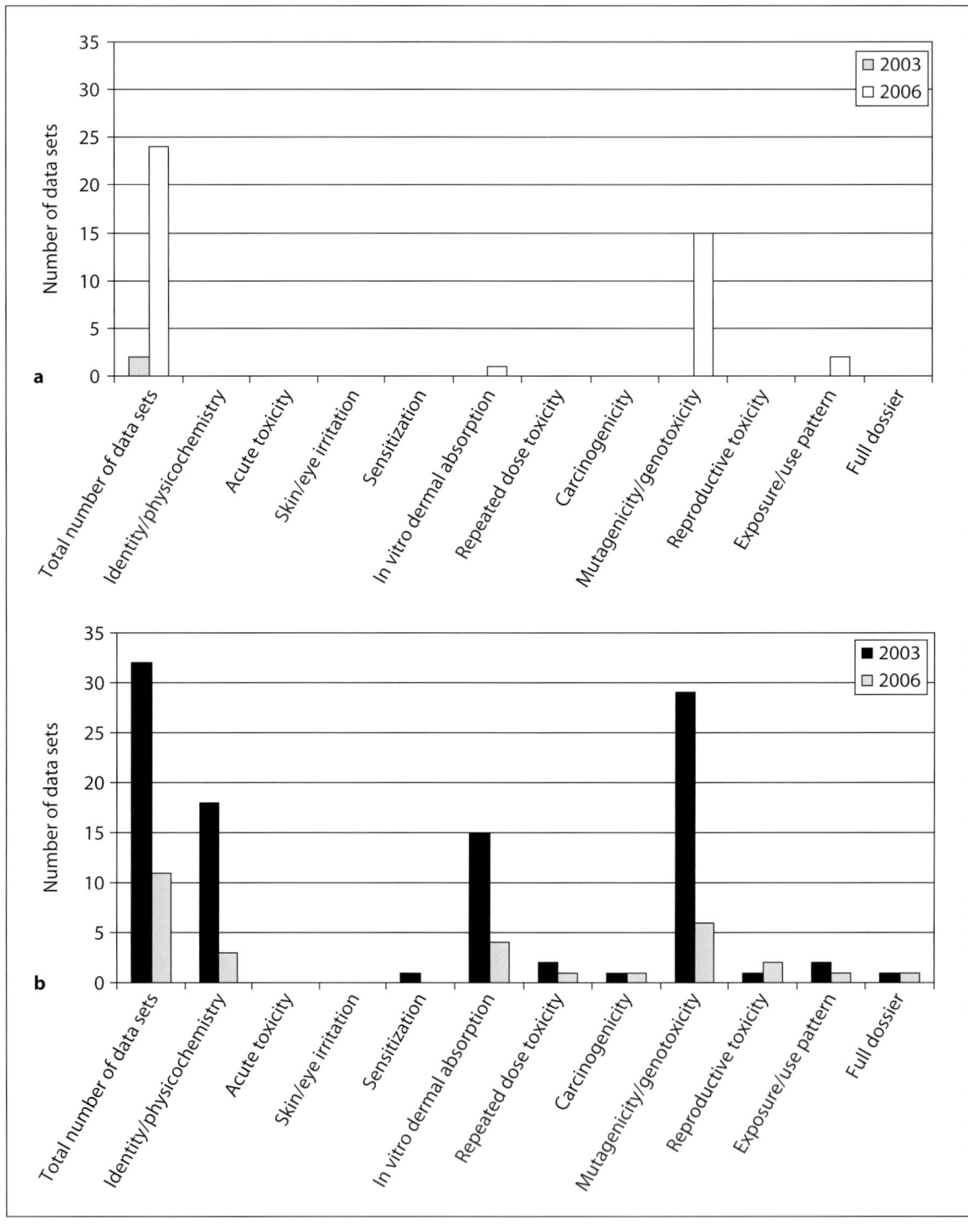

Fig. 4. Additional data requested by the SCC(NF)P in 2003 and 2006 for compounds found safe for use (**a**) or those that failed to do so (**b**).

Rogiers · Pauwels

reason resides in the increasing concern for the protection of experimental animals. From an ethical point of view, it does not appear acceptable to request additional studies that consume such a high number of animals if not absolutely necessary to safeguard human health. For DA, an in vitro alternative [OECD, 2004c] is available, which is not the case for carcinogenicity.

As far as data acceptance is concerned, two important findings can be extracted:

1 Some studies occurring in more than 85% of the dossiers declared safe for use show remarkably low acceptance levels. More specifically identity/physicochemistry and mutagenicity/genotoxicity score below par, with acceptance levels of 8% and 32%, respectively, for the positive opinions issued in 2006.

2 Comparison between data availability and data acceptance related to negative and positive opinions reveals statistically significant lower acceptance ratios for skin sensitisation studies, in vitro DA studies, mutagenicity/genotoxicity data, toxico-kinetics and human data in case of negative opinions. The shortlist of mostly requested additional data can be found back in the above-observed differences.

3.2.6. The Interplay between Industry and the SCC(NF)P over the Years

a) Observations

Although considered as a rather delicate subject, it cannot be denied that the overall acceptance of a submission may be influenced by the quality of the interplay between industry (e.g. Colipa) and the SCC(NF)P. Under ideal conditions, industry should be perfectly aware of the standards imposed by the Scientific Committee, whereas the Scientific Committee should, whenever possible, take into consideration the technical, ethical and logistic constraints with which the industry is confronted. Table 4 presents a flavour of some differences in points of view between both parties (out of discussions with senior scientists from both sides).

The discussion points of table 4 are not restricted to the safety assessment of cosmetic ingredients by the SCCP, but can, in our opinion, rather be encountered in any registration/authorisation/notification procedure which involves industry data submission to a competent authority.

In addition, bureaucracy at both sides aggravates the situation. Submissions often need to go through different steps and administrations at the Commission level before they reach the scientific experts. It is not unthinkable that this process may contribute to longer delays and in the worst case to loss of information or documents. Simultaneously, industry's delivery of additionally requested information often is perceived as taking too much time and in some cases there even is no follow-up at all. Another reoccurring problem is that submissions are regularly supported by different industrial partners, who, independently from each other, introduce new elements, which inevitably may increase the risk for regrettable misunderstandings.

Table 4. Some potential differences in points of view between industry and the SCC(NF)P

Topic	Point of view of SCC(NF)P	Point of view of industry
Delay for study of dossiers (see also table 3)	mean period of 1 year is quite acceptable	1 year is acceptable, but the few dossiers that take 3 years still may have a large economical impact
Changes in requirements over the years	new requirements enter into force immediately, they are necessary to follow the most recent advances in toxicological knowledge	dossiers should not need to fulfil requirements which were not yet into force on the date of submission, unless a serious health risk can be identified
Wording of opinions	opinions have been formulated with care and in the correct wording	many of the statements may become problematic when taken out of context (e.g. 'cannot be declared as safe' or 'safe use cannot be guaranteed') and the exact requirements and/or expectations are not always clear
Additional data requested	experts have the right to ask for additional data if they estimate them indispensable for the final safety assessment	all the missing data should by preference be listed after a first study of the dossier by the secretariat, unless the additional data themselves trigger further requests; moreover, experts should justify the necessity of the additional data with scientific arguments
Importance of hearings	hearings are useful, but also time-consuming, wherefore they need to be restricted to important dossiers and to discussions at the scientific level (no lobbying)	face to face hearings allow to clear up misinterpretation from both sides in the shortest possible time span

There is no simple solution to the above problems, but both at the Commission and at the industrial level, some considerable efforts were made over the past 5 years.

b) Actions Taken by Colipa for Submitting Hair Dye-Related Dossiers
Viewing the magnitude of the number of submissions required to fulfil the demands of the Commission's strategy on hair dyes[8], industry decided to set up an organised consortium, thus outsourcing the compilation of the hair dye and hair dye components dossiers. Although open to any hair dye supplier/manufacturer, the work is reported to be performed by the largest economic players on the European market. They made up a set of specific criteria and introduced some harmonisation in the

---

8   All details available through http://europa.eu.int/comm/enterprise/cosmetics/html/cosm_ongoing_init.htm (consulted December 2007).

format of the dossiers. As the first dossiers prepared by this industry consortium were introduced in the year 2003, their outcome should be reflected in the 2005–2006 opinions (according to table 3).

c) Organisation within the SCCP

In order to guide industry as much as possible, the SCC(NF)P updates its Notes of Guidance on a regular basis [SCCNFP, 2000b, 2003b; SCCP, 2006g]. This document not only displays the basic requirements for the inclusion of a substance in the Annexes to the Cosmetic Products Directive, but it also contains chapters dealing with specific problems and/or product types, together with a structured standard format of the opinions.

With the aim of ensuring transparency, SCC(NF)P opinions are published on the Committees' Websites[9–11]. In some cases, public consultation is foreseen before the final opinion is formulated. These public consultations are announced through the cosmetic section of the Website of DG Enterprise[12].

The specific working group on hair dyes within the SCC(NF)P has tackled the increased workload by dividing the different parts of the dossiers among chosen experts and by outsourcing a part of the work to neutral experts in order to reduce the delays for industry (information from SCCP secretariat).

d) Steps Taken by the EU Commission

To improve exchange of information between EU scientific committees in the field of consumer safety, the ICCG was founded. Made up of the chairs and vice-chairs of the SCCP, SCHER and SCENIHR, the ICCG aims at ensuring the harmonisation of risk assessment procedures and the efficient exchange of information between scientific committees. As can be deduced from its minutes[13], the ICCG also collaborates with other Community agencies and institutions such as EFSA, EMEA and the European Parliament.

In addition, to assess the value of its existing scientific committees in the Commission's decision making, DG SANCO recently outsourced a study on the rules of procedure and the activities of inter alia the SCCP [Levitt, 2006]. Among the recommendations mentioned in the report, the advice is present to ensure that the responsibility of the follow-up of timely reception of data and of the necessary literature searches is clearly defined. Furthermore, it is advised that the Commission increases time and human resources in order to improve scientific quality and better divide the technical handling of dossiers. It is also recommended that the tasks of the secretariats should be reviewed.

---

9   http://ec.europa.eu/health/ph_risk/committees/sccp/sccp_opinions_en.htm (consulted December 2007).

10 http://ec.europa.eu/health/ph_risk/committees/04_sccp/sccp_opinions_en.htm (consulted December 2007).

11 http://ec.europa.eu/health/ph_risk/committees/04_sccp/sccp_statements_en.htm (consulted December 2007).

12 http://ec.europa.eu/enterprise/cosmetics/index_en.htm (consulted December 2007).

13 http://ec.europa.eu/health/ph_risk/committees/coordination/coor_minutes_en.htm (consulted December 2007).

3.3 Analysis of Three Contentious Areas in the EU Safety Assessment of Cosmetic Ingredients

The study described in section 3.2 was partly designed to identify the main problem areas in the past and current EU safety assessments of cosmetic ingredients. It therefore examined general content of industry submissions studied by the SCC(NF)P between 2000 and 2006, together with the perceived quality of the individual studies and the type of additional data that were mostly requested by the Committees. As already mentioned, the results of the analysis indicate that identity/physicochemistry, DA and mutagenicity/genotoxicity are areas which require some in-depth investigation, as they show to have influenced the overall outcome of the SCC(NF)P opinions over the years.

Therefore, the database was extended to enable detailed searches in these three particular fields.

3.3.1. Methodology

Use was made of the Microsoft Access database present at the Vrije Universiteit Brussel, Department of Toxicology, as described in section 3.2. It contains information extracted from 185 SCC(NF)P opinions issued between 2000 and 2006, dealing with 175 substances in total.

The Microsoft Access database and the Microsoft Excel files linked to it were extended with the following features:

For identity/physicochemistry:
– presence of individual data (Log P_{ow}, density, molecular weight, purity, etc.)
– identification and occurrence of flaws reported

For DA and mutagenicity/genotoxicity:
– details on individual tests performed (in vivo/in vitro, species involved)
– dates of individual tests and numbers of animals used (in vivo)
– identification and occurrence of flaws reported
– details on use of DA in calculations of MoS

3.3.2. Identity and Physicochemistry

a) Detailed SCC(NF)P Requirements
The SCCP Notes of Guidance [SCCP, 2006g] emphasise that physical and chemical properties of ingredients are considered as crucial information, since they may be able to predict certain toxicological properties.

Table 5. Shortcomings in identity/physicochemical data packages as mentioned in the SCC(NF)P opinions (2002–2006)

Flaws reported	Data sets	
	n	%
Incomplete stability data	84	50
Impurities not stated for all batches	72	43
Inadequate basic physicochemical properties set	65	39
Sum of purity and impurities ≠ 100%	29	17
Incomplete solubility data	27	16

The minimal specifications for any ingredient to be evaluated by the SCCP are stated to be: (1) chemical identity, (2) physical form, (3) molecular weight, (4) characterisation and purity of the chemical, (5) characterisation of the impurities or accompanying contaminants, (6) solubility, (7) partition coefficient (Log P_{ow}).

Already in earlier versions of the SCCNFP Notes of Guidance [SCCNFP 2000b; SCCNFP, 2003b], it was emphasised that small changes in the nature of impurities can considerably alter the toxicity of substances. Therefore, the degree of purity has always been asked to be specified, as well as an identification of the nature of any toxicologically significant impurities that may be present and their concentration.

b) Mostly Reported Shortcomings in SCC(NF)P Reports

Although identity and physicochemical data form part of every submitted dossier, they display extremely low acceptance levels (8 and 3% in submissions leading to a positive or negative opinion, respectively).

A more in-depth search reveals that of the 194 industry submissions discussed by the SCC(NF)P between 2002 and 2006, 167 identity/physicochemical data packages were declared incomplete and/or of inferior quality. Frequently reoccurring remarks are displayed in table 5.

Incomplete stability data refer to the stability in envisaged finished products, in the receptor fluid used in DA studies, or in specific solvents used in toxicity tests.

As far as the identification/characterisation of the compound under study is concerned, the impurity profile appears to be a major problem. In first instance, the sum of purity and impurities does not always result to 100% (17% of the data sets). Secondly, and more importantly, impurity profiles are often not reported for every batch mentioned in the submission. The latter showed to be a problem in 43% of the data sets.

With regard to basic physicochemical properties, a commonly encountered remark is that the stated properties (pH, density, Log P_{ow}, etc.) were not measured, but extracted from the literature. Especially the Log P_{ow} is a parameter that is required to be measured according to an officially accepted methodology [EU, 1992; OECD, 1995, 2000c, 2004b, 2006].

In addition to the flaws mentioned in table 5, the SCC(NF)P regularly (23 data sets) requested additional data with regard to the exact nitrosamine content in the final formulation (for secondary amines) or for data on the potential release of p-phenylene diamine by azo compounds. The occurrence of these requests is directly linked to the dominance of hair dyes in the product types studied between 2002 and 2006, since secondary amines or azo structures are common features in hair dye substances.

3.3.3. The in vitro Dermal Absorption Study

a) Official Guidance, Including SCC(NF)P Requirements
At the European level, official guidance was given in the 'Basic Criteria for the in vitro assessment of percutaneous absorption of cosmetic ingredients' of the SCCNFP [SCCNFP, 1999] and the 'Guidance document on dermal absorption' of the DG SANCO, [1999]. Whereas the former document specifically addressed DA of cosmetic ingredients, the latter was issued to support the EU risk assessment process of plant protection products. Both documents have been updated over the years until their most recent versions became available in 2006 [SCCP, 2006c] and 2004 [DG SANCO, 2004], respectively. Within that same period of time the OECD published the general 'Technical Guideline 428: the in vitro skin absorption method' [OECD, 2000b, 2004c], accompanied by its 'Guidance document for the conduct of skin absorption studies' [OECD, 2000a, 2004a]. Joining on to the OECD, the IPCS drafted its 'Environmental Health Criteria EHC 235: Dermal Absorption' in 2006 [IPCS, 2006]. This multitude of guidelines and their updates inevitably induced some uncertainties with regard to the correct performance of the in vitro DA assay. Although the SCCP, DG SANCO, OECD and the IPCS describe the same type of study, there are some differences in the protocol details and there have been some changes over the past 8 years.

b) General Principles of the in vitro Dermal Absorption Study
The purpose of the in vitro DA study is to obtain information on the passage of a chemical compound across the skin. In the common experimental setting (fig. 5), a skin sample is placed between the upper and lower chambers of a diffusion cell. An in-use mimicking (finite) or excessive (infinite) dose of the test sample is subsequently applied on top of the skin (upper chamber or donor compartment), which on its turn is in contact with the receptor fluid filling the lower chamber of the cell (receptor compartment).

Diffusion cells may display static or flow-through designs, meaning that the receptor fluid either remains in the lower chamber as a static phase, or is continuously renewed by flowing through the chamber. Although for full details reference is

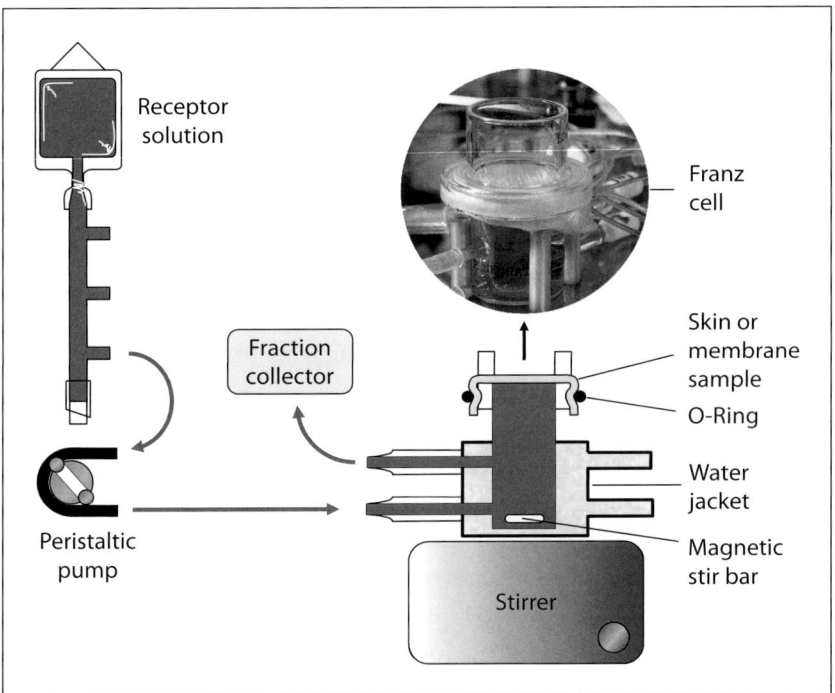

Fig. 5. Schematic representation of the experimental setting of an in vitro dermal absorption study making use of a Franz cell. Adapted from Steiling [2007].

made to the official guidance documents, some relevant features are mentioned below.

– With regard to the type of skin sample used, all guidelines express preference for human or pig skin, ideally split-thickness (200–500 μm) or full-thickness skin (up to 1,000 μm).

– The number of skin samples to be tested is by far the most fluctuating parameter in the available protocols, going from 4 replicates per test preparation [OECD, 2000a, b] to minimum 6 evaluable samples from each of at least 3 donors [SCCP, 2006c].

– The test substance should ideally be radio-labelled and needs to be well characterised.

– There is general agreement that the amount of substance applied is 2–10 mg/cm^2 for solids or 10 μl/cm^2 for liquids in finite dose experiments and >10 mg/cm^2 or 100 μl/cm^2 in infinite dose experiments. Hair dyes are normally applied at 20 mg/cm^2 [SCCP, 2006c].

– All guidelines advise testing of different concentrations in different typical formulations. Due to the supposed inverse relation between the compound's concentration and the percentage of absorption, the lowest in-use concentration is mentioned [DG SANCO, 2004], whereas the highest in-use concentration is considered necessary to cover the complete range of human exposure [SCCP, 2006c].

- The contact time with the skin sample mimics in-use conditions. In most cases it is 24 h. For cosmetic rinse-off products and hair dyes, a contact time of 15–45 min is often encountered [SCCP, 2006c].
- Every guidance describes the nature and composition of the receptor fluid to be of key importance. It should not only be physiologically conducive and not affect the skin sample's integrity, but the test substance must be sufficiently soluble in it.
- No preference is expressed for the static or flow through design. Both are acceptable, with the knowledge that in static systems the concentration of the compound in the receptor fluid must at all times remain 10 times below its saturation level and that flow-through systems may be less sensitive for poorly absorbed compounds.
- As far as sampling frequency is concerned, an average of 6–12 time points in 24 h should allow the requested graphical representation of the absorption profile.
- At the end of the test, skin measurements are ideally performed separately for stratum corneum (usually by tape stripping), epidermis (without stratum corneum) and dermis. The amount of test substance retrieved in the stratum corneum is generally not considered as dermally absorbed.
- The sum of the percentages measured in donor chamber, rinsing solution, skin surface, skin preparation and full apparatus rinse should lead to a recovery of the applied substance of $100 \pm 15\%$.
- Expression of the final results usually is in $\mu g/cm^2 \cdot h$ (steady state flux J_{ss}, i.e. the rate of compound transfer through the skin per skin surface area and time unit) or in cm/h (permeability coefficient K_p, i.e. the steady-state flux divided by the concentration of the test substance). Both parameters assume the achievement of a steady state (equilibrium) in the DA diffusion process, meaning that an infinite dose has been applied. In finite dose experiments, DA will most frequently be expressed in percent (percentage of the applied dose) or in $\mu g/cm^2$ (the amount of substance absorbed per skin surface area).

c) Mostly Reported Shortcomings in SCC(NF)P Reports
In order to analyze the specific problems related to the SCC(NF)P assessment of DA studies, the 194 industry submissions discussed by the SCC(NF)P between 2002 and 2006 were screened for the presence and acceptance of the study. The results are displayed in table 6.

This first analysis shows that the majority of DA studies submitted to the SCC(NF)P were in vitro assays. More than 45% of these studies were considered scientifically unacceptable.

The main part (>75%, individual data not shown) of those in vitro studies were performed after 1999, thus after the publication of the first SCCNFP basic criteria for the performance of in vitro DA studies [SCCNFP, 1999].

The major comments expressed by the SCC(NF)P and their occurrence are displayed in table 7.

Table 6. DA studies mentioned in SCC(NF)P opinions (2002–2006), their occurrence and acceptance level

Type of test	Data sets	DA data accepted
In vitro study (human skin)	61	40
In vitro study (pig skin)	35	12
In vitro study (rat skin)	1	0
In vivo study (human)	16	5
In vivo study (rat)	37	17

Table 7. Flaws in the 45 data sets with non-accepted in vitro DA studies, as mentioned in SCC(NF)P opinions (2002–2006)

Flaws mentioned	Data packages	
	n	%
Other than the in-use concentration tested	16	36
Solubility in receptor fluid unknown	15	33
Skin compartments not separated for individual measurement	14	31
Dosage too high	13	29
Wrong receptor fluid	12	27
Insufficient skin samples tested	11	24
High variability/lacking or inappropriate statistics	9	20
Overall inadequate test description	8	18
Lack of recovery data	7	16
Composition of formulation not given	6	13
Insufficient contact time	6	13

Lack of testing with the in-use concentration and an exaggerated dosage level are flaws that reoccur over the whole study period (2002–2006) for pig and human in vitro DA studies. All other flaws can predominantly be retrieved in opinions expressed after 2003. This observation is quite unexpected, since both the original SCCNFP 'Basic Criteria for the in vitro assessment of percutaneous absorption of cosmetic ingredients' [SCCNFP, 1999] and its first update [SCCNFP, 2003] draw the attention to those particular points and contain guidance to avoid these.

The incorrect separation of the skin samples was mainly encountered with pig skin.

Table 8. Types of DA values used for MoS calculations in SCC(NF)P opinions (2002–2006)

Value	Opinions	
	DA expressed in $\mu g/cm^2$	DA expressed as a % of the applied dose
Mean	7	6
Highest value	20	2
Mean $\pm$ 2 SD	1	0
100% assumed	–	4
SCCP estimate	0	1
SUM	28	13

d) The Use of Dermal Absorption Data in Margin of Safety Calculations

In the safety assessment of cosmetic ingredients, DA may be expressed as a percentage of the applied dose (%) and/or as the amount that may be absorbed per skin surface unit ($\mu g/cm^2$). These values are subsequently used to calculate the compound's SED and its MoS. On a case by case basis, the SCC(NF)P decides which numeric value of the in vitro DA study is used for further calculation.

The SCCP Notes of Guidance also mention that 'in case an insufficient number of skin samples has been tested, the highest absorption value will be taken into account, otherwise the mean value $\pm$ 2 SD will be used and if results are derived from an inadequate in vitro study, the default value of 100% absorption could be applied' [SCCP, 2006g].

Of the 41 cases in which in vitro DA was used for the calculation of the MoS, the SCC(NF)P expressed the DA value as the amount per surface unit in 28 cases and as a percentage of the applied dose in 13 cases. Table 8 provides some more detail.

Overall, DA was more often expressed in $\mu g/cm^2$ than in percent. In the former case, the highest value measured in the in vitro assay was mostly used for calculation, whereas for the latter, the mean value was preferred.

Nevertheless, in the event of a well-performed finite dose study, the choice between the $\mu g/cm^2$ and the percent value to be used for the calculation of the MoS is not expected to significantly influence the outcome. To challenge this hypothesis, the SCC(NF)P opinions for which the MoS was calculated and both percent and $\mu g/cm^2$ DA values were available, were gathered. The second calculation of the MoS (based upon the value that was not chosen by the SCC(NF)P was systematically performed and compared with the original value (see MoS expressed in percent and in $\mu g/cm^2$ in table 9). This exercise shows that in the majority of the cases, both MoS values were in the same order of magnitude or at least both >100, thus classifying the ingredient under study in the same category (safe-unsafe).

Two exceptions (factor >200 of difference) were linked to in vitro pig skin studies where the amount applied was excessively high (1,000 mg/cm^2). As stated in the SCCP Notes of Guidance, the use of a percent value from assays in which the intended use conditions are exceeded leads to an underestimation of the systemic exposure [SCCP, 2006g]. This is indeed the case in the two exceptions of table 9 where the MoS is clearly overestimated when using the percent value.

A third exception concerned a compound that appeared to be readily absorbed through the skin ($\pm$64 µg/cm^2 or 55%). Here, the use of the µg/cm^2 value generates a lower MoS value. The test description in the concerned opinion, however, was not detailed enough to explain the observed difference [SCCP, 2006i].

e) Additional in vitro Dermal Absorption Issues

Despite having obtained regulatory acceptance by worldwide official instances, the in vitro DA test has never been formally validated according to the principles followed by ECVAM (see 2.3.1). With respect to the OECD Guideline 428, it was reported that studies undertaken using appropriate in vitro experimental conditions had produced data for a wide range of chemicals that demonstrated the usefulness of the method [OECD, 2004a]. Nevertheless, the organisation acknowledges that the in vitro method may not be applicable for all situations and classes of chemicals and that in certain cases an in vivo follow-up study may be necessary [OECD, 2004c].

Besides the different points of importance mentioned by the SCCP, a multitude of variables that affect the in vivo and/or in vitro DA rate of a chemical, can be identified by going through the current literature. They are manifold and include variables related to as well test compounds as skin samples and external influences [van de Sandt et al., 2004; Nohynek et al., 2005; Buist et al., 2005; Wilkinson et al., 2006; Akomeah et al., 2007; Basketter et al., 2007; van de Sandt et al., 2007].

Under the wings of a 3-year European project called EDETOX[14], 10 European laboratories independently measured the in vitro DA of three compounds with diverging physicochemical properties. The intra-laboratory coefficients of variation were determined for the maximum absorption rate and for the percentage of test compound measured in the receptor fluid. They reached levels up to 111%. Also the recovery rate of 100 $\pm$ 15% appeared impossible to reach in some cases. According to the authors, the high coefficients of variations were mainly attributed to human interindividual variability in skin (sample)-related variables and anatomical site. The text mentioned that 'at least three samples are recommended and if an outlier is present, up to six samples are needed' [EDETOX, 2004]. However, it is not specified whether this concerns three samples per donor, per concentration or simply per experiment.

For lipophilic compounds, skin thickness proved to be an additional critical variable. With regard to the failing of matching the recovery requirements, it is explained

---

14 EU Framework Programme 5, Evaluations and predictions of DA of toxic chemicals, Project Number: QLKA-2000-00196, 2001–2004.

Table 9. Overview of MoS calculations in SCC(NF)P opinions (2002–2006): cases where DA values were available both in % and in $\mu g/cm^2$

DA method	DA %	DA $\mu g/cm^2$	mg/cm² applied	Thickness skin	DA used by SCC(NF)P	MoS DA in $\mu g/cm^2$	DA in %	Difference (factor)
In vivo human	0.19	4.47	no data	n.a.	$\mu g/cm^2$	77	210	2.7
In vitro human	5.00	1.27	no data	epidermal membrane	%	405	150	2.5^{-1}
In vitro pig	0.04	0.10	2	full thickness	$\mu g/cm^2$	6,667	15,873	2.3
In vitro human	4.72	0.09	2	split thickness	%	128	257	2.0
In vitro pig	0.26	13.20	1,000	split thickness	$\mu g/cm^2$	17,143	3,481,319	**203.1**
In vitro pig	0.60	35.50	1,000	full thickness	$\mu g/cm^2$	1,522	360,000	**236.5**
In vitro human	1.26	3.87	20	full thickness	$\mu g/cm^2$	1,111	1,488	1.3
In vitro human	0.90	0.89	20	not stated	$\mu g/cm^2$	20,000	76,191	3.8
In vitro human	3.00	4.01	20	split thickness	$\mu g/cm^2$	106	147	1.4
In vitro human	1.70	4.56	20	full thickness	$\mu g/cm^2$	4,150	5,176	1.3
In vitro human	1.02	4.33	20	split thickness	$\mu g/cm^2$	392	588	1.5
In vitro human	1.30	1.00	20	split thickness	$\mu g/cm^2$	125	309	2.5
In vitro human	0.50	1.04	20	split thickness	$\mu g/cm^2$	833	1,200	1.4
In vitro human	0.07	0.25	20	split thickness	$\mu g/cm^2$	1,667	2,143	1.3
In vitro human	6.10	3.22	20	split thickness	$\mu g/cm^2$	1,331	1,967	1.5
In vitro pig	1.10	2.07	10	split thickness	$\mu g/cm^2$	4,167	3,030	1.4^{-1}
In vitro human	1.26	2.52	20	split thickness	$\mu g/cm^2$	170	680	4.0
In vitro human	0.80	2.73	5	split thickness	$\mu g/cm^2$	109	619	5.7
In vitro human	55.20	63.80	5	not stated	%	10	102	**10.2**
In vitro human	1.31	8.21	20	not stated	$\mu g/cm^2$	1,042	1,527	1.5
In vitro human	0.01	0.04	20	not stated	$\mu g/cm^2$	250,000	874,636	3.5
In vitro human	1.90	1.01	20	split thickness	$\mu g/cm^2$	8,333	12,632	1.5
In vitro human	3.10	7.14	20	split thickness	$\mu g/cm^2$	241	323	1.3

Exceptions are indicated in **bold**.

that $25\ \mu l/cm^2$ is considered the minimum volume to produce a homogeneous distribution on the skin surface. The technical difficulty of evenly spreading small volumes on the skin surface, as commonly requested for regulatory purposes to mimic in-use conditions, is considered a potential cause for low recovery values. Overall, the in vitro method for skin absorption was considered to be relatively robust [van de Sandt et al., 2004; EDETOX, 2004].

With regard to the use of the study results for risk assessment, it is acknowledged that the in vitro study is unable to take into account repeated exposure effects, such as gradual skin damage due to long-term exposure to low concentrations of skin irritants [Buist et al., 2005] and that skin metabolism is absent in the majority of the skin samples tested [Nohynek et al., 2005], which usually were stored frozen before use. Biotransformation is only expected in freshly isolated skin [Diembeck et al., 1999].

Rogiers · Pauwels

Finally, discussions are ongoing with regard to potential reservoir effects of the substance remaining in the stratum corneum. In the currently applied calculations this amount is not considered to be dermally absorbed, but in case of a reservoir effect it may be released into the systemic circulation and thus the DA is underestimated [Williams, 2006; Capt, 2007]. Although the reservoir effect is mostly pronounced for lipophilic compounds, hydrophilic substances may also be involved through receptor or protein binding [Williams, 2006].

The inter-individual variability of skin samples used in in vitro DA studies appears to reflect the natural variability occurring in the human population. This in vitro system is therefore difficult to standardise as inevitably reflected in the variability of the results. Although it seems reassuring that both types of MoS calculations in table 9 are of the same order of magnitude, the question could be raised whether results obtained through an in vitro DA test are good enough to be used in a quantitative exercise. An in-depth statistical analysis of all available variability data may shed some light on this issue, though it has not been performed to date.

f) Alternatives for in vitro Dermal Absorption Studies
A possible alternative would be to gradually replace the test with newly developed mathematical models and/or QSARs, or to make use of conservative default values for DA. Proposals in this field can be summarised as follows:
- For many years, mathematical models have attempted to translate the DA process into a series of equations each describing the expected mass flows from one skin layer to another. They use the physicochemical data of the compound under study (mainly P_{ow} and molecular weight) as input parameters and take into account some default physiological parameters such as blood flow and thickness of individual skin layers [Krüse et al., 2007]. These models are expected to allow extrapolation from infinite dose scenarios to in-use mimicking (finite dose) applications. Mathematical models are, however, not considered ready to be used for regulatory purposes [van de Sandt et al., 2007].
- QSAR approaches are theoretical models that predict the physicochemical, biological and/or environmental properties of chemicals. They express in a mathematical form the quantitative relationship that may exist between the chemical structure of a series of chemicals and their measured effect or activity. The 3-dimensional chemical structure and the available physicochemical data of the compound under study constitute typical input parameters for QSARs [Netzeva et al., 2005]. Unfortunately QSAR's are currently not considered fit enough to be used in a regulatory setting [van de Sandt et al., 2007].
- Conservative default values for DA. In the absence of experimental DA data, the most extreme worst-case scenario is assuming that 100% of the chemical at a relevant dose will be absorbed [Kroes et al., 2007]. If this still results in a risk assessment indicating that the exposure level is acceptable, a DA test is not required [IPCS, 2006].

In the framework of the evaluation of DA for plant protection products, it is proposed that, based on theoretical considerations on skin permeation, an optimum in Log P_{ow} and a maximum in molecular weight for facilitating DA exist. More specifically, a default value of 10% DA is proposed in case the molecular weight exceeds 500 Da and the Log P_{ow} is smaller than –1 or higher than 4. Otherwise, 100% DA is assumed. By expert judgment, however, a deviation from 100 and 10% DA can be chosen, on a case by case basis taking into account all data available (e.g. data on water solubility, ionogenic state, 'molecular volume', oral absorption and dermal area dose in exposure situations in practice) [DG SANCO, 2004].

This approach is also taken up in a proposal for a tiered risk assessment under REACH (details available through http://www.ecb.jrc.it/reach/rip, consulted February 2008) and is under discussion by the SCCP.

3.3.4. Mutagenicity/Genotoxicity

a) Detailed SCC(NF)P Requirements
The SCC(NF)P expressed the opinion that, for the evaluation of the potential for mutagenicity/genotoxicity of any cosmetic ingredient to be included in the Annexes to the Cosmetic Products Directive, tests are required that provide information on three major genetic endpoints, namely (a) mutagenicity at a gene level, (b) chromosome breakage and/or rearrangements (clastogenicity), and (c) numerical chromosome aberrations (aneugenicity). Thus, the following base set is defined [SCCNFP, 2004a; SCCP, 2006g]:

1 Tests for gene mutation: (i) Bacterial Reverse Mutation Test [EU, 2000b; OECD, 1997a]; (ii) In Vitro Mammalian Cell Gene Mutation Test [EU, 2000c; OECD, 1997c].
2 Tests for clastogenicity and aneugenicity: (i) In vitro micronucleus test [OECD, 2007].

Since a possible correlation was reported between the use of hair dyes and the occurrence of bladder cancer [SCCNFP, 2001d], the SCCNFP defined some additional requirements for the in vitro mutagenicity/genotoxicity testing battery of hair dyes [SCCNP, 2002d] by also requesting the in vitro unscheduled DNA synthesis study [EU, 1988c; OECD, 1986d]. Over the past 6 years, the hair dye testing battery was updated twice [SCCNFP, 2003c; SCCP, 2006d] to adapt the base set to newly acquired knowledge (overview in table 10).

Especially the introduction of the 6test in vitro battery in 2003 [SCCNFP, 2003c] resulted in a pronounced reaction from industry, since neither for pharmaceuticals, plant protection products, biocides, food additives or industrial chemicals, the requirements of the in vitro mutagenicity/genotoxicity testing base set were so extensive [Müller et al., 2003; Kirkland et al., 2005b]. The necessity of the UDS and the SHE cell transformation assay was challenged through an extensive screening of available test results [Kirkland et al., 2005a, b]. This comprehensive study was one of

Table 10. Overview of SCC(NF)P requirements with regard to the mutagenicity/genotoxicity data packages for hair dyes [SCCNFP 2002d, 2003c; SCCP 2006d]

Test	SCCNFP/0566/02 June 2002	SCCNFP/0720/03 June 2003	SCCP/0971/06 March 2006
Bacterial reverse mutation test [EU, 2000b; OECD, 1997a]	+	+	+
In vitro mammalian chromosome aberration test [EU, 2000a; OECD, 1997b]	+ (1 of 2 tests)	+	+ (1 of 2 tests)
In vitro micronucleus test [OECD, 2007]		+	
In vitro mammalian cell gene mutation test [EU, 2000c; OECD, 1997c]	+	+	+
Unscheduled DNA synthesis in mammalian cells in vitro [EU, 1988c; OECD, 1986d]	+	+	−
In vitro SHE cell transformation assay [EU, 1988e]	−	+	−

the arguments leading the SCCP to reduce the mutagenicity/genotoxicity base set for oxidative hair dyes back to the three in vitro assays [SCCP, 2006d] recommended for the safety testing of any cosmetic ingredient to be included in the Annexes to Directive 76/768/EEC [SCCNFP, 2004a].

In addition to the opinions on the data requirements related to the mutagenic/genotoxic properties of hair dyes, the SCCP also identified three separate categories of hair dye substances, namely temporary, semi-permanent and permanent hair dye substances [SCCP, 2006b]. The latter category comprises the oxidative hair dyes, which generally consist of complex mixtures of dye precursors, couplers and hydrogen peroxide. For this specific type of hair dyes, the SCCP added some additional remarks and an assessment scheme [SCCP, 2006d].

Although the in vitro mutagenicity/genotoxicity testing battery is widely used in many sectors, it still suffers from the frequent occurrence of 'false positive' results [Kirkland et al., 2005a, 2007] and the need for optimisation of existing protocols [Kirkland et al., 2007; Kirsch-Volders and Lombaert, 2008]. International expert working groups are concerned with specialised subjects such as the problem of negative predictivity (i.e. the issue of 'false positives'), refinement of the mutagenicity/genotoxicity testing battery with the aim of reducing animal testing, combination of standard genotoxicity tests and toxicogenomics, etc. [Ku et al., 2007; Thybaud et al., 2007]. Going into more detail on the complex problems related to the in vitro mutagenicity/genotoxicity testing battery, however, goes beyond the scope of this book.

The subject will appear again in chapter 6, where the in vitro and in vivo test results for individual cosmetic ingredients studied by the SCC(NF)P are compared.

Table 11. Presence and outcome of the performed in vitro mutagenicity/genotoxicity studies as reported by the SCC(NF)P (2002–2006)

Test	Data sets	Data accepted	Result negative[1]	Result positive[2]	Result equivocal[3]
Bacterial mutation test [EU, 2000b, 1988a; OECD, 1986b, 1997a]	115	95	60	31	4
In vitro mammalian cell gene mutation test [EU, 2000c; OECD, 1997c]	82	67	44	11	12
In vitro mammalian chromosome aberration test [EU, 2000a; OECD, 1997b]	82	63	23	35	5
In vitro micronucleus test [OECD, 2007]	17	17	3	13	1
In vitro UDS [EU, 1988c; OECD, 1986d]	18	8	4	4	0
In vitro SCE assay [EU, 1988d; OECD, 1986a]	11	7	3	4	0
Mitotic recombination assay in *Saccharomyces cerevisiae* [EU, 1988b; OECD, 1986c]	1	1	1	0	0
In vitro mammalian cell transformation assay [EU, 1988e]	4	3	3	0	0

[1]Substance failed to induce mutagenic/genotoxic effect under employed test conditions.
[2]Substance induced mutagenic/genotoxic effect under employed test conditions.
[3]No final conclusion (positive or negative) could be drawn based upon the test results.

b) Presence of Individual Studies in SCC(NF)P Reports

As all data on the same substances were assembled to obtain one combined data package per substance, the overall content of the individual mutagenicity/genotoxicity testing batteries per cosmetic ingredient, could be analyzed.

The information provided (194 industry submissions, 164 data packages) revealed 115 substances with mutagenicity/genotoxicity data. The in vitro mutagenicity/genotoxicity tests performed are displayed in table 11.

None of the mutagenicity/genotoxicity data packages, irrespective of their ingredient type, contained all 6 required in vitro assays as requested by the SCCNFP in June 2003.

Sixty-five substances (56%), however, were accompanied by the base set of 3 in vitro mutagenicity tests as required. For 40 (35% of all data packages) of those, the experts considered all 3 tests scientifically acceptable. Nevertheless, for 13 of the latter category, additional mutagenicity/genotoxicity data were still requested. This shows the complexity of the field. Evaluating mutagenicity/genotoxicity dossiers is performed on a case by case basis, taking into account the availability and quality of the individual studies, but also the results of the in vitro studies and the chemical structure of the test compound. Structural alerts may trigger additional testing [Ashby and

Table 12. Mostly reported flaws in the mutagenicity/genotoxicity data packages submitted to the SCC(NF)P

Flaws reported	Occurrence
Incomplete testing battery	74 out of 123 data packages (60%)
In vitro UDS: inappropriate choice of analytical method	7 out of 18 data packages (39%)
In vivo micronucleus: lack of proof that the compound reached the bone marrow	27 out of 94 data packages (29%)
All studies: insufficient identification of the test compound	21 out of 123 data packages (17%)

Tennant, 1991]. Unlike other toxicological endpoints, mutagenicity/genotoxicity is not addressed by a single test, but requires a whole battery of in vitro (and potentially in vivo) testing.

The determination of the exact content of this battery requires extensive knowledge and experience in the field.

c) Mostly Reported Shortcomings in SCC(NF)P Reports

The 123 mutagenicity/genotoxicity data packages (resulting from 194 individual evaluations) were screened for the mostly reported flaws (table 12).

The mostly made remark (in 74 cases or 60%) is that the proposed testing battery was insufficient with regard to number and type of tests. In 59% of those cases, the 3-test base set was available but nevertheless considered insufficient. With regard to the specific additional data required, only in a quarter of the cases the SCC(NF)P mentioned which tests were needed. In all other instances, general reference was made to relevant SCC(NF)P opinions [SCCNFP, 2002d, 2003c] and the Notes of Guidance [SCCNFP, 2000b, 2003b].

With respect to the in vitro unscheduled DNA synthesis assay (occurring in 15% of all data sets), the use of liquid scintillation counting was seen as being inferior to autoradiographic scoring because of potential interference from cells undergoing replicative DNA synthesis [e.g. SCCNFP, 2003d].

For the in vivo micronucleus tests, in more than a fifth of the cases the test sponsors failed to prove that the test compound had reached the actual target organ, the bone marrow. Although this assay was present in many data packages (76%), it is not a part of the base set requirements.

In 17% of all cases, the test compound was not sufficiently identified.

Thus, insufficient data availability appears to be the major remark. However, as already pointed out under 3.3.4.b, this cannot be anticipated by using a thick box approach and providing a pre-defined testing battery, but requires an expert opinion.

3.4 **Discussion and Conclusions**

Studying the safety assessment of cosmetic ingredients in the EU without making use of the large amount of data made publicly available through the web pages of the SCC(NF)P, would be a missed opportunity. Over the years, the scientific committee has published guidance on numerous risk assessment-related topics and detailed safety evaluations of more than 200 cosmetic ingredients. These so-called ad hoc opinions, however, have never been gathered for a critical evaluation. For the purpose of this book, the information contained in the SCC(NF)P reports issued between 2000 and 2006 was extracted and translated into a structured and searchable database. The goal was to gain deeper insight in the safety assessment process of cosmetic ingredients at the EU level and to contribute to a higher level of safety and transparency.

A first observation is that the Commission's strategy on hair dyes (officially issued in 2003) has led to a clear dominance of hair dyes and hair dye components in the SCC(NF)P opinions. The obtained results are also of relevance for product types outside the hair dye sector, since a hair dye-related safety dossier does not significantly differ from that of other cosmetic ingredients on the annexes, with the exception of the mutagenicity/genotoxicity data package.

With regard to data availability (content of individual submissions for cosmetic ingredients present on the annexes or for which concern exists) it was found that the following set of tests formed part of nearly every cosmetic ingredient dossier, irrespective of the outcome of the opinion: identification and physicochemical properties; acute oral toxicity, skin and eye irritation; skin sensitisation; in vitro DA; 90-day oral toxicity; mutagenicity/genotoxicity; reproductive toxicity.

The only exception is the in vitro DA study, which was more often lacking in submissions leading to a negative opinion. When this type of study was not available, the worst case of 100% absorption was assumed for exposure in the risk assessment calculations. For several compounds this was no problem since they were so innocuous that the MoS calculations still resulted in values higher than 100.

With respect to data acceptance (evaluation of the quality of the presented tests), our study could identify three problem areas, namely physicochemical properties, DA and mutagenicity/genotoxicity.

Indeed, data acceptance was found the lowest in the sections dealing with the identity and physicochemical properties of the compounds under study. This is rather surprising as it appears to be the 'easiest' part of the dossier which requires a limited number of tests which are usually animal free.

The mostly reported flaws included identification of purity and impurity profiles of all batches used and the fact that the majority of stated physicochemical properties (pH, density, Log P_{ow}, etc.) were not measured, but extracted from the current literature. These low acceptance levels, however, did not seem to affect the overall outcome of the SCC(NF)P opinions.

Data whose non-acceptance did have a major impact on the overall outcome were those of skin sensitisation studies, in vitro DA assays, mutagenicity/genotoxicity dossiers, toxicokinetics and human data.

The fact that in vitro DA and mutagenicity/genotoxicity studies also frequently occurred on the lists of additionally required data by the SCC(NF)P, highlights the importance of a sound pre-check by industry of these particular parts of the dossier before submission to the SCC(NF)P.

Although a multitude of guidelines are available for in vitro DA, the studies presented were afflicted by a considerable number of flaws, including the application of a concentration deviating from in-use conditions, problems related to the receptor fluid (solubility of test substance unknown or wrong choice), failure to separate skin compartments for individual measurements, excess dosage, insufficient skin samples tested and inappropriate statistics or high variability rates. The issue of the variability in the in vitro DA study was also taken up in an EU project investigating the robustness of the in vitro DA study (EDETOX). Although this project concluded that the study could be considered robust, interindividual variability of the results ranged up to 111%, raising the question whether results obtained by an in vitro DA study are fit enough for being used in quantitative calculations.

The problem is that there is no real alternative besides the existing in vivo DA test, which will be forbidden after 11 March 2009. Indeed, the currently investigated mathematical models and/or QSARs are not ready to go into the regulatory acceptance phase. As a last resort, the use of conservative default values could be considered and this approach is currently under study by the SCCP.

Therefore, we believe that, at this stage, the best proposal consists of harmonisation of the existing guidelines. Currently, an in vitro DA study performed for a substance under the chemical legislation according to OECD Guideline 428 combined with the ECB guidance may not be acceptable for a cosmetic ingredient. A harmonised protocol with the minimum requirements per sector in one document would significantly help the laboratories involved to deliver adequate results.

With regard to the mutagenicity/genotoxicity data packages, some test-specific remarks reoccurred in a number of SCC(NF)P opinions, such as the use of an inferior detection method in the in vitro UDS assay and the lack of proof that the compound reached the bone marrow in the in vivo micronucleus test. However, the main problem in this area is that the mutagenicity/genotoxicity data set was often considered incomplete.

Due to the complexity of the mechanisms involved, the interpretation of mutagenicity/genotoxicity studies is performed on a case-by-case basis and largely depends on expert judgment. On the other hand, it must be acknowledged that, especially for the category of hair dyes, industry had to deal with frequently changing data requirements. For various substances, the requirements changed between the time of the industry submission and the SCC(NF)P discussions, which is not an easy situation to deal with. To this respect, it is notable that the most extensive set of 6 tests (introduced in June 2003) was not present in any hair dye submission discussed between 2002 and 2006.

Based on the data extracted from the database, it is impossible to define a specific set of mutagenicity/genotoxicity tests that would guarantee a positive judgment of the SCC(NF)P, even in case they are all scientifically acceptable. The only certainty is that three in vitro assays form the base set to be performed for any cosmetic ingredient. Any further decision will be based upon expert judgment, since it depends upon the detailed results of the in vitro tests, the chemical structure of the compound, physicochemical data, etc. In our opinion, however, it seems fair towards the cosmetic industry that the SCC(NF)P would take into account the data requirements of the date of submission, although it is clear that in case of a serious health concern, deviations may be necessary.

Finally, it is interesting that an evolution took place in the SCC(NF)P strategy over time. More specifically, from a situation in which a minor lack of data caused the refusal of a compound, the committee evolved towards the application of a 'milder' strategy of temporary acceptance based not only upon the availability of data, but also taking into consideration the expectation of requested additional data. On the other hand, multiple changes in dossier requirements (e.g. in the fields of DA and mutagenicity/genotoxicity) and some unfortunate long delays between industry submission and final SCC(NF)P opinion were not always appreciated by industry. Nevertheless, over the past couple of years, both industry and the SCC(NF)P have done considerable efforts to improve submission quality and efficiency, and timing and transparency of the opinions, respectively. Although the situation still is far from ideal and some controversy probably always will exist, it would be appreciated by all parties to see this constructive trend continued in the following years.

3.5 References

Akomeah FK, Martin GP, Brown MB: Variability in human skin permeability in vitro: comparing penetrants with different physicochemical properties. J Pharm Sci 2007;96:824–834.

Ashby J, Tennant RW: Definitive relationships among chemical structure, carcinogenicity and mutagenicity for 301 chemicals tested by the U.S. NTP. Mutat Res 1991;257:229–306.

Basketter D, Pease C, Kasting G, Kimber I, Casati S, Cronin M, Diembeck W, Gerberick F, Hadgraft J, Hartung T, Marty JP, Nikolaidis E, Patlewicz G, Roberts D, Roggen E, Rovida C, van de Sandt J: Skin sensitisation and epidermal disposition: the relevance of epidermal disposition for sensitisation hazard identification and risk assessment. The report and recommendations of ECVAM workshop 59. Altern Lab Anim 2007;35:137–154.

Box G, Hunter W, Hunter J: Statistics for Experimenters, an Introduction to Design, Data Analysis and Model Building. New York, Wiley, 1978, pp 306–418.

Buist HE, van de Sandt JJ, van Burgsteden JA, de Heer C: Effects of single and repeated exposure to biocidal active substances on the barrier function of the skin in vitro. Regul Toxicol Pharmacol 2005;43:76–84.

Capt A, Luzy AP, Esdaile D, Blanck O: Comparison of the human skin grafted onto nude mouse model with in vivo and in vitro models in the prediction of percutaneous penetration of three lipophilic pesticides. Regul Toxicol Pharmacol 2007;47:274–287.

DG SANCO: Sanco/222/2000: Guidance Document on Dermal Absorption. European Commission, Health and Consumer Protection Directorate-General, Doc. Sanco/222/2000 revision 1 of June 1999.

DG SANCO: Sanco/222/2000: Guidance Document on Dermal Absorption. European Commission, Health and Consumer Protection Directorate-General, Doc. Sanco/222/2000 revision 7 of 19 March 2004.

Diembeck W, Beck H, Benech-Kieffer F, Courtellemont P, Dupuis J, Lovell W, Paye M, Spengler J, Steiling W: Test guidelines for in vitro assessment of dermal absorption and percutaneous penetration of cosmetic ingredients. Food Chem Toxicol 1999;37:191–205.

Dong F: On the identification of active contrasts in unreplicated fractional factorials. Stat Sin 1993;3:209–217.

EDETOX: Evaluations and predictions of dermal absorption of toxic chemicals. Final Report for Dissemination, Contract No. QLK4-2000-00196, 2004. Available through http://www.ncl.ac.uk/edetox/index.html (consulted December 2007).

EU: Council Directive 76/768/EEC of 27 July 1976 on the approximation of the laws of the Member States relating to cosmetic products. Off J 1976;L262:169–200.

EU: B.15. Mutagenicity testing and screening for carcinogenicity. Gene mutation – *Saccharomyces cerevisiae*. Commission Directive 88/302/EEC of 18 November 1987 adapting to technical progress for the ninth time Council Directive 67/548/EEC on the approximation of laws, regulations and administrative provisions relating to the classification, packaging and labelling of dangerous substances. Off J 1988a;L133:55–57.

EU: B.16. Mitotic recombination – *Saccharomyces cerevisiae*. Commission Directive 88/302/EEC of 18 November 1987 adapting to technical progress for the ninth time Council Directive 67/548/EEC on the approximation of laws, regulations and administrative provisions relating to the classification, packaging and labelling of dangerous substances. Off J 1988b;L133:58–60.

EU: B.18. DNA damage and repair – unscheduled DNA synthesis – mammalian cells in vitro. Commission Directive 88/302/EEC of 18 November 1987 adapting to technical progress for the ninth time Council Directive 67/548/EEC on the approximation of laws, regulations and administrative provisions relating to the classification, packaging and labelling of dangerous substances. Off J 1988c;L133:64–67.

EU: B.19. Sister Chromatid Exchange assay in vitro. Commission Directive 88/302/EEC of 18 November 1987 adapting to technical progress for the ninth time Council Directive 67/548/EEC on the approximation of laws, regulations and administrative provisions relating to the classification, packaging and labelling of dangerous substances. Off J 1988d;L133:68–70.

EU: B.21. In vitro mammalian cell transformation tests. Commission Directive 88/302/EEC of 18 November 1987 adapting to technical progress for the ninth time Council Directive 67/548/EEC on the approximation of laws, regulations and administrative provisions relating to the classification, packaging and labelling of dangerous substances. Off J 1988e;L133:73–75.

EU: A.8. Partition coefficient. Commission Directive 92/69/EEC of 31 July 1992 adapting to technical progress for the seventeenth time Council Directive 67/548/EEC on the approximation of laws, regulations and administrative provisions relating to the classification, packaging and labelling of dangerous substances. Off J 1992;L383A:63–73.

EU: B.10. Mutagenicity – in vitro mammalian chromosome aberration test. Commission Directive 2000/32/EC of 19 May 2000 adapting to technical progress for the 26th time Council Directive 67/548/EEC on the approximation of the laws, regulations and administrative provisions relating to the classification, packaging and labelling of dangerous substances. Off J 2000a;L136:35–42.

EU: B.13/14. Mutagenicity – reverse mutation test bacteria. Commission Directive 2000/32/EC of 19 May 2000 adapting to technical progress for the 26th time Council Directive 67/548/EEC on the approximation of the laws, regulations and administrative provisions relating to the classification, packaging and labelling of dangerous substances. Off J 2000b;L136:57–64.

EU: B.17. Mutagenicity – in vitro mammalian cell gene mutation test. Commission Directive 2000/32/EC of 19 May 2000 adapting to technical progress for the 26th time Council Directive 67/548/EEC on the approximation of the laws, regulations and administrative provisions relating to the classification, packaging and labelling of dangerous substances. Off J 2000c;L136:65–72.

IPCS: International Programme on Chemical Safety, Environmental Health Criteria 235 (2006): Dermal Absorption. WHO, Geneva, 2006, available through http://www.who.int/ipcs/features/2006/ehc235/en/index.html (consulted Dec 2007).

Kirkland DJ, Aardema M, Hendersen L, Müller L: Evaluation of the ability of a battery of three in vitro genotoxicity tests to discriminate rodent carcinogens and non-carcinogens I. Sensitivity, specificity and relative predictivity. Mutat Res 2005a;584:1–256.

Kirkland DJ, Henderson L, Marzin D, Müller L, Parry JM, Speit G, Tweats DJ, Williams GM: Testing strategies in mutagenicity and genetic toxicology: an appraisal of the guidelines of the European Scientific Committee for Cosmetics and Non-Food Products for the evaluation of hair dyes. Mutat Res 2005b;588:88–105.

Kirkland D, Pfuhler S, Tweats D, Aardema M, Corvi R, Darroudi F, Elhajouji A, Glatt H, Hastwell P, Hayashi M, Kasper P, Kirchner S, Lynch A, Marzin D, Maurici D, Meunier JR, Müller L, Nohynek G, Parry J, Parry E, Thybaud V, Tice R, van Benthem J, Vanparys P, White P: How to reduce false positive results when undertaking in vitro genotoxicity testing and thus avoid unnecessary follow-up animal tests: Report of an ECVAM Workshop. Mutat Res 2007;628:31–55.

Kirsch-Volders M, Lombaert N: In vitro genotoxicity/ mutagenicity-requirements, strategies and problems; in Rogiers V, Pauwels M (eds): Proceedings of Safety Assessment of Cosmetics in the EU – Follow-up Course, 4–6 February 2008. Brussels, Belgium, 2008, p 387.

Kroes R, Renwick AG, Feron V, Galli CL, Gibney M, Greim H, Guy RH, Lhuguenot JC, van de Sandt JJ: Application of the threshold of toxicological concern (TTC) to the safety evaluation of cosmetic ingredients. Food Chem Toxicol 2007;45:2533–2562.

Ku WW, Bigger A, Brambilla G, Glatt H, Gocke E, Guzzie PJ, Hakura A, Honma M, Martus HJ, Obach RS, Roberts S, Strategy Expert Group, IWGT: Strategy for genotoxicity testing–metabolic considerations. Mutat Res 2007;627:59–77.

Levitt R, Hoorens S, Hallsworth M, Rubin,J, Klautzer L: Intermediate evaluation of Directorate-General Health and Consumer Protection non-food scientific committees. Final Report. Eds. RAND Corporation, Santa Monica, USA, 2006.

Müller L, Blakey D, Dearfield KL, Galloway S, Guzzie P, Hayashi M, Kasper P, Kirkland D, MacGregor JT, Parry JM, Schechtman L, Smith A, Tanaka N, Tweats D, Yamasaki H, IWGT Expert Group: Strategy for genotoxicity testing and stratification of genotoxicity test results-report on initial activities of the IWGT Expert Group. Mutat Res 2003;540:177–181.

Netzeva TI, Worth A, Aldenberg T, Benigni R, Cronin MT, Gramatica P, Jaworska JS, Kahn S, Klopman G, Marchant CA, Myatt G, Nikolova-Jeliazkova N, Patlewicz GY, Perkins R, Roberts D, Schultz T, Stanton DW, van de Sandt JJ, Tong W, Veith G, Yang C: Current status of methods for defining the applicability domain of (quantitative) structure-activity relationships. The report and recommendations of ECVAM Workshop 52. Altern Lab Anim 2005;33:155–173.

Nohynek GJ, Duche D, Garrigues A, Meunier PA, Toutain H, Leclaire J: Under the skin: Biotransformation of para-aminophenol and para-phenylenediamine in reconstructed human epidermis and human hepatocytes. Toxicol Lett 2005;158:196–212.

OECD: OECD Guideline for testing of chemicals – Guideline 479 (1986a): Genetic Toxicology: In vitro Sister Chromatid Exchange Assay in Mammalian Cells. Organization for Economic Cooperation and Development, Paris, original guideline adopted 23 October 1986.

OECD: OECD Guideline for testing of chemicals – Guideline 480 (1986b): Saccharomyces cerevisiae, Gene Mutation Assay. Organization for Economic Cooperation and Development, Paris, original guideline adopted 23 October 1986.

OECD: OECD Guideline for testing of chemicals – Guideline 481 (1986c): Genetic Toxicology: Saccharomyces cerevisiae, Mitotic Recombination Assay. Organization for Economic Cooperation and Development, Paris, original guideline adopted 23 October 1986.

OECD: OECD Guideline for testing of chemicals – Guideline 482 (1986d): Genetic Toxicology: DNA Damage and Repair, Unscheduled DNA Synthesis in Mammalian Cells in vitro. Organization for Economic Cooperation and Development, Paris, original guideline adopted 23 October 1986.

OECD: OECD Guideline for testing of chemicals – Guideline 107 (1995): Partition Coefficient (n-octanol/water): Shake Flask Method. Organization for Economic Cooperation and Development, Paris, updated guideline adopted 27 July 1995.

OECD: OECD Guideline for testing of chemicals – Guideline 471 (1997a): Bacterial Reverse Mutation Test. Organization for Economic Cooperation and Development, Paris, adopted 26 May 1983, last updated 21 July 1997.

OECD: OECD Guideline for testing of chemicals – Guideline 473 (1997b): In vitro Mammalian Chromosomal Aberration Test. Organization for Economic Cooperation and Development, Paris, updated 21 July 1997.

OECD: OECD Guideline for testing of chemicals – Guideline 476 (1997c): In vitro Mammalian Cell Gene Mutation Test. Organization for Economic Cooperation and Development, Paris, adopted 4 April 1984, last updated 21 July 1997.

OECD: Draft Guidance Document for the Conduct of Skin Absorption Studies. Organization for Economic Cooperation and Development (OECD), Environment Directorate, OECD Environmental Health and Safety Publications, Series on Testing and Assessment No. 28, Paris, 2000a.

OECD: Draft Guideline 428 (2000b): Skin absorption: In vitro method. Organization for Economic Cooperation and Development, Paris, draft approved December 2000.

OECD: OECD Guideline for testing of chemicals – Guideline 122 (2000c): Partition Coefficient (n-Octanol/Water) pH-Metric Method for Ionisable Substances. Organization for Economic Cooperation and Development, Paris, draft guideline approved November 2000.

OECD (2004a): Guidance Document for the Conduct of Skin Absorption Studies. Document number ENV/JM/MONO(2004)2. Organization for Economic Cooperation and Development (OECD), Environment Directorate, OECD Environmental Health and Safety Publications, Series on Testing and Assessment No. 28, Paris, 5 March 2004.

OECD: OECD Guideline for testing of chemicals – Guideline 117 (2004b): Partition Coefficient (n-octanol/water), HPLC Method. Organization for Economic Cooperation and Development, Paris, updated guideline adopted 13 April 2004.

OECD: OECD Guideline for testing of chemicals – Guideline 428 (2004c): Skin absorption: In vitro method. Organization for Economic Cooperation and Development, Paris, adopted 13 April 2004.

OECD: OECD Guideline for testing of chemicals – Guideline 123 (2006): Partition Co-efficient (1-Octanol/Water): Slow-Stirring method. Organization for Economic Cooperation and Development, Paris, adopted 23 March 2006.

OECD: OECD Guideline for testing of chemicals – Draft Guideline 487 (2007): In Vitro Mammalian Cell Micronucleus Test (MNvit). Organization for Economic Cooperation and Development, Paris, draft (3rd version) approved 13 December 2007.

SCCNFP: SCCNFP/0167/99 (1999): Basic Criteria for the in vitro assessment of percutaneous absorption of cosmetic ingredients, adopted by the SCCNFP during the 8th plenary meeting of 23 June 1999.

SCCNFP: SCCNFP/0320/00 (2000a): Opinion concerning an initial list of perfumery materials which must not form part of fragrances compounds used in cosmetic products, adopted by the SCCNFP during the 12th plenary meeting of 3 May 2000.

SCCNFP: SCCNFP/0321/00 (2000b): Notes of Guidance for Testing of Cosmetic Ingredients for Their Safety Evaluation, 4th revision, adopted by the SCCNFP during the plenary meeting of 24 October 2000.

SCCNFP: SCCNFP/0392/00 (2001a): Opinion concerning an Initial List of Perfumery Materials which must not form part of Cosmetic Products except subject to the restrictions and conditions laid down, adopted by the SCCNFP during the 18th plenary meeting of 25 September 2001.

SCCNFP: SCCNFP/0450/01 (2001b): Memorandum on the SCCNFP opinion concerning fragrance allergy in consumers, adopted by the SCCNFP during the 16th plenary meeting of 16 March 2001.

SCCNFP: SCCNFP/0474/01 (2001c): Opinion concerning chemical ingredients in cosmetic products classified as carcinogenic, mutagenic or toxic to reproduction according to the Chemicals Directive 67/548/EEC, adopted by the SCCNFP during the 18th plenary meeting of 25 September 2001.

SCCNFP: SCCNFP/0484/01 (2001d): Opinion on the use of permanent hair dyes and bladder cancer risk, adopted by the SCCNFP during the 17th plenary meeting of 12 June 2001.

SCCNFP: SCCNFP/0495/01 (2002a): Opinion concerning the safety review of the use of certain azo-dyes in cosmetic products, adopted by the SCCNFP during the 19th plenary meeting of 27 February 2002.

SCCNFP: SCCNFP/0546/02 (2002b): Memorandum concerning the actual status of alternative methods to the use of animals in the safety testing of cosmetic ingredients, adopted by the SCCNFP during the 20th plenary meeting of 4 June 2002.

SCCNFP: SCCNFP/0557/02 (2002c): Position statement on the calculation of the Margin of Safety of ingredients incorporated in cosmetics which may be applied to the skin of children, adopted by the SCCNFP during the 19th plenary meeting of 27 February 2002.

SCCNFP: SCCNFP/0566/02 (2002d): Proposal for a strategy for testing hair dye cosmetic ingredients for their potential genotoxicity/mutagenicity, adopted by the SCCNFP during the 20th plenary meeting of 4 June 2002.

SCCNFP: SCCNFP/0588/02 (2002e): Position statement concerning fragrance chemicals in detergents and other household products, adopted by the SCCNFP during its 20th plenary meeting of 4 June 2002.

SCCNFP: SCCNFP/0635/03 (2003a): Opinion concerning request for a re-evaluation of hair dyes listed in Annex III to Directive 76/768/EEC on Cosmetic Products, adopted by the SCCNFP during the 23rd plenary meeting of 18 March 2003.

SCCNFP: SCCNFP/0690/03 (2003b): Notes of Guidance for the testing of cosmetic ingredients and their safety evaluation, adopted by the SCCNFP during the 25th plenary meeting of 20 October 2003.

SCCNFP: SCCNFP/0720/03 (2003c): Updated recommended strategy for testing hair dyes for their potential genotoxicity/mutagenicity/carcinogenicity, adopted by the SCCNFP during the 24th plenary meeting of 24–25 June 2003.

SCCNFP: SCCNFP/0732/03 (2003d): Opinion concerning 2-chloro-6-methyl-3-aminophenol hydrochloride (Colipa n° A 94), adopted by the SCCNFP during the 25th plenary meeting of 20 October 2003.

SCCNFP: SCCNFP/0740/03 (2003e): Opinion concerning Bergamottin, adopted by the SCCNFP during the 25th plenary meeting of 20 October 2003.

SCCNFP: SCCNFP/0750/03 (2003f): Basic Criteria for the in vitro assessment of dermal absorption of cosmetic ingredients – updated November 2003, adopted by the SCCNFP during the 25th plenary meeting of 20 October 2003.

SCCNFP: SCCNFP/0761/03 (2003g): Opinion concerning Isopimpinellin, adopted by the SCCNFP during the 26th plenary meeting of 9 December 2003.

SCCNFP: SCCNFP/0770/03 (2003h): Opinion concerning an update of the initial list of perfumery materials which must not form part of cosmetic products except subject to the restrictions and conditions laid down, adopted by the SCCNFP during the 26th plenary meeting of 9 December 2003.

SCCNFP: SCCNFP/0771/03 (2003i): Opinion concerning an update of the initial list of perfumery materials which must not form part of fragrance compounds used in cosmetic products, adopted by the SCCNFP during the 26th plenary meeting of 9 December 2003.

SCCNFP: SCCNFP/0755/03 (2004a): Recommended Mutagenicity/Genotoxicity tests for the safety testing of cosmetic ingredients to be included in the annexes to Council Directive 76/768/EEC (SCCNFP Notes of Guidance), adopted by the SCCNFP on 23 April 2004 by means of the written procedure.

SCCNFP: SCCNFP/0797/04 (2004b): Opinion concerning use of permanent hair dyes and bladder cancer, adopted by the SCCNFP on 23 April 2004 by means of the written procedure.

SCCNFP: SCCNFP/0825/04 (2004c): Opinion concerning chemical ingredients in cosmetic products classified as carcinogenic, mutagenic or toxic to reproduction according to the Chemicals Directive 67/548/EEC, adopted by the SCCNFP during the 28th plenary meeting of 25 May 2004.

SCCNFP: SCCNFP/0834/04 (2004d): Opinion concerning 'Report for establishing the timetable for phasing out animal testing for the purpose of the cosmetics directive' issued by ECVAM (30/04/2004), adopted by the SCCNFP on 1 July 2004 by means of the written procedure.

SCCP: SCCP/0838/04 (2004a): Opinion on Hydroxyisohexyl 3-cyclohexene Carboxaldehyde (sensitisation only), adopted by the SCCP during the 2nd plenary meeting of 7 December 2004.

SCCP: SCCP/0847/04 (2004b): Opinion on Atranol and chloroatranol present in natural extracts (e.g. oak moss and tree moss extract), adopted by the SCCP during the 2nd plenary meeting of 7 December 2004.

SCCP: SCCP/0868/05 (2005a): Opinion on Cresylpropionaldehyde (p-Methyldihydrocinnam-aldehyde) (sensitisation only), adopted by the SCCP during the 3rd plenary meeting of 15 March 2005.

SCCP: SCCP/0869/05 (2005b): Opinion on Opinion on Tagetes erecta, T. minuta and T. patula Extracts and Oils (phototoxicity only), adopted by the SCCP during the 4th plenary meeting of 21 June 2005.

SCCP: SCCP/0871/05 (2005c): Opinion on Commiphora Erythrea Glabrescens Gum Extract and Oil (Opoponax) (sensitisation only), adopted by the SCCP during the 3rd plenary meeting of 15 March 2005.

SCCP: SCCP/0872/05 (2005d): Opinion on Liquidambar spp. Balsam Extracts and Oils (Storax) (sensitisation only), adopted by the SCCP during the 3rd plenary meeting of 15 March 2005.

SCCP: SCCP/0882/05 (2005e): Opinion on the safety of fluorine compounds in oral hygiene products for children under the age of 6 years, adopted by the SCCP during the 5th plenary meeting of 20 September 2005.

SCCP: SCCP/0883/05 (2005f): Opinion on 2-Mercaptobenzothiazole (MBT) (sensitisation only), adopted by the SCCP during the 4th plenary of 21 June 2005.

SCCP: SCCP/0888/05 (2005g): Opinion concerning request for confirmation of the SCCNFP opinion 0474/01 on chemical ingredients in cosmetic products classified as carcinogenic, mutagenic or toxic to reproduction according to Council Directive 67/548/EEC, adopted by the SCCP during the 3rd plenary meeting of 15 March 2005.

SCCP: SCCP/0913/05 (2005h): Opinion concerning request for confirmation of the SCCNFP opinion 0474/01 on chemical ingredients in cosmetic products classified as carcinogenic, mutagenic or toxic to reproduction according to Council Directive 67/548/EEC, adopted by the SCCP during the 4th plenary meeting of 21 June 2005.

SCCP: SCCP/0919/05 (2005i): Memorandum on the classification and categorisation of skin sensitisers and grading of test reactions, adopted by the SCCP during the 5th plenary meeting of 20 September 2005.

SCCP: SCCP/0930/05 (2005j): Opinion on personal use of hair dyes and cancer risk, adopted by the SCCP during the 5th plenary meeting of 20 September 2005.

SCCP: SCCP/0935/05 (2006a): Opinion on Coumarin (sensitisation only), adopted by the SCCP during the 8th plenary meeting of 20 June 2006.

SCCP: SCCP/0959/05 (2006b): Review of the SCCNFP opinion on Hair Dye Strategy in the light of additional information, adopted by the SCCP during the 8th plenary meeting of 20 June 2006.

SCCP: SCCP/0970/06 (2006c): Opinion on basic criteria for the in vitro assessment of dermal absorption of cosmetic ingredients – updated February 2006, adopted by the SCCP during the 7th plenary meeting of 28 March 2006.

SCCP: SCCP/0971/06 (2006d): Updated recommended strategy for testing oxidative hair dye substances for their potential mutagenicity/genotoxicity (SCCP's Notes of Guidance), adopted by the SCCP during the 7th plenary meeting of 28 March 2006.

SCCP: SCCP/0984/06 (2006e): Opinion on Vetiveryl Acetate (sensitisation only), adopted by the SCCP during the 7th plenary meeting of 28 March 2006.

SCCP: SCCP/0986/06 (2006f): Opinion on Sclareol (sensitisation only), adopted by the SCCP during the 7th plenary meeting of 28 March 2006.

SCCP: SCCP/1005/06 (2006g): The SCCP's Notes of Guidance for the Testing of Cosmetic Ingredients and their Safety Evaluation, adopted by the SCCP during the 10th plenary meeting of 19 December 2006.

SCCP: SCCP/1023/06 (2006h): Opinion on clarifications to SCCNFP/0392/00 'An initial list of perfumery materials which must not form part of cosmetic products except subject to the restrictions and conditions laid down', adopted by the SCCP during the 8th plenary meeting of 20 June 2006.

SCCP: SCCP/1068/06 (2006i): Opinion on methyl-n-methylanthranilate (photo-toxicity only), adopted by the SCCP during the 10th plenary meeting of 19 December 2006.

Steiling W: Dermal absorption/percutaneous penetration – Bioavailability of dermal exposed cosmetic ingredients. Intensive course in dermatocosmetic sciences. Brussels, Vrije Universiteit Brussel, 2007.

Thybaud V, Aardema M, Casciano D, Dellarco V, Embry MR, Gollapudi BB, Hayashi M, Holsapple MP, Jacobson-Kram D, Kasper P, MacGregor JT, Rees R: Relevance and follow-up of positive results in in vitro genetic toxicity assays: an ILSI-HESI initiative. Mutat Res 2007;633:67–79.

van de Sandt JJ, van Burgsteden JA, Cage S, Carmichael PL, Dick I, Kenyon S, Korinth G, Larese F, Limasset JC, Maas WJ, Montomoli L, Nielsen JB, Payan JP, Robinson E, Sartorelli P, Schaller KH, Wilkinson SC, Williams FM: In vitro predictions of skin absorption of caffeine, testosterone, and benzoic acid: a multi-centre comparison study. Regul Toxicol Pharmacol 2004;39:271–281.

van de Sandt JJ, Dellarco M, Van Hemmen JJ: From dermal exposure to internal dose. J Expo Sci Environ Epidemiol 2007;17:S38–S47.

Wilkinson SC, Maas WJ, Nielsen JB, Greaves LC, van de Sandt JJ, Williams FM: Interactions of skin thickness and physicochemical properties of test compounds in percutaneous penetration studies. Int Arch Occup Environ Health 2006;79:405–413.

Williams F: In vitro studies – how good are they at replacing in vivo studies for measurement of skin absorption? Environ Toxicol Pharmacol 2006;21:199–203.

4 **Safety Assessment of Cosmetic Ingredients Present in Technical Information Files of Finished Products**

Rogiers V, Pauwels M (eds): Safety Assessment of Cosmetics in Europe.
Curr Probl Dermatol. Basel, Karger, 2008, vol 36, pp 94–114

4.1 Introduction

As explained in detail in section 1.2.7, two distinct channels are operative for the safety evaluation of cosmetic ingredients, namely the safety evaluation of cosmetic ingredients of direct relevance to Council Directive 76/768/EEC [EU, 1976a], currently taken care of by the SCCP, and the safety evaluation of all ingredients present in finished cosmetic products, carried out by a qualified safety assessor.

The most extensive list of data requirements imposed by the SCCP consists of: (1) acute toxicity (if available), (2) irritation and corrosivity, (3) skin sensitisation, (4) dermal/percutaneous absorption, (5) repeated dose toxicity, (6) mutagenicity/genotoxicity, (7) carcinogenicity, (8) reproductive toxicity, (9) toxicokinetics, (10) photo-induced toxicity, (11) human data.

Points 1–6 are generally considered the minimal base set requirements, whereas points 7–9 may become necessary when considerable oral intake is expected or when the data on dermal/percutaneous absorption indicate a considerable DA. Photo-induced toxicity data (point 10) are specifically required when the cosmetic product is expected or intended to being used on sunlight-exposed skin [SCCP, 2006b]. In the previous chapter, we have seen that the majority of SCC(NF)P submissions indeed contained points 1–6, but equally point 8 (see 3.2.5.a).

As opposed to cosmetic ingredients taken up in the Annexes of the Cosmetic Products Directive, there is no official framework providing clear guidelines for the safety assessment of ingredients used in finished cosmetic products. The cosmetic legislation only states that the safety of a cosmetic product needs to be assessed 'by taking into consideration the general toxicological profile of the ingredients, their chemical structure and their level of exposure' [EU, 1993]. Experience has learnt that the retrieval of sound and sufficient toxicological data on individual ingredients of cosmetic products often constitutes a major obstacle for safety assessors. In many cases, they will turn to the respective raw material suppliers to obtain physicochemical specifications and minimal toxicological data packages on their ingredients.

Although the SCCP is not responsible for the safety assessment of ingredients not taken up in the Annexes to Dir. 76/768/EEC [EU, 1976a], some general considerations are provided in the SCCP Notes of Guidance. Inter alia, the Committee alleges that acute toxicity, skin and eye irritation, skin sensitisation and a basic set of mutagenicity data, form the minimal data package to enable a scientifically sound safety evaluation of a cosmetic ingredient.

The SCCP advises that suppliers should be encouraged to deliver at least these data to all their customers in the cosmetic industry, especially since some substances are so-called 'actives' and are not necessarily safe at all concentrations used [SCCP, 2006b].

In a real-life situation, the aforementioned minimal toxicological data package can not always be obtained, e.g. when a cosmetic company wants to develop a 'new' cosmetic product and needs certain ingredients from a raw material supplier. The latter may be reluctant to disclose all information on these substances, in particular since in this early phase no commercial links yet exist. Another example is the typical situation of SMEs, which may be put at a disadvantage because of reduced spending power towards suppliers. Sometimes, only important clients receive all available toxicological information.

In cases where the requested data are difficult to obtain or are incomplete, it may be necessary to consult external sources of physicochemical and toxicological data that can be accessed independently from raw material suppliers.

Before such an extensive search is initiated, it is useful to know which data can be found on specific types of compounds. Since Dir. 76/768/EEC [EU, 1976a] does not impose specific data requirements for the majority of cosmetic ingredients that are no candidates for inclusion in one of the Annexes of the Cosmetic Products Directive, we have to refer to the complex web of EU regulations mentioned in chapter 1 of this book. Besides safety tests carried out (on a voluntary basis) for certain cosmetic ingredients, the availability of data will depend upon the requirements and data accessibility measures laid down in the other legislation(s) governing these substances. A useful evaluation of expected data availability is given in section 1.3.

Finally, it must be emphasised that the accessible parts of available toxicological data not necessarily consist of full study reports. In general, summaries and study results are described, while the details and raw data of the studies remain property of the company involved.

The list of available sources is long and includes websites of official organisations, freely accessible databases and their commercial counterparts. Out of our own experience, an overview of useful data sources is compiled in order to assist the cosmetic safety assessor in her/his comprehensive task.

4.2 Database Search for Safety Information on Cosmetic Ingredients

4.2.1. General Considerations

From a practical point of view, potentially relevant safety data for cosmetic ingredients usually are a combination of:

- the standard toxicological data package available for chemical substances, typically consisting of LD_{50} values, irritation and sensitisation data, NOAEL values out of repeated dose toxicity studies, results of mutagenicity, carcinogenicity and/or reproductive toxicity studies, etc.,
- additional relevant data including official classifications and industrial threshold limit values, data on analogous substances, relevant data in the public literature, etc.

Besides official documents and websites at the EU and non EU level, free and commercial databases and websites all over the world have proven to be storehouses of information. As the number of data sources containing safety data is very diverse, they need to be compiled in a structured overview in order to obtain, within a limited time frame, the key information that exists on a particular cosmetic ingredient. In addition, a general and realistic overview of the usefulness of the available data sources and points of strength and weaknesses forms the basis of a good search, followed by a scientific evaluation of the quality of the obtained information.

Our own experience in safety assessment of cosmetics will be the guide through the quest for safety data in practice and the judgment of their quality and relevance.

Although the focus of this section clearly resides on the search for human toxicity data, the same channels as those mentioned hereunder may equally be explored to search for physicochemical and/or ecotoxicological data.

4.2.2. Useful Data Sources

a) Types of Data Sources
Relevant information can be extracted from worldwide official instances' websites, industry-governed websites and freely available and commercial databases. As far as the latter are concerned, it is important to distinguish between bibliographical databases containing citations from extended lists of periodicals, journals, books, etc., and factual databases containing the actual data on a specific subject. Most interesting for our purpose are factual databases comprising fields with physicochemical, toxicological and/or ecotoxicological data, by preference accompanied by plain references.

Companies such as the Scientific and Technical Network (STN®)[1] and Thomson Dialog Datastar[2] commercialise sets of bibliographical and factual databases by selling CD-ROMs and/or allowing registered users to consult the databases through the Internet.

---

1 http://www.stn-international.de/ (consulted July 2007).
2 http://www.dialog.com/products/datastar/ (consulted July 2007).

b) Free Information Sources on the Internet

Google[TM3], Yahoo![®4] and MSN Search[5]

Coverage: the World Wide Web, generating lists of Internet links that match the entered keyword(s).

Comment:
- the number of hits gives a general idea on the amount of available data;
- reliability of data cannot be guaranteed.

EUR-Lex[6]

Coverage: European treaties, legislation, case-law and legislative proposals[7], including consolidated versions[8] of EU Directives.

Comment: without the correct search items (literal wording in the legislative texts), it may be unexpectedly hard to retrieve existing information.

Directorate-General (DG) Enterprise, Cosmetic Section[9]

Coverage: existing and upcoming cosmetic-related legislation[10], discussions on legislative aspects and many useful links.

Comment: the website has significantly improved over the past years and has become a key tool to follow up the EU cosmetic legislation.

Directorate-General Health and Consumer Protection (DG SANCO)[11]

Coverage: overview of EU laws on safety of food and other products, on consumers' rights and on the protection of people's health, including links to individual opinions of scientific committees such as the SCCP, previously called SCCNFP[12, 13].

Comment: an information source of major importance due to the presence of the SCC(NF)P opinions, the website's practical search value is impaired by the fact that cosmetic ingredients are not necessarily designated by their INCI names.

European Chemicals Bureau (ECB)[14]

Coverage: wide range of information related to the EU risk assessment procedures of dangerous substances and preparations, with direct links to consolidated pieces of

---

3   http://www.google.be/ (consulted July 2007).
4   http://www.yahoo.com/ (consulted July 2007).
5   http://www.msn.com/ (consulted July 2007).
6   http://europa.eu.int/eur-lex/ (consulted July 2007).
7   http://europa.eu.int/eur-lex/lex/RECH_menu.do?ihmlang = en (consulted July 2007).
8   http://europa.eu.int/eur-lex/accessible/en/consleg/index1.html (consulted July 2007).
9   http://ec.europa.eu/enterprise/cosmetics/index_en.htm (consulted July 2007).
10 http://ec.europa.eu/enterprise/cosmetics/html/cosm_ongoing_init.htm (consulted July 2007).
11 http://ec.europa.eu/dgs/health_consumer/index_en.htm (consulted July 2007).
12 http://ec.europa.eu/health/ph_risk/committees/04_sccp/sccp_opinions_en.htm (consulted July 2007).
13 http://ec.europa.eu/health/ph_risk/committees/sccp/sccp_opinions_en.htm (consulted July 2007).
14 http://ecb.jrc.it/ (consulted July 2007).

legislation in the chemical field and to the most recent versions of the physicochemical, toxicological and ecotoxicological test protocols[15].

Comment: user-friendly website with broad coverage of existing and future developments in EU chemical legislation.

CIR (Cosmetic Ingredient Review) Conclusions – US CTFA[16]
Coverage: conclusions of safety reviews and assessments of cosmetic ingredients.

Comment: the relevance of the conclusions is high due to the cosmetic focus; however, they usually do not provide the level of detail required for a full risk assessment.

US National Library of Medicine[17]
Coverage: medical library covering a large number of freely available databases[18], such as:
- PubMed[19]: a widely used bibliographic database including over 16 million citations from Medline and other life science journals for biomedical articles,
- TOXNET[20]: collection of databases on human environmental health, covering:
  - ChemIDplus[21]: names, synonyms and structures of more than 370,000 chemicals,
  - HSDB[22]: comprehensive, peer-reviewed factual toxicological data for about 5,000 chemicals, together with their human exposure, industrial hygiene, environmental fate and regulatory requirements,
  - TOXLINE[23]: broad bibliographic database in the field of toxicology,
  - CCRIS[24]: compilation of carcinogenicity and mutagenicity test results for over 8,000 chemicals,
  - DART[25]: bibliographic database in the field of developmental and reproductive toxicology,
  - Multi-Database Search[26]: search engine allowing to explore the available NLM chemical databases.

Comment: due to its convenient mix of identification, factual and bibliographical databases, TOXNET shows to be an appropriate starting point for an extended toxicological data search.

---

15 Annex V to Directive 67/548/EEC through http://ecb.jrc.it/testing-methods/ (consulted July 2007).
16 http://www.cir-safety.org/ (consulted July 2007).
17 http://www.nlm.nih.gov/ (consulted July 2007).
18 http://www.nlm.nih.gov/databases/ (consulted July 2007).
19 http://www.ncbi.nlm.nih.gov/entrez/query.fcgi?db = PubMed (consulted July 2007).
20 http://toxnet.nlm.nih.gov/ (consulted July 2007).
21 http://toxnet.nlm.nih.gov/cgi-bin/sis/htmlgen?CHEM (consulted July 2007).
22 http://toxnet.nlm.nih.gov/cgi-bin/sis/htmlgen?HSDB (consulted July 2007).
23 http://toxnet.nlm.nih.gov/cgi-bin/sis/htmlgen?TOXLINE (consulted July 2007).
24 http://toxnet.nlm.nih.gov/cgi-bin/sis/htmlgen?CCRIS (consulted July 2007).
25 http://toxnet.nlm.nih.gov/cgi-bin/sis/htmlgen?DARTETIC (consulted July 2007).
26 http://toxnet.nlm.nih.gov/cgi-bin/sis/htmlgen?Multi (consulted July 2007).

US Environmental Protection Agency (US EPA)[27]
Coverage:

- links to existing laws, regulations and dockets in the US[28];
- IRIS[29], a database of human health effects resulting from exposure to various substances found in the environment;
- HPVIS[30], providing access to (eco)toxicological data on chemicals manufactured in exceptionally large amounts in the US;
- documentation on individual aspects of the risk assessment procedure, such as exposure data[31], information on human toxicity in general[32], test methods and guidelines[33] and much more.
  Comment:
- a reliable source for information related to chemicals on the US market;
- some care is required while extrapolating classifications and regulations to the European situation, which often is quite different.

US National Toxicology Program (NTP)[34]
Coverage: reports on the evaluation of agents of public health concern, including development and application of modern toxicology and molecular biology.
  Comment:

- a reliable source of information, since the NTP has built up its own testing program and houses large experience in the overall field of risk assessment;
- includes the possibility to follow up the actual testing status of substances.

International Programme on Chemical Safety (IPCS)[35]
Coverage: information on the scientific basis for the safe use of chemicals, offering access to reviews on the human health and environmental effects caused by chemicals[36].

  Comment: especially the so-called Concise International Chemical Assessment Documents[37] are worth to consult.

27 http://www.epa.gov/ (consulted July 2007).
28 http://www.epa.gov/epahome/lawregs.htm (consulted July 2007).
29 http://www.epa.gov/iris/ (consulted July 2007).
30 http://www.epa.gov/hpvis/index.html (consulted July 2007).
31 http://www.epa.gov/ebtpages/humaexposure.html (consulted July 2007).
32 http://www.epa.gov/ebtpages/humatoxicity.html (consulted July 2007).
33 http://www.epa.gov/epahome/Standards.html (consulted July 2007).
34 http://ntp-server.niehs.nih.gov/ (consulted July 2007).
35 http://www.who.int/ipcs/en/ (consulted July 2007).
36 http://www.who.int/ipcs/publications/cicad/en/index.html (consulted July 2007).
37 http://www.who.int/ipcs/publications/cicad/en/index.html (consulted July 2007).

Australian National Industrial Chemicals Notification and Assessment Scheme (NICNAS) – Chemical Assessment Reports[38]
Coverage: reports containing physicochemical, (eco)toxicological and exposure data, followed by recommendations for safe use.

Comment: the full reports can be downloaded and contain useful descriptions of and full references to useful (eco)toxicological studies.

European Centre for Ecotoxicology and Toxicology of Chemicals[39] (ECETOC)
Coverage: fundamental research, manufacturing, risk assessment, toxicological and ecotoxicological testing of chemicals, including reports on individual chemical substances.

Comment: ECETOC reports incorporate the know-how of a large number of leading chemical companies and represents reliable and useful information.

The International Fragrance Association (IFRA) Code and Standards[40]
Coverage: IFRA recommendations on more than 130 fragrance components, in some cases accompanied by toxicological information.

Comment: this data source has proven impact in the cosmetic world, but improvement is possible as some entries only consist of a short mention of the results of an unpublished study.

Human and Environmental Risk Assessment[41] (HERA)
Coverage: risk assessments of ingredients used in household cleaning products.

Comment: this source provides insight in a number of industry-governed data which are not available through other data sources, but the number of compounds studied is rather restricted.

International Agency for Research on Cancer (IARC)[42]
Coverage: monographs on the carcinogenicity of the compounds studied, with detailed information on research on causes of human cancer, mechanisms of carcinogenesis and development of scientific strategies for cancer control.

Comment: important information source but of limited impact for cosmetics as only few of the studied substances are present in cosmetic products.

---

38 http://www.nicnas.gov.au/publications/car/New.asp (consulted July 2007).
39 http://www.ecetoc.org/Content/Default.asp?PageID = 32 (consulted July 2007).
40 http://www.ifraorg.org/GuideLines.asp (consulted July 2007).
41 http://www.heraproject.com/RiskAssessment.cfm (consulted July 2007).
42 http://www.iarc.fr/ (consulted July 2007).

Occupational Safety and Health Administration (OSHA)[43]
Coverage: reports on occupational safety, with emphasis on the continuous improvement of safety and health in the workplace.

Comment: this database only offers secondary information as its emphasis resides on occupational safety.

c) Commercial Data Sources
A Selection of Factual Databases
SciFinder[44] – Chemical Abstracts Service, USA
Coverage: biochemistry, biotechnology, organic and inorganic chemistry, macromolecular and applied chemistry, physical and analytical chemistry, toxicology and environmental science.

Comment: useful database to locate information on a wide variety of chemistry-related topics, offering a software package that makes searches easy to perform.

CIR (Cosmetic Ingredient Review) Full Reports – US CTFA[45]
Coverage: detailed safety reviews and assessments of cosmetic ingredients.
Comment:
- full CIR reports have the significant advantage of containing company-sensitive information that can not be retrieved through any other public information channel;
- CIR is supported by industry, but it consists of an independent expert panel.

CTFA International Cosmetic Legal and Regulatory Database – CTFA
Coverage:
- US health laws, including cosmetic-related regulations;
- industry guidelines and other documents related to the personal care products industry;
- CIR evaluations;
- European INCI list.

Comment: useful database when investigating the global status of a cosmetic ingredient, though restricted to subscribing CTFA members only.

Note: CTFA has recently changed its name into Personal Care Products Council.

---

43 http://www.osha.gov/ (consulted July 2007).
44 http://www.cas.org/SCIFINDER/ (consulted July 2007).
45 http://www.ctfa-international.org/ (consulted July 2007).

RTECS (Registry of Toxic Effects of Chemical Substances) – US NIOSH
Coverage: toxicological information such as irritation data, mutagenicity, carcino-genicity, reproduction toxicity, long-term toxicity, officially recommended human exposure limits, legislative restrictions, ...

Comment: submitted data are included without peer review and should therefore be looked at critically.

Beilstein – Beilstein Chemical Data and Software, Germany
Coverage:
- organic chemistry, including chemical name, molecular and structural formula, prepa-ration methods, physicochemical and biological properties, occurrence in nature, ...
- the information provided is extracted out of critically reviewed documents from the Beilstein Handbook of Organic Chemistry and 176 journals.
  Comment: good data source for organic molecules, large coverage.

Gmelin – Gmelin Institute of Inorganic Chemistry, Germany
Coverage: similar to Beilstein, but for the inorganic and organometallic chemistry, including critically reviewed documents from the Gmelin Handbook of Inorganic and Organometallic Chemistry and 110 journals.

Comment: a negative point is that no update exists since 1997.

MSDS-OHS (Material Safety Data Sheet – Occupational Health and Safety) – MDL
Information Systems, USA
Coverage: full texts of MSDSs, summary sheets and label data for more than 59,000 substances and/or mixtures.

Comment: MSDSs are no major data sources for toxicological information.

Chemlist – Chemical Abstracts Service, USA
Coverage: national listings such as TSCA, DSL, NDSL, ECL, ENCS, EINECS, ELINCS and AICS.

Comment: the mentioned lists are useful for regulatory purposes, but do not rep-resent (eco)toxicological data sources.

A Selection of Bibliographical Databases

Kosmet (Cosmetic and Perfume Science and Technology) – IFSCC, UK
Coverage: cosmetic product development, knowledge on healthy skin, trading of cos-metics, raw materials research and development, manufacture, analysis, safety aspects, physicochemical and biological properties, stability and packaging.

Comment: very useful due to the cosmetic focus, though slightly impaired by the frequent occurrence of conference proceedings, which are hard to retrieve.

On the following pages, 11 bibliographical databases are listed with their individual fields of coverage. They may provide useful references to secondary information and thus form good candidates for inclusion in a cluster search.

TOXCENTER (Toxicology Center) – Chemical Abstracts Service, USA
- Pharmacological, biochemical, physiological and toxicological effects of drugs and other chemicals,
- references to published materials in an area going from environmental toxicology of chemicals to human toxicity of medicinal products,
- also covering CA Plus, Biosis and Medline.

Medline[46] – US National Library of Medicine (NLM)
Information on every area of medicine, corresponding to the *Index Medicus, Index to Dental Literature, Health STAR database* and *International Nursing Index.*

EMBASE (Excerpta Medica[47] Database) – Elsevier Science B.V., The Netherlands
Literature in the biomedical and pharmaceutical fields, including biological science, biochemistry, human medicine, forensic science, paediatrics, pharmacy, pharmacology and drug therapy, pharmaco-economics, psychiatry, public health, biomedical engineering and instrumentation and environmental science.

IPA (International Pharmaceutical Abstracts) – ASHP, USA
Pharmacy and health-related topics, including pharmaceutical technology, drug stability, pharmaceutical education, the practice of pharmacy and the legal aspects of pharmacy and drugs.

HEALSAFE (Health and Safety Science Abstracts) – Cambridge Scientific Abstracts, US
Information on general, environmental, industrial, occupational and medical safety, transportation, aviation and aerospace.

SciSearch – Institute for Scientific Information, USA
- Scientific literature covering the broad field of science, technology, and biomedicine,
- contains records published in *Science Citation Index* and additional records from the *Current Contents* series of publications.

CA (Chemical Abstracts) Plus/Search – Chemical Abstracts Service, USA[48]
Guide to the chemical literature, referencing over 25 million documents and covering worldwide literature from all areas of chemistry, biochemistry and chemical engineering.

---

46 Possesses a freely accessible counterpart called PubMed [http://www.ncbi.nlm.nih.gov/PubMed/ (consulted July 2007)].
47 http://www.excerptamedica.com/ (consulted July 2007).
48 http://www.info.cas.org/ (consulted July 2007).

CSNB (Chemical Safety NewsBase) – The Royal Society of Chemistry, UK
Chemical-related information such as fire and explosions, storage, transport, waste removal, laboratory animal studies and health and safety.

LIFESCI (Lifescience Collection) – Cambridge Scientific Abstracts, USA
More than 20 different fields of life sciences, including animal behavior, biochemistry, biotechnology, ecology, genetics and immunology.

Biosis – Biosis, USA
Original research reports, reviews, selected US patents in biological and biomedical areas, with subjects ranging from aerospace biology to zoology.

AGRICOLA – National Agricultural Library, US Department of Agriculture
Agricultural economics and rural sociology, agricultural production, animal sciences, chemistry, entomology, food and human nutrition, forestry, national resources, pesticides, plant science, soils and fertilisers, water resources, biology and biotechnology, botany, ecology and natural history.

Some Useful Database Combinations on CD-ROM

Chembank – US Department of Transportation, EPA, NIOSH and NLM
Coverage: IRIS, RTECS, HSDB, OHMTADS, CHRIS and TSCA.
    Comment: Historically the most commonly used CD-ROM by safety assessors.

IUCLID (International Uniform ChemicaL Information Database) – ECB[49]
Coverage: details of all the data sets for existing substances submitted to the ECB, including general substance information, labelling, use, occupational exposure limits, physicochemical properties, (eco)toxicological data.
    Comment: many data sets are restricted in content and level of detail.

d) Information Provided by the Ingredients' Manufacturer(s)
The Material Safety Data Sheet
The MSDS usually is encountered as the first information source on a particular chemical substance or preparation. It is, however, not designed to represent a source of detailed toxicological information. The emphasis lies on occupational safety and the dangerous-to-health effects from exposure to the substance or preparation [EU,

---

49 http://ecb.jrc.it/iuclid/ (consulted July 2007).

1999, 1991a]. There is no obligation to mention all available toxicological data. Moreover, the MSDS itself is not always obligatory, e.g. when a preparation does not contain dangerous substances exceeding pre-defined concentration levels.

Additional Information and Confidentiality

In the specific case of cosmetic products, where the safety assessment is based upon the intrinsic properties of the individual ingredients and their level of exposure, the availability of physicochemical and toxicological data is indispensable.

Basically, the following information is needed:

- Details on the identity of the substance (including INCI and chemical name, CAS number, EINECS/ELINCS/NLP (No Longer Polymer) number).
- Purity/impurities of the ingredient.
- In case of a mixture, the quantitative composition or at least the concentration ranges of the individual constituents (including additives).
- Physicochemical data, with emphasis on pH value, solubility in different solvents, molecular weight and octanol/water partition coefficient (K_{ow}).
- All available toxicological data on the chemicals/mixtures, including study summaries, LD_{50} values, NOAEL values, etc. As suggested by the SCCP [SCCP, 2006b], acute oral/dermal toxicity, skin and eye irritation, skin sensitisation, DA and mutagenicity data are considered a minimal data package to enable a scientifically sound safety evaluation.

Since they do not commonly figure in toxicological data lists of chemicals outside the cosmetic field, DA values are often lacking. Nevertheless, they may be crucial in the calculation of the margin of safety of cosmetic ingredients.

Suppliers often consider the above-mentioned information as confidential. Therefore it is important to foresee confidentiality agreements which ensure that the provided information will only be used for the purpose of compiling the cosmetic product's dossier and thus will only be disclosed upon inspection by the competent authorities of the EU Member States.

It should be emphasised that obtaining the specific physicochemical and toxicological information on the delivered substances and/or mixtures, with their own particular purity/impurities profile, from the supplier, forms the basis of reliable and safe cosmetics. Furthermore, it may be necessary to perform an additional in vitro DA study. In case this is envisaged, it is highly advised to consult the SCCP opinion on the basic criteria for the in vitro assessment of dermal absorption of cosmetic ingredients [SCCP, 2006a].

4.2.3. The Quest for Safety Data in Practice

When a cosmetic ingredient is purchased in significant volumes from a supplier, the latter is expected to provide the required level of (eco)toxicological information. In case an independent search for the existing safety data on the compound is considered, the following sequence of search actions is proposed.

a) Identification of the Substance/Mixture

An often neglected step is the correct identification of the substance or mixture. Notwithstanding this identity will often be introduced as a search item and thus will significantly contribute to the efficiency and the outcome of the search.

The most common possibilities of identity display are:
- CAS[50] registry number
- IUPAC[51] name
- CA Index Name from the CAS Chemical Registry System[52]
- INN
- common name
- INCI name
- EINECS or ELINCS number

Since not all databases use the same identifiers, it is advisable to first use an identification database such as SciFinder[53] (payable) or ChemIDplus[54] (free of charge) in order to identify as much synonyms/numbers as possible. On-line commercial databases offer the advantage that the search can be performed by the intermediate of such an identification database, thus immediately searching on all possible identifiers.

The best identification tool is, in our experience, the CAS registry number, which is recognised by the majority of bibliographical and factual databases.

b) A Free of Charge Internet Search

A general Internet search through the classic World Wide Web search engines (Google[TM55], Yahoo!®[56], MSN Search[57]) may deliver a number of hits, but their quality and relevance requires careful assessment. A more valuable approach consists of the systematic consultation of a pre-defined set of reliable Websites.

---

50 http://www.cas.org/EO/regsys.html (consulted July 2007).
51 http://www.iupac.org/index_to.html (consulted July 2007).
52 http://www.cas.org (consulted July 2007).
53 http://www.cas.org/scifinder/ (consulted July 2007).
54 http://toxnet.nlm.nih.gov/cgi-bin/sis/htmlgen?CHEM (consulted July 2007).
55 http://www.google.be/ (consulted July 2007).
56 http://www.yahoo.com/ (consulted July 2007).
57 http://www.msn.com/ (consulted July 2007).

Check for Legal Restrictions

Before considering the use of a cosmetic ingredient, it is useful to consult the legislation in place for potential classification / restrictions through:

– the European legislation on cosmetics[58] [EU, 1976a], in particular its Annexes,

– the European legislation on dangerous substances, more specifically Annex I to Dir. 67/548/EEC [EU, 1967] on classification[59] and Dir. 76/769/EEC [EU, 1976b] on restrictions[60].

Useful side information may be obtained through:

– lists of approved food additives in Europe[61],

– Annexes I, IA and IB to the Biocidal Products Directive[62] [EU, 1998] and Annex I to the Plant Protection Products Directive[63] [EU, 1991b].

A joint remark for all the official websites is that the choice of the search items will determine the rate of success. The more identifiers are screened, the lower the chance of overlooking important information.

The Quest for Toxicological Data

(i)   In the European situation, a first check should be whether the compound under study has been discussed by the experts of the SCC(NF)P through the Committees' websites[64, 65]. Again, identification of the test compound needs to be as broad as possible.

(ii) Subsequently, the compound can be introduced in TOXNET[66] with the CAS number as identifier and the corresponding database entries can be further explored. In particular, the HSDB database is highly appreciated for its level of peer-reviewed information.

(iii) Additionally, a bibliographical search through the PubMed system[67], followed by full text document retrieval through Internet, order companies and/or libraries, can be performed. It must be admitted that this search often results in few relevant publications.

(iv) A screening of some additional websites such as IARC[68], IPCS[69], US EPA[70] and US NTP[71], may provide some additional data, but often all information obtained is covered by TOXNET.

---

58   http://europa.eu.int/eur-lex/en/consleg/main/1976/en_1976L0768_index.html (consulted July 2007).

59   http://ecb.jrc.it/classification-labelling/ (consulted July 2007).

60   http://europa.eu.int/eur-lex/en/consleg/main/1976/en_1976L0769_index.html (consulted July 2007).

61   http://www.elc-eu.org/html/alphalist.htm (consulted July 2007).

62   http://ecb.jrc.it/biocides/ (consulted July 2007).

63   http://europa.eu.int/eur-lex/en/consleg/main/1991/en_1991L0414_index.html (consulted July 2007).

64   http://ec.europa.eu/health/ph_risk/committees/04_sccp/sccp_opinions_en.htm (consulted July 2007).

65   http://ec.europa.eu/health/ph_risk/committees/sccp/sccp_opinions_en.htm (consulted July 2007).

66   http://toxnet.nlm.nih.gov/ (consulted July 2007).

67   http://www.ncbi.nlm.nih.gov/entrez/query.fcgi?db = PubMed (consulted July 2007).

68   http://www.iarc.fr/ (consulted July 2007).

69   http://www.who.int/ipcs/en/ (consulted July 2007).

70   http://www.epa.gov/ (consulted July 2007).

71   http://ntp-server.niehs.nih.gov/ (consulted July 2007).

c) The Search in Commercial Databases (Payable)

An on-line search in a set of commercial databases may either confirm the lack of availability of toxicity data, or supplement the data that have been found in the open domain. It must be emphasised that training is required to perform this type of search. Knowledge on special features such as the definition of a cluster of databases, the automatic removal of duplicate bibliographical results, individual databases' structures, their lexicon and specific display costs, is indispensable to reduce the costs of a search action.

CIR and KOSMET constitute a highly recommended factual and bibliographical database, respectively. Being cosmetically oriented, they efficiently supplement the freely available HSDB and PubMed.

4.2.4. Evaluation of Data Quality

Toxicological data can be encountered under different formats, ranging from full study reports to on-line quotes. Abundance of data on a single substance is not always favourable, since frequently contradictory results are found. Therefore, it is indispensable to examine reliability and relevance of the data retrieved.

Reliability covers the inherent quality of the performed study relating to the test methodology, its description and the presentation of the results [ECB, 2003]. Klimisch et al. [1997] published an approach for the attribution of reliability scores (categories) to (eco)toxicological data, principally based upon the level of detail provided, the level of accordance with internationally accepted guidelines or protocols, and the fact whether the study was performed under GLP or not.

The concept of relevance covers the appropriateness of the study for the particular risk assessment exercise [ECB, 2003]. A typical example is the acceptance or rejection of the use of a certain species for the prediction of human toxicity. More than anything else, relevance needs to be determined on a case by case basis and strongly relies on expert judgment.

An additional factor to take into consideration when processing results from (eco)toxicological data searches is the reliability of the data source itself. Every factual database has its own policy with regard to the acceptance and inclusion of data. This policy is useful to refer to when formulating an opinion on the quality of the information found. Peer review and the involvement of independent expert groups automatically inspire more confidence in the presented information. To this respect HSDB, SCC(NF)P opinions and CIR reports are considered dependable toxicological data sources. This additional factor may be considered together with the reliability categories as defined by Klimisch et al. [1997].

It is common practice to subject cosmetic ingredients to a WoE methodology for risk assessment. As described by Weed et al. [2005], such an approach typically takes into account all the retrieved (eco)toxicological data accompanied by their reliability categories, the latter indicating the weight attributed to them. Since information packages in the cosmetic field may display disappointing reliability scores, it might be useful to take into account the factor of reliability of the source of information in the overall reliability score.

4.3 Risk Assessment of Cosmetic Ingredients in Finished Cosmetic Products in the EU

The risk assessment of the ingredients included in a cosmetic product is done by a qualified safety assessor.

Since no official EU guidance is available, the safety assessor will rely upon personal and existing experience in the fields of EU risk assessment in general (as commonly performed in other sectors) and of cosmetic safety assessment in particular (as performed by the SCC(NF)P). Therefore, the presented analysis of SCC(NF)P opinions in chapter 3 of this book may be used to identify some areas that might need special consideration and to identify the data one should by preference have available in order to perform a sound risk assessment.

The SCCP Notes of Guidance mention that at least a minimal set of toxicity studies need to be available per ingredient to enable a scientifically sound safety evaluation [SCCP, 2006b]. Our analysis of the SCC(NF)P opinions shows that the typical data packages studied by the Committee are nearly all supplemented with in vitro dermal absorption, 90-day oral toxicity and reproduction toxicity (see 3.2.5.a). For the calculation of the MoS (= NO(A)EL/SED), these particular types of studies show to be of key importance, since they provide the substance-related parameters in the equation, being the NO(A)EL and the dermal absorption value (see 2.2.3 and 2.2.4).

This means that, with only the minimal data package available, the safety assessor will not be able to calculate the MoS for the ingredients under study.

Special consideration needs to be given to products intended for use on children under the age of 3 and for cosmetic products intended exclusively for use in external intimate hygiene [EU, 2003]. This legal provision is in our opinion spontaneously picked up by a qualified safety assessor. Also the target population of the finished cosmetic product, the application site and the intended use are important factors that have to be taken into consideration when assessing individual ingredients.

It should be clear that the safety assessor is free to express his/her personal expert opinion on the use of default dermal absorption values based upon physicochemical data and/or on alternative approaches, such as making use of the TTC [Kroes et al., 2000]. Tailored exposure scenarios may need to be developed on a case by case basis, since not all product types, combinations or new developments (e.g. nanoparticles) are included in the exposure data table taken up in the SCCP Notes of Guidance [SCCP, 2006b].

Commonly used cosmetic products consist of a substantial number of individual ingredients. Assessing them, one by one, in view of their intended use in a cosmetic product, is a careful exercise, taking into consideration:

– All available data on the individual constituents (either provided by raw material suppliers or searched for in the public or commercial domain).
– The relevance of those data for the specific batches used (taking into consideration the impurity profiles of the ingredients or mixtures used).
– The likelihood that local effects may be caused by the ingredient in its final concentration in the cosmetic product. To this end, the safety assessor needs to apply his/her expertise to evaluate whether the presence of an ingredient, in combination with the other constituents of the cosmetic product, may be at the basis of a skin or eye irritating or skin sensitising effect.
– The likelihood that systemic effects may be caused by an ingredient in its final concentration in the cosmetic product. Depending on the available data, the MoS will be calculated or not. If not, some assumptions can be formulated based upon acute toxicity data in combination with physicochemical and structural properties of the compound under study.
– The intended use of the product, including its frequency of use, the target population, anatomical site, body surface area involved and expected skin condition (e.g. potentially damaged skin in the diaper zone of babies).
– An evaluation of all potential routes of exposure (e.g. besides dermal absorption, inhalation of deodorant spray products, ingestion of oral care products).
– Available data on reported undesired effects on human health. A good complaint system, in place for a number of years, showing that a particular product has not caused adverse health effects, contains very useful information and may to a certain extent compensate for the lack of data on some ingredients.
– Whenever available, full descriptions and results from performed in vitro studies with the finished cosmetic product and/or human tests such as compatibility and in-use tests. In vitro studies mainly allow to classify the product in relation to a well-known benchmark product, whereas human tests can provide direct information on the compatibility of the product with human skin.
– Claims and other mentions on the label that may have an impact on the product's safety for human health.
– The potential benefit caused by the cosmetic product. Especially in the case of sunscreen products, it should not be forgotten that unprotected excessive exposure to sunlight may be at the basis of the development of skin cancer [IARC, 1992].
– As far as possible, reactions potentially occurring in the finished cosmetic products. Typical examples include nitrosamine formation by mixing secondary amines with nitro-group containing compounds and formaldehyde release by e.g. bronopol or other so-called formaldehyde releasers. Stability data may provide an

indication with respect to the occurrence of unexpected and unwanted reactions between constituents and should therefore also be looked at by the safety assessor.

Taking all the above together, it is possible that, when two independent safety assessors evaluate the safety of the same finished cosmetic product, two different reports are obtained. However, both assessors should have picked up the same discussion points and should express the same concerns. It is readily understood that the task of the competent authority's inspectors to accept and understand all aspects of cosmetic safety assessments, is complex and requires appropriate training.

As a final note, it should be mentioned that the prohibition of testing cosmetic ingredients on animals, represents one of the greatest challenges a cosmetic safety assessor could be faced with.

4.4 Discussion and Conclusions

Due to the fact that the safety assessment of finished cosmetic products is based upon the intrinsic properties of its individual ingredients and their level of exposure, the need for retrieving toxicological information on cosmetic ingredients is imminent.

Although cosmetics are exempted from the European legislations on dangerous substances, dangerous preparations, food additives, biocides, detergents, medicinal products, plant protection products and medical devices, a lot of useful safety information on cosmetic ingredients may have become available through their provisions. Therefore, spending some time to get familiar with the European legislation into force is worth the effort. It not only leads to a realistic picture of data expectations, but equally supports negotiations for obtaining (non-)confidential data from manufacturers and suppliers.

A topic that merits continuing attention is the legislation on dangerous substances and, more specifically, the new road taken with REACH. Monitoring the implementation and practical realisation of REACH is key in maintaining a realistic view on safety data availability for a large number of cosmetic ingredients.

The process of collecting relevant safety data for cosmetic ingredients in databases is not an easy task, but with some training and experience a lot of information can be found. A good database search starts with the adequate identification of the compound under study. Subsequently, these identifiers can be run through some pre-defined free and commercial databases in order to obtain as much information as possible. In a final step before the actual safety assessment, it is important to evaluate the reliability and relevance of the retrieved data. To this respect, it must be emphasised that the set of databases and Internet links mentioned in this chapter is based upon our years of experience and is as such not exhaustive. More information sources exist and, depending on personal preference and the selected study field, searchers involved will select their own preferred set.

Finally, once all available data on the ingredients of the finished cosmetic product have been collected, it is up to the competent safety assessor to investigate their safe use in the finished product. Many different factors are to be considered and a number of assumptions are involved. For the major part of the safety assessment procedure, no official guidance is available, meaning that a qualified safety assessor needs to rely on personal experience and scientific skills. As it is already difficult to base a judgment upon animal data that are commonly used for risk assessment, it will undoubtedly become an even greater challenge to assess the safety of cosmetic ingredients based upon replacement alternative methods and to correctly interpret the results obtained. In the coming years, we expect to be confronted with product dossiers containing a mosaic of in vivo and in vitro data, often not related with each other (e.g. in vivo data on an original product and in vitro data on a modified form, without knowing the relationship between in vivo and in vitro for the modified product) and not focusing on the relevant endpoints needed for risk assessment.

4.5 References

ECB: European Chemicals Bureau. Technical Guidance Document on Risk Assessment in support of Commission Directive 93/67/EEC on Risk Assessment for new notified substances, Commission Regulation (EC) No 1488/94 on Risk Assessment for existing substances and Directive 98/8/EC of the European Parliament and of the Council concerning the placing of biocidal products on the market. Doc. EUR 20418 EN/1, European Communities, 2003.

EU: Council Directive 67/548/EEC of 27 June 1967 on the approximation of laws, regulations and administrative provisions relating to the classification, packaging and labelling of dangerous substances. Off J 1967;P196:1–98.

EU: Council Directive 76/768/EEC of 27 July 1976 on the approximation of the laws of the Member States relating to cosmetic products. Off J 1976a;L262: 169–200.

EU: Council Directive 76/769/EEC of 27 July 1976 on the approximation of the laws, regulations and administrative provisions of the Member States relating to restrictions on the marketing and use of certain dangerous substances and preparations. Off J 1976b;L262:201–203.

EU: Commission Directive 91/155/EEC of 5 March 1991 defining and laying down the detailed arrangements for the system of specific information relating to dangerous preparations in implementation of Article 10 of Directive 88/379/EEC. Off J 1991a;L076:35–41.

EU: Council Directive 91/414/EEC of 15 July 1991 concerning the placing of plant protection products on the market. Off J 1991b;L230:1–32.

EU: Council Directive 93/35/EEC of 14 June 1993 amending for the sixth time Directive 76/768/EEC on the approximation of the laws of the Member States relating to cosmetic products. Off J 1993;L151:32–37.

EU: Directive 98/8/EC of the European Parliament and of the Council of 16 February 1998 concerning the placing of biocidal products on the market. Off J 1998;L123:1–63.

EU: Directive 1999/45/EC of the European Parliament and of the Council of 31 May 1999 concerning the approximation of the laws, regulations and administrative provisions of the Member States relating to the classification, packaging and labelling of dangerous preparations. Off J 1999;L200:1–68.

EU: Directive 2003/15/EC of the European Parliament and of the Council of 27 February 2003 amending Council Directive 76/768/EEC on the approximation of the laws of the Member States relating to cosmetic products. Off J 2003;L066:26–35.

IARC: Monograph on solar and ultraviolet radiation. International Agency for Research on Cancer, World Health Organisation. Lyon, France, 1992, vol 55.

Klimisch H-J, Andreae M, Tillmann U: A systematic approach for evaluating the quality of experimental toxicological and ecotoxicological data. Regul Toxicol Pharmacol 1997;25:1–5.

Kroes R, Galli C, Munro I, Schilter B, Tran L, Walker R, Wurtzen G: Threshold of toxicological concern for chemical substances present in the diet: a practical tool for assessing the need for toxicity testing. Food Chem Toxicol 2000;38:255–312.

SCCNFP: SCCNFP/0834/04 (2004): Opinion concerning 'Report for establishing the timetable for phasing out animal testing for the purpose of the cosmetics directive' issued by ECVAM (30/04/2004), adopted by the SCCNFP on 1 July 2004 by means of the written procedure.

SCCP: SCCP/0970/06 (2006a): Opinion on basic criteria for the in vitro assessment of dermal absorption of cosmetic ingredients – updated February 2006, adopted by the SCCP during the 7th plenary meeting of 28 March 2006.

SCCP: SCCP/1005/06 (2006b): The SCCP's Notes of Guidance for the Testing of Cosmetic Ingredients and their Safety Evaluation, adopted by the SCCP during the 10th plenary meeting of 19 December 2006.

Weed DL: Weight of Evidence: A Review of Concepts and Methods. Risk Anal 2005;25:1545–1557.

The Cosmetic Technical Information File in Practice

5

Rogiers V, Pauwels M (eds): Safety Assessment of Cosmetics in Europe.
Curr Probl Dermatol. Basel, Karger, 2008, vol 36, pp 115–128

5.1 Introduction

As already mentioned in chapter 1, Art. 7a.1 of the Cosmetic Products Directive [EU, 1976] forms the legal basis for the compilation of a so-called cosmetic dossier (TIF, PIR, or any other denomination used). It states that the following information should be readily accessible to the Member States' Competent Authorities [EU, 1993, 2003]:

a the qualitative and quantitative composition of the product,
b physicochemistry, microbiology and purity of the ingredients and the cosmetic product,
c the manufacturing method,
d safety assessment of the finished cosmetic product,
e name and address of the safety assessor,
f existing data on undesirable effects on human health,
g proof of the effects claimed,
h data on animal testing.

In most companies, the dossier is available electronically, but for small companies with a limited number of products, it can be more useful to keep a paper dossier per product.

Official guidance on how to fill in the above-mentioned requirements is not available at the European level. The only available official additional information can be found in the further wording of Art. 7a.1, but only few details are provided.

A survey among the competent authorities of the EU Member States revealed that there is a general agreement among the inspectors that the directive is not explicit enough regarding the TIF. Consequently, Member States are not provided with the information they need to effectively monitor industry and to perform inspections in a harmonised way all over Europe [GHK, 2007].

Therefore, we here propose, based upon our own experience, a TIF framework that has been shown to be successful for a series of cosmetic products in real life. It tackles points a–h of Art. 7a.1 with respect to the exact nature of the information that could be provided. The detailed workable framework for a TIF, structuring the above points in an inspection-friendly way, is provided in appendix 3.

Table 1. Representation of how the qualitative and quantitative composition of a finished cosmetic product may be presented in its TIF

Internal code	Supplier	Trade name	INCI name	Function	Concentration % w/w	
abcd	Company 1	Demi water	Aqua	Solvent	70.3	
efgh	Company 2	Mineral oil B	Paraffinum Liquidum	Solvent	15.0	
ijkl	Company 3	Glycerine C	Glycerin	Humectant	6.0	
mnop	Company 4	Emulsifier D	Glyceryl Stearate	Weak w/o emulsifier, part of o/w emulsifying complex	1.6	
qrst	Company 5	Preserving mixture E	Phenoxyethanol Methylparaben Ethylparaben Butylparaben Propylparaben Isobutylparaben	Preservative	0.30 0.10 0.02 0.02 0.02 0.02	0.4
uvwx	Company 6	Perfume F	Parfum code xxxx	perfume	1.000	
...	...	...	...	...	...	

5.2 The Legal Requirements in Practice: A Proposal

5.2.1. Qualitative and Quantitative Composition of the Product

In practice, we propose to visualise the quantitative composition of a cosmetic product in the form of a table (table 1).

The different items of importance in table 1 can be summarised as follows:
– Internal codes usually are appointed by the cosmetic company and allow rapid in-house retrieval of information related to the ingredient concerned. In case the production of the finished product is performed externally, the cosmetic companies' internal codes and/or the ones given by the manufacturing site may be indicated in the table.
– All possible suppliers are specified in the composition table. In the case of mixtures, compositions may differ from one supplier to another (e.g. the presence or absence of a preservative, different solvents used). In that case, all information is reflected in such a way that the table gives a complete overview of every component the formulation might contain.

- The INCI name is the preferred denomination of a cosmetic ingredient. However, since the INCI list is neither a closed nor a restrictive list, common names and/or chemical names may also be used in case of absence of the INCI name. For the specific case of perfumes, commercial names and code numbers are commonly mentioned.
- The function of all ingredients is clearly indicated, since it can have direct legal implications. Some preservatives are, for example, allowed for other than preserving purposes outside the legal restrictions laid down in Annex VI to Dir. 76/786/ EEC [EU, 1976].
- Finally, the concentration is by preference expressed as an unambiguous weight per weight percentage. It is acknowledged that sometimes only a semi-quantitative composition is provided by raw material suppliers. Typically, concentration ranges are stated. In that case, it is advised to indicate the maximum possible concentrations of the constituents concerned in the composition table, since that percentage will potentially be present in the finished cosmetic product. Obtaining exact compositions for all the mixtures is ideal, but because of the suppliers' trade secrets, this is not always possible.

5.2.2. Physicochemistry, Microbiology and Purity of Ingredients and of the Finished Product

a) Physicochemical Data

For every raw material and the finished product, the TIF is expected to contain a physicochemical data set. Not only are a number of parameters determined, but, in the light of sound quality control, they should be checked on a regular basis. Usually, these measurements and checks are performed at the level of the manufacturing plant or unit. Unfortunately, there is no clear-cut official guidance of which parameters to be defined. The SCCP Notes of Guidance [SCCP, 2006] mention physical state, organoleptic properties (colour, odour, taste if relevant), solubility in water and relevant solvents, partition coefficient (Log P_{ow}, at ...°C), density (at ...°C), viscosity (at ...°C), pKa (at ...°C), flash point, boiling point, melting point, ignition point, vapour pressure (at ...°C), ...

Depending on the nature of the ingredient, certain parameters are relevant whereas others are not applicable. It is up to the cosmetic company and/or the manufacturing site to make up a list of relevant parameters for each ingredient and for the finished cosmetic product. In the TIF, this list is displayed, accompanied by the frequency of inspection of the particular property (e.g. per batch, every 6 months) and the accepted result range (specification). In some cases, raw materials are not pre-checked before they are incorporated in finished cosmetic products. The certificates of analysis and the specification sheets provided by the raw material suppliers are then considered as a reliable quality statement and those data are copied into the TIF.

For finished products, on the other hand, we have to date not encountered a manufacturing site that did not perform a set of physicochemical quality checks.

b) Microbiological Checks

Microbiological checks are indispensable for substances susceptible to contamination. Some raw materials, such as preservatives and fats are not necessarily considered being susceptible.

As was the case for physicochemical control, the tests are sometimes only performed on the finished product. Most commonly investigated are total bacterial count (total viable aerobic mesophylic count), *Staphylococcus aureus* (Gram-positive bacteria), *Pseudomonas aeruginosa* (Gram-negative bacteria) and *Candida albicans* (yeast giving chlamydospores) [Colipa, 1997]. Again, the frequency of the performed checks is indicated in the TIF, together with the acceptance limits (e.g. the number of colony-forming units).

c) Physicochemical and Microbiological Stability

The physical stability of a cosmetic product is commonly tested through so-called accelerated stability tests. Herein, substances are typically exposed to fluctuating external temperatures (4, 20, 40°C) during 6 weeks. The setup and the relevance of such testing are chosen on a case by case basis and depend upon the cosmetic product category and the composition. Usually, an accelerated stability test is performed as a precursor of a full stability test at ambient conditions. This is started from the moment the product is commercialised and it is expected to confirm the estimated shelf-life of the product.

Microbiological stability testing of finished cosmetic products can be looked at from two different angles. As stated in the SCCP Notes of Guidance [SCCP, 2006], microbial contaminants may either be introduced during production and filling, or they may come from the permanent, variable and additive microbial contamination during the use of the cosmetic by the consumer. The first type of contamination is usually checked through classical microbiological determinations after filling of the product in its final packaging (see 5.2.2.b). The second type of contamination is typically excluded through the performance of a so-called challenge test [Colipa, 1997]. This consists of an artificial contamination of the finished product, followed by an evaluation of the decrease in contamination to levels ensuring pre-defined microbial limits [European Directorate for the Quality of Medicines, 2001].

Finally, the introduction of the period after opening in the cosmetic labelling provisions [EU, 2003] constitutes quite a challenge for the development of appropriate stability tests. To date, most companies follow an in-house knowledge-based set of rules.

d) Purity and Impurity Profile

As also emphasised by the SCCP [2006], small changes in the nature of impurities of cosmetic ingredients can considerably alter their toxicity. Therefore, it is important to obtain as much information as possible on the purity of the cosmetic ingredient under its commercially supplied form. Sometimes economic interests (cheaper ingredients) are considered of higher importance than a high level of knowledge on the purity and impurity profile of an ingredient. However, the TIF should contain purity data for every ingredient incorporated in the finished product under study.

5.2.3. Manufacturing Method

Already in 1994, Colipa published guidelines for the manufacturer of cosmetic products. The document deals with a multitude of aspects, such as designation of responsibilities, appropriate training of the personnel, adapted testing premises, equipment and machinery, description and careful filing of procedures and finally the different steps of the manufacturing process itself (materials receipt, storage, processing, filling and packaging). The necessity for a good quality control system is emphasised [Colipa, 1994]. Recently, these principles were translated into ISO/FDIS 22716, Guidelines on Good Manufacturing Practice for Cosmetics.

Although all related documents to any applied cosmetic GMP need to be filed in a transparent way, we advise not to include these in the TIF. Instead, a summary of the manufacturing process can be included, specifying the composition of premixes, describing heating processes (with temperature ranges) and the conditions under which different phases are mixed together. Throughout this summary, reference to the detailed documentation usually is made.

5.2.4. Safety Assessment of the Finished Cosmetic Product

The major part of the process of safety assessment of finished cosmetic products has already been discussed under section 4.4. Indeed, Art. 2 of the Cosmetic Products Directive requests that in order to assess the safety for human health of the finished product, the general toxicological profile of the ingredients, their chemical structure and their level of exposure need to be taken into consideration [EU, 1993].

In practice, this means that the safety assessor assembles the available data on all ingredients present in the cosmetic product, and repeats the risk assessment exercise for every one of them. It is important to know that any additive to a cosmetic ingredient is also considered to be a separate ingredient in the final cosmetic formulation. The only exceptions are impurities in the raw materials used, subsidiary technical materials used in the preparation but not present in the final product, and materials used in strictly necessary quantities as solvents or as carriers for perfume and aromatic compositions. Overall, an open communication with the manufacturers is important, since they are able to provide information on composition, purity, additives, and the summaries of performed toxicological tests on the specific ingredients they supply. Inevitably, there are ingredients with very restricted data packages (e.g. substances taken up on EINECS, natural ingredients, …) and others displaying an abundance of toxicological data.

In the final step, the safety assessor translates the entirety of toxicological properties of individual compounds into a substantiated, detailed declaration of safety for the finished product. Since cosmetics often are very complex mixtures consisting of a large number of ingredients (>20), this exercise requests a great deal of experience and a large dose of common sense. In the best case, the decision can be backed up by a number of in vitro assays and/or human compatibility studies performed with the finished cosmetic product, but often those are not available.

For cosmetic products that are on the market for a certain amount of time, the archives of the complaint system may also give additional reassurance, but this is of course not applicable for new products.

5.2.5. Name and Address of the Safety Assessor

The Safety Assessor must hold a higher education or university degree (min. 3 years of study) in the field of pharmacy, toxicology, dermatology, medicine or a similar discipline (e.g. a chemist with the right experience, …) [EU, 1989, 1993]. To enable the authorities to check the competence of the safety assessor, it is advised to include a copy of the curriculum vitae in the TIF.

5.2.6. Existing Data on Undesirable Effects on Human Health

The cosmetic legislation not only requires that existing data on undesirable human health effects resulting from use of the cosmetic product are included in the TIF, but these data should also be made easily accessible to the public by any appropriate means, including electronic ones [EU, 1993, 2003]. As a consequence, two aspects of the complaint system are important: (i) it must be well-elaborated and readily accepted by the competent authorities and (ii) a procedure must be installed that makes the information publicly available.

The first aspect can be tackled by the elaboration of an in-house SOP, describing every step to be taken from the moment a consumer complaint is received until the final action related to that complaint is undertaken. This SOP needs to clearly define what is understood by an undesirable effect. This may differ from one cosmetic product type to another. The employees dealing with complaints must be appropriately trained so that they can distinguish a serious health complaint from any other one. Subsequently, it is important that the right questions are asked in order to obtain objective information to evaluate the complaint. We advise to prepare pre-printed questionnaires per cosmetic product type. Getting accurate information from the consumer is key, since it gives a first and sometimes conclusive indication of the presence or absence of a link between the experienced health effect and the use of the cosmetic product under consideration. Responsibilities must be clearly defined for deciding upon certain actions to be taken, e.g. to involve a dermatologist or MD to follow up a complaint. Finally, it is crucial that every single complaint, as insignificant as it may seem, is registered. In case in-depth investigation seems necessary, every step is carefully documented and filed under a unique archiving number related to the complaint. Although some guidance on the elaboration of a sound complaint system exists [Colipa, 2005], it remains a highly individual exercise within the cosmetic industry.

This is even more the case for the second step, where every company should make the information on its complaint system publicly available. Since there are no strict legal requirements, the majority of companies keep the information as restricted as possible, highlighting the fact that only very few adverse effects occur on a large amount of units of cosmetic products sold [De Groot et al., 1994], indicating that the products can be considered as safe. Upon request, they have to provide the full data.

5.2.7. Proof of the Effects Claimed

According to the cosmetic legislation [EU, 1976], it is industry's responsibility not to mislead the consumer. This principle was already enforced through the general rules on misleading advertising [EU, 1984].

With regard to the efficacy of sunscreen products and the claims made thereto, Commission Recommendation 2006/647/EC imposes some clear minimum efficacy criteria for sun products [EU, 2006b]. Outside the sunscreen area, however, no legal framework for claim substantiation is in place. There are recommendations from the industry side [Colipa, 2001] and from scientific organisations such as EEMCO. The latter has published a number of non-binding strategies and methodologies to substantiate in a scientific way some specific cosmetic claims. Efficacy measurements in the fields of skin hydration, hair shedding and alopecia and antiperspirants and deodorants, are just a couple of examples [Rogiers, 2001; Piérard et al., 2003, 2004].

In general, it is considered that for individual ingredients, claim substantiation can be achieved through literature searches or by contacting the manufacturer. Claims on the label and any form of advertisement for the product must be carefully formulated so that the claimed effects remain related to the ingredients and are not automatically attributable to the finished product. For example, a clear distinction can be made between the claims 'This product contains hydrating compound x' and 'Due to the presence of compound x, this product will hydrate the skin'.

For the finished product, in use tests are envisaged, as well as laboratory experiments and clinical trials, depending on the nature of the product and the specific claims made.

Nevertheless, claim substantiation remains a grey zone as far as data requirements and appropriate testing methods are concerned [Lodén, 2007].

5.2.8. Data on Animal Testing

Art. 7a.1 of the Cosmetic Products Directive requests that every TIF should contain 'data on any animal testing performed by the manufacturer, his agents or suppliers, relating to the development or safety evaluation of the product or its ingredients, including any animal testing performed to meet the legislative or regulatory requirements of non-member countries' [EU, 2003]. In a real life situation, it is quite impossible to find out which experiments have ever been performed for whatever purpose on a particular cosmetic ingredient. Therefore, it is very unclear how this requirement can be filled in. Moreover it will be very hard to be double-checked by any competent authority. In the context of REACH, the EChA is expected to administer a new, freely accessible internet database of registered chemicals, including their safety characteristics [Warhurst, 2006]. This may be the way forward for the Commission to obtain the requested information on performed tests and the involvement of experimental animals. However, the relevance of a list of performed animal tests on cosmetic ingredients in a TIF is not immediately clear.

When the claim for a cosmetic product is made that no animal testing was carried out during its development, some major hurdles still must be overcome.

According to the 7th Amendment of Dir. 76/768/EEC, this claim is allowed in case 'the manufacturer and his suppliers have not carried out or commissioned any animal tests on the finished product, or its prototype, or any of the ingredients contained in it, or used any ingredients that have been tested on animals by others for the purpose of developing new cosmetic products' [EU, 2003]. In order to further explain this provision, a Commission Recommendation states that proof needs to be provided that 'the manufacturer and his suppliers, including all suppliers in the supply chain, have not directly carried out the animal tests or have not requested or paid for animal tests by means for instance of sponsorship of research by academic institutions'. Equally 'the manufacturer and his suppliers should not have used ingredients for which data resulting from animal tests made by others for the purpose of developing a new cosmetic product are available for instance in scientific literature' [EU, 2006a]. The underlined words make it impossible to ever substantiate such a claim, unless a worldwide central database would be available assembling all possible safety data of all compounds used in cosmetic products. Since this seems quite unrealistic, it is assumed that the claim 'no animal testing was carried out' will not easily be applied.

5.3 Some Practical Remarks

This section contains practical additional remarks related to the compilation of TIFs and the marketing of cosmetic products in general.

1 A TIF is a dynamic set of data: it must be updated with every (minor) modification to the cosmetic product (new manufacturer of an ingredient, different colour for the product, any change in the production process, any minor change in the composition, …). Care should be taken that, in case of a significant change, the safety assessor is requested to update the undersigned safety assessment.

2 The presentation of the information strongly depends on the kind of inspection.

In case inspection is performed at random, the presented information is best kept quite general, since it is supposed to cover all possible combinations of ingredient types and sources that may be included in the finished product.

In case inspection is performed after a complaint, it is possible that the suspicious batch number has been identified. In that case, batch-specific data should be assembled, from the specific production process sheet for possible deviations to the protocol, to detailed information on batch-specific data for the individual ingredients used. In this stage, batch traceability is crucial and should be rapidly and effectively effectuated.

3 Our experience is that, usually, one product is inspected and not a complete product line. In the latter case, the company is allowed to ask for some more time to constitute the TIFs. Some documents mention time limits of 48 or 72 h to assemble the product information, but the European legislation only mentions that the information should be 'readily accessible', which leaves some room for discussion with the competent authority.

4 A TIF is required for all cosmetic products, including products that have been on the market for a long time, products not manufactured but 'only' imported into Europe, cosmetic products for professional use and promotional campaigns and gifts. For the latter, due to their common small size, the labelling requirement often constitutes a major problem.

5 According to Art. 7a.3 [EU, 1976], the TIF must be available in one of the national languages of the Member State concerned or in a language readily understood by the competent authorities. It is common practice to make TIFs in English.

6 Three different responsibilities are commonly defined in the TIF:
(i) the marketer: overall responsible for the product and its placing on the market,
(ii) the file coordinator: responsible for assembling the different parts of the TIF and for keeping it up to date,
(iii) the safety assessor: having the required qualifications, this person makes up and signs the safety assessment but is not responsible for other parts of the TIF.

7 The place of manufacture or the place of initial importation of cosmetic products must be notified to the competent authority of the Member State concerned.

8 National legislations must be carefully consulted when exploring the market in other European Member States. Every Member State has transposed the Cosmetic Products Directive into national legislation, and there are some significant differences with regard to notification requirements to governmental institutions and/or national poison control centres. In order to be in compliance with all legal provisions,

it is worth the effort to contact the individual competent authorities of the EU Member State. A list of competent national authorities in the cosmetic sector has been officially published [EU, 2004].

5.4 Proposed Framework for a TIF

The data mentioned in the previous section must be available in a structured and inspection-friendly way. A practical proposal is included in appendix 3. It was presented to industry during several 'Safety Assessment of Cosmetics in the EU' training courses, yearly held at the Vrije Universiteit Brussel. The framework proposed is currently being successfully used by a number of Belgian and Dutch SMEs.

Please note that the name 'dossier' does not imply the use of a hard paper copy, but may as well be an electronic version of the information.

The proposed framework divides the technical information into three parts:

1 An administrative part:
– Trade name of the product and responsible company, manufacturer or distributor.
– Product category (Annex I).
– Integral quantitative composition of the product.
– Identification of persons with ultimate responsibility.
2 An ingredients part:
A separate section for every ingredient, containing:
– Identity(ies), supplier(s) and composition(s) of the ingredient.
– Details on manufacturer(s) and supplier(s) of the ingredient.
– Physicochemistry and microbiology of the ingredient (including the physicochemical and microbiological inspections).
– Toxicity data: acute oral, dermal and/or inhalation toxicity, skin irritation, eye irritation, sensitisation, photo-allergy and photo-irritation when relevant, repeated dose toxicity and additional relevant toxicological data.
– First aid measures.
– Risk and safety instructions with EU labelling according to Dir. 67/548/EEC [EU, 1967] and specific labelling according to Dir. 76/768/EEC [EU, 1976] and/ or national legislation(s).
– List of animal tests performed with the ingredient.
3 A finished product part:
– Fabrication of the product with place(s) of manufacturing, methodology, identification of person responsible for manufacturing.
– Stability of the product including physical and microbiological stability.
– Physicochemical properties and microbiological data on the finished product, including examinations.

- Safety data concerning the finished product including an overview of the toxicological data of the ingredients, the communication done with the national competent authorities and the poison control centres, toxicological animal testing performed on the finished product, toxicological tests using alternative methods, human tests performed on the finished product, an undersigned safety evaluation with the identification of the safety assessor and the appropriate credentials (CV).
- Efficacy of the finished product: a summing up of the claims made, efficacy tests that have been carried out, additional information or argumentation.
- Packaging and labelling: this part, starting with an overview of the data on packaging and labelling of the ingredients, provides the labelling of the finished product, gives information on packaging materials and weight/volume, packaging procedures, identification of the batch number, checks on the end products and finally identifies the person responsible for packaging.

Not mentioned above but indispensable is the follow-up dossier of the market, which contains all the details related to the complaint system.

Finally, the last key part of the finished product dossier is the safety evaluation of the product, signed by the safety assessor.

5.5 Discussion and Conclusions

The current chapter results from the imminent need for guidance related to the practical problems when trying to assemble a TIF according to the EU regulatory requirements. It offers a set of recommendations for all safety-related items that are required by the legislation for compiling a cosmetic TIF.

Firstly, the qualitative and quantitative composition of the product is unravelled with special attention for potential complexity due to possible combinations of slightly different mixtures supplied by different companies. Physicochemical/microbiological properties, stability data, the manufacturing method, the complaint system and finally also the claim substantiation need to be fully documented. However, viewing the dynamic character of a TIF, not all available information is included in full. Generally, summaries are given with clear references to detailed test descriptions and results, and/or to archived SOP's and internal protocols. Therefore, appointing a file coordinator within a cosmetic company is important. Keeping a TIF up to date is a task that requires good knowledge of the legal requirements and of a large number of technical aspects. This chapter assists file coordinators and safety assessors in their respective tasks.

This brings us to the final important part of the TIF, namely the safety assessment. Ideally, this document is included in the TIF, but it should also be readable without additional information. It contains all the arguments that the safety assessor has used to come to his/her conclusion and ideally, it is revised on a regular basis, taking into account the most recent knowledge and information (e.g. the results of the market follow-up procedure, including the complaint system). In case the TIF is inspected, the presence of the safety assessor is not mandatory, but may help to answer a number of crucial questions posed by the competent authorities.

The order in which the requirements are displayed in the Cosmetic Products Directive is not perceived as a structured overview for the inspector. Therefore, a blank proposal of a structured framework for a TIF is included in appendix 3. It is subdivided in three major sections: one mainly containing administrative information, one fully describing the cosmetic ingredients used and a final part providing all relevant details on the finished cosmetic product. This allows the inspector to first check the administrative compliance of the company, after which he or she can analyze in more depth the technical and toxicological information. Over the years, our framework proposed here has proven its usefulness and has been appreciated by Dutch and Belgian inspectors.

5.6 **References**

5

Colipa: Cosmetic Good Manufacturing Practices – Guideline for the Manufacturer of Cosmetic Products. The European Cosmetic Toiletry and Perfumery Association, 1994, available through http://www.colipa.com/site/download.cfm?SAVE = 28500&LG = 1 (consulted December 2007).

Colipa: Guidelines on Microbial Quality Management (MQM). The European Cosmetic Toiletry and Perfumery Association, 1997, available through http://www.colipa.com/site/download.cfm?SAVE = 28506&LG = 1 (consulted December 2007).

Colipa: Guidelines for the Evaluation of the Efficacy of Cosmetic Products, ed 2. The European Cosmetic Toiletry and Perfumery Association, 2001.

Colipa: The European Cosmetic Toiletry and Perfumery Association (Colipa) and the Cosmetic, Toiletry and Frangrance Association (CTFA) Guidelines on Stability Testing of Cosmetic Products. Document No. 03/094 – MC, 2004, available through www.colipa.com/site/download.cfm?SAVE = 28511&LG = 1 (consulted December 2007).

Colipa: Guidelines on the Management of Undesirable Event Reports. The European Cosmetic Toiletry and Perfumery Association, 2005.

De Groot AC, Weyland JW, Nater JP (eds): Unwanted Effects of Cosmetics and Drugs Used in Dermatology, ed 3. Amsterdam, Elsevier Science, 1994.

EU: Council Directive 67/548/EEC of 27 June 1967 on the approximation of laws, regulations and administrative provisions relating to the classification, packaging and labelling of dangerous substances. Off J 1967;P196:1–98.

EU: Council Directive 76/768/EEC of 27 July 1976 on the approximation of the laws of the Member States relating to cosmetic products. Off J 1976;L262:169–200.

EU: Council Directive 84/450/EEC of 10 September 1984 concerning misleading and comparative advertising. Off J 1984;L250:17–23.

EU: Council Directive 89/48/EEC of 21 December 1988 on a general system for the recognition of higher-education diplomas awarded on completion of professional education and training of at least three years' duration. Off J 1989;L019:16–23.

EU: Council Directive 93/35/EEC of 14 June 1993 amending for the sixth time Directive 76/768/EEC on the approximation of the laws of the Member States relating to cosmetic products. Off J 1993; L151:32–37.

EU: Directive 2003/15/EC of the European Parliament and of the Council of 27 February 2003 amending Council Directive 76/768/EEC on the approximation of the laws of the Member States relating to cosmetic products. Off J 2003;L066:26–35.

EU: Communication 2004/C 278/02. Competent national authorities in the cosmetics sector. Off J 2004;C278:2–8.

EU: Commission Recommendation 2006/406/EC of 7 June 2006 establishing guidelines on the use of claims referring to the absence of tests on animals pursuant to Council Directive 76/768/EEC. Off J 2006a;L158:18–19.

EU: Commission Recommendation 2006/647/EC of 22 September 2006 on the efficacy of sunscreen products and the claims made relating thereto. Off J 2006b;L265:169–200.

GHK (2007): Evaluation on DG Enterprise and Industry legislation – Cosmetics Directive. Final report submitted by the EEC (GHK, Technopolis) within the framework of ENTR/04/093-FC-Lot 1, Special contract reference ENTR/R5/04/093/1/06/10, DG Enterprise and Industry, European Commission, 21 September 2007.

Lodén M: Changes in European legislation make it timely to introduce a transparent market surveillance system for cosmetics. Acta Derm Venereol 2007;87:485–492.

European Directorate for the Quality of Medicines: European Pharmacopoeia, ed 4, suppl 4.2. Strassbourg, Council of Europe, 2001.

Piérard GE, Elsner P, Marks R, Masson P, Paye M: EEMCO group (European Expert Group on Efficacy Measurement of Cosmetics and other Topical Products) – EEMCO guidance for the efficacy assessment of antiperspirants and deodorants. Skin Pharmacol Appl Skin Physiol 2003;16:324–342.

Piérard GE, Piérard-Franchimont C, Marks R, Elsner P: EEMCO group (European Expert Group on Efficacy Measurement of Cosmetics and other Topical Products) – EEMCO guidance for the assessment of hair shedding and alopecia. Skin Pharmacol Physiol 2004;17:98–110.

Rogiers V: EEMCO group (European Expert Group on Efficacy Measurement of Cosmetics and other Topical Products) – EEMCO guidance for the assessment of transepidermal water loss in cosmetic sciences. Skin Pharmacol Appl Skin Physiol 2001; 14:117–128.

SCCP: SCCP/1005/06 (2006): The SCCP's Notes of Guidance for the Testing of Cosmetic Ingredients and their Safety Evaluation, adopted by the SCCP during the 10th plenary meeting of 19 December 2006.

The Use of Alternative Methods in the Safety Assessment of Cosmetic Ingredients

6

Rogiers V, Pauwels M (eds): Safety Assessment of Cosmetics in Europe.
Curr Probl Dermatol. Basel, Karger, 2008, vol 36, pp 129–165

6.1 Introduction

A common problem shared by the SCCP and the individual safety assessor, is the foreseen animal testing ban on cosmetic ingredients. The lack of replacement alternatives for the endpoints that are commonly assessed in the current risk/safety assessment paradigm, is reason for concern. On several occasions, academics and members of scientific committees have stressed the need to check the adequacy of 3R alternative methods, not only for hazard determination but in particular for quantitative risk assessment [CSTEE, 2004; SCCNFP, 2004g; Rogiers and Pauwels, 2005; ICCG, 2006; Greim et al., 2006; Greim, 2007]. The combination of the abolition of animal testing and the continuous requirement to safeguard human health calls for the development of new hazard and risk assessment paradigms.

A complicating factor may be that individual sector legislations apply other standards and use specific terminology. For cosmetic ingredients, the outcome from an alternative method can only be used in case the method is either officially validated or taken up in Annex IX to the Cosmetic Products Directive [EU, 2003]. For the purpose of testing under REACH, on the other hand, results from 'suitable' alternative methods are equally accepted. REACH defines 'suitable' as 'sufficiently well developed according to internationally agreed test development criteria (e.g. the European Centre for the Validation of Alternative Methods (ECVAM) criteria for the entry of a test into the pre-validation process)' [EU, 2006].

In order to extend the usefulness to some aspects related to the animal testing ban, the previously described VUB database (see chapter 3) was extended with information on animal numbers and the use of alternative methods as occurring in the SCC(NF)P dossiers.

This allowed investigation of the extent to which alternative methods have advanced into the safety assessment of cosmetic ingredients present on the annexes. In addition, it was verified how well the requirement to use the validated alternative method, from the moment it is available [EU, 1993, 2003], has been respected in the dossiers examined.

Finally, the obtained animal numbers are compared with the projected animal toll of REACH, thus placing the number of animals tested for cosmetics in a broader European context.

6.2 **Materials and Methods**

Use was made of the Microsoft Access database present at the Vrije Universiteit Brussel, Department of Toxicology, as described in sections 3.2 and 3.3. It contains information extracted from 185 SCC(NF)P opinions issued between 2000 and 2006, dealing with 175 substances in total.

The Microsoft Access database and the Microsoft Excel files linked to it were extended with the following features:
- species involved per specific toxicological endpoint,
- indication of the date of animal testing[1], most commonly the date of test report,
- numbers of animals involved[2],
- separate entries for 3R alternatives,
- details on obtained results.

Since the aim of the current study was to obtain a general view on which types of tests (alternative methods or not) form part of a complete data package introduced for a single substance, the data gathered through subsequent industry submissions on a same ingredient were systematically taken together as one single data set. Viewing the restricted number of detailed opinions available from the years 2000 and 2001, the information presented in this chapter is limited to the 2002–2006 SCC(NF)P opinions.

6.3 **Animal Testing and 3-R Alternatives in SCC(NF)P Dossiers**

6.3.1. **Acute Toxicity**

a) Background

For many years, acute oral/dermal/inhalation toxicity was assessed through the so-called lethal dosage LD_{50} tests, of which the acute oral LD_{50} assay was most commonly performed [EU, 1992a; OECD, 1981a]. The purpose of the test was to determine the dosage that had a lethal effect on 50% of the tested animals and therefore typically three dose levels of a test substance were administered to groups of 5–10 rats or mice.

---

1   In a restricted number of cases, some studies were repeated in the same species. In those instances, the date of the most recent study was introduced in the database.

2   If not specified in the report, an estimation was made based upon the number of animals required according to the general description of the animal assays in Annex V of Dir. 67/548/EEC, Part B and/or OECD testing guidelines.

Viewing the cruelty of this procedure and considering the fact that substances with an oral LD_{50} value above 2,000 mg/kg did not require any classification or labelling, the so-called 'limit test' was introduced. Herein, the high dose of 2,000 mg/kg was administered to a small number of animals. If no lethality was observed, further testing was redundant and the LD_{50} value could be considered higher than the classification limit of 2,000 mg/kg.

Although it was a good reduction measure, the limit test did not offer an ethically acceptable alternative for substances with lower LD_{50} values. Therefore, three reduction and refinement alternatives were developed:

- The fixed dose method [EU, 2004a; OECD, 2001c], which abandons lethality as an endpoint, but instead relies on the observation of clear signs of toxicity at one of a series of fixed dose levels. As such, pain and distress in the animals is significantly reduced and the goal of refinement is achieved.
- The acute toxic class method [EU, 2004b; OECD, 2001d], which does not aim to calculate a precise LD_{50} value. Instead, it allows the determination of defined exposure ranges where lethality is expected since death of a proportion of the animals is still the major endpoint. The test follows a complex stepwise dosage scheme, using three animals of a single sex per step, thus offering a reduction in the number of animals.
- The up-and-down procedure [OECD, 2001e], in which only one animal is dosed at a time. Depending on the outcome of the previous animal, the dose for the next animal is adjusted up or down: if an animal survives, dosage is increased, if it dies, dosage is decreased. This is continued until reversal occurs. With this procedure, the number of animals is significantly reduced.

Since the existing alternative methods still involve the use of experimental animals, their performance on cosmetic ingredients in Europe will be prohibited from 11 March 2009 on. A currently running EU project called 'A-Cute Tox[3]' was set up with the goal of developing an in vitro testing strategy that is sufficiently robust and powerful to completely replace in vivo testing of acute toxicity of chemicals.

As stated in the reports of the individual Working Parties of the project[4], the following activities have been completed:

- Generation of an in vivo acute toxicity database for 97 selected reference chemicals, including LD_{50} values, data from acute poisoning cases and physicochemical data.
- Testing of the 97 selected chemicals in in vitro cytotoxicity assays, making use of three different basal cytotoxicity assays and five different cell lines.

---

3   EU Framework Programme 6 Integrated Project (contract No. LSHB-CT-2004-512051, 2005–2009), more information through: http://www.acutetox.org (consulted February 2008).
4   http://www.acutetox.org/results/index.php (consulted February 2008).

Rogiers · Pauwels

Table 1. Reported use of alternative acute oral toxicity assays in SCC(NF)P opinions (2002–2006)

Alternative method used	Year of alternative assay	Year of 'classic' B.1 assay for the same substance	Reference
Up and down procedure	1989	1993	SCCNFP, 2002
Acute toxic class method	2000	1995	SCCNFP, 2003a
	2000	None	SCCP, 2005a
Fixed dose method	1997	1984	SCCP, 2006a
	2004	1990	SCCP, 2006o
	2004	1994	SCCP, 2005d
	2004	None	SCCP, 2006f
	2004	None	SCCP, 2006q
	2005	1977	SCCP, 2006l
	2005	None	SCCP, 2006g
	2005	None	SCCP, 2006h
	2005	None	SCCP, 2006p

- Introduction of all in vivo/in vitro/physicochemical data in a databank called AcuBase.
- In vitro/in vivo comparison, extraction of the best test systems and identification of outliers.
- Research into new cell systems and new endpoints and in the development of in vitro systems/computer models that can predict metabolism-dependent toxicity.

A-Cute Tox is nearly in its final stage, aiming at pre-validating the in vitro testing strategy to demonstrate the reproducibility and relevance of each of its building blocks. This work is expected to start in May–June 2008.

It should be mentioned that in the fields of dermal and inhalation acute toxicity testing no alternatives are available to date or within the near future. The A-Cute Tox project will not offer a solution in these particular fields. The OECD has drafted three proposals:
- Acute Inhalation Toxicity-Fixed Dose Procedure [OECD, 2004d],
- Acute Dermal Toxicity-Fixed Dose Procedure [OECD, 2004e],
- Acute Inhalation Toxicity – Acute Toxic Class Method [OECD, 2004f].
  These, however, still await final approval.

b) Acute Oral Toxicity Data in SCC(NF)P Opinions
Between 2002 and 2006, the SCC(NF)P studied data on 164 individual substances. In total, 12 alternative assays for acute oral toxicity testing were reported. In 6 cases, they were used as a stand-alone test (table 1). Compared to a total of 101 substances for

which the classical LD_{50} assay was presented, this appears to be a low number. However, it needs to be emphasised that the vast majority (94%) of the LD_{50} tests were performed before the year 2001 (publication of the OECD guidelines) and that many of them consist of limit tests (only testing the highest dosage level).

It can be concluded that gradually the fixed dose method starts to appear in SCCP submissions. However, for many substances old classical LD_{50} studies appear to be available, making additional testing redundant.

6.3.2. Skin Irritation

a) Background

For more than 60 years, skin irritation has been assessed through the so-called 'Draize skin irritation test' [Draize et al., 1944]. The method was taken up in EU legislation in 1984 and initially involved the use of 3–6 rabbits [EU, 1984a]. Gradually, refinement and reduction measures were introduced, including the obligation to check the following parameters before initiating an in vivo skin irritation test with the rabbit [EU, 1992b, 2004c]:
– existing human and animal data,
– structure activity relationships,
– relevant physicochemical properties and chemical reactivity (e.g. substances with a pH ≤ 2.0 or ≥ 11.5 are automatically considered corrosive),
– available dermal toxicity data,
– results from in vitro and ex vivo tests.

For the specific endpoint of skin corrosion, three validated alternative methods are available, making use of either excised rat skin or human skin models [EU, 2000g; OECD, 2004a, b]. Since corrosion is not often encountered in cosmetic ingredients, let alone in finished cosmetic products, these assays are mainly useful outside the cosmetic field [SCCP, 2007a].

In 2007, the ESAC recognised the Episkin™ method as a reliable and relevant stand-alone test for predicting rabbit skin irritation.

It is considered appropriate for the purpose of distinguishing between R38[5] skin irritating and non-skin irritating substances [ESAC, 2007c].

Although it appeared an ideal alternative method in the cosmetic field, the SCCP recently expressed some concerns with regard to the applicability domain of the Episkin™ replacement test. More specifically, the Committee pointed out that the endpoint of the test is MTT[6] reduction, in which colour formation is essential.

---

5   R38: Irritating to skin.
6   3-(4,5)-dimethyl-2-thiazolyl-2,5-dimethyl-2H-tetrazolium bromide.

Objective observations may thus be affected in case hair dyes and colourants are added to the system and influence colouration [SCCP, 2007b]. As also noticed by the SCCP, the MTT colourimetric method was equally described as problematic for dyes in another setting, namely in the use of the Episkin™ model for the assessment of in vitro phototoxicity [Lelièvre et al., 2007].

As such, it appears that the Episkin™ methodology needs some further study before its use as a skin irritation replacement method for cosmetic ingredients will be generally accepted. Nevertheless, it is a promising development that most probably will find its use for many cosmetic ingredient types, potentially with the exception of some colourants and hair dye substances.

b) Skin Irritation Data in SCC(NF)P Opinions

Since reduction and refinement measures were gradually introduced into official protocols, it was impossible to check the availability of 'alternative methods' for skin irritation in SCC(NF)P reports. Nevertheless, the database shows useful to provide general data on performed skin irritation studies, their results and potential problems encountered in vivo.

On the 164 individual substances evaluated by the SCC(NF)P, 107 were accompanied by in vivo skin irritation data. Out of these, 91% were considered acceptable. The tests were mainly performed in the rabbit with an average of 6 animals per tested cosmetic ingredient. The test substance was either used undiluted (in 64% of the cases) or diluted in an appropriate solvent for an in vivo skin irritation study. Concentrations ranged from 0.1 to 40%.

The 97 in vivo skin irritation data packages that were considered acceptable by the SCC(NF)P can now be considered candidates for further in vivo/in vitro comparison. They can be subdivided in four different categories with regard to their irritating potential (table 2).

Overall, the problem of skin colouration was encountered in 22% of the in vivo irritation data sets presented for hair dyes.

As such, the database allows the drawing of a list of candidate reference compounds to be included in an in vivo/in vitro comparison study, including:
– Representative substances for each skin irritation category.
– Especially the non-irritating, slightly/mildly irritating and moderately irritating compounds are of importance, since for skin corrosion, validated replacement alternatives are already available.
– Representative substances for different ingredient types.

The discolouration of the animals' skin in the in vivo study was reported for hair dye substances only. Therefore, within each skin irritation category, one could distinguish:
(i)   hair dye substance(s) reported to cause skin colouration in the rabbit,
(ii) hair dye substance(s) not reported to cause skin colouration in the rabbit,
(iii) other than hair dye substance(s).

Table 2. Summary of results from in vivo dermal irritation studies considered acceptable by the SCC(NF)P

Classification by the SCC(NF)P	Data sets	Problems encountered in the in vivo study
Non-irritating	66	in 11 cases[1], discolouration of the animal's skin made readings difficult
Slightly/mildly irritating	19	in 4 cases[1], discolouration of the animal's skin made readings difficult
Severely/moderately irritating	11	none reported
Corrosive	1	none reported
None	10	data were not scientifically acceptable; in 2 cases[1], discolouration of the animal's skin made readings difficult/impossible

[1]Hair dye substances.

6.3.3. Eye Irritation

a) Background

The classical Draize eye irritation test was developed together with the original skin irritation assay described above [Draize et al., 1944]. It is an in vivo test method that initially involved the use of 3–6 rabbits [EU, 1984b]. The eye irritation test was heavily criticised because of the subjectivity of the method, the overestimation of human responses, but above all because of the method's cruelty [Vinardell and Mitjans, 2007]. Instilling a substance in the rabbit's eye is a procedure that inevitably causes pain and distress to the animal.

Therefore, the test method has repeatedly been subject to refinement and reduction measures, including:
– The introduction of the LVET, in which only 10% of the original dose is applied to the rabbit eye, and a reduction of the number of animals from 6 to 3 [Bruner et al., 1992].
– As is the case for skin irritation studies, the obligation to check available physico-chemical, in vitro and in vivo data before moving to the animal [EU, 1992c, 2004d].

To date, there is not yet a validated alternative method for eye irritation available.

In 2006, the US ICCVAM completed an evaluation of the validation status of four in vitro eye irritation test methods [ICCVAM, 2006]:

- the BCOP assay,
- the HET-CAM assay,
- the ICE assay,
- the IRE assay.

BCOP, ICE and IRE typically use tissues from slaughterhouses [Gautheron et al., 1992; Prinsen, 1996; Prinsen and Koëter, 1993], whereas the HET-CAM assay involves the use fertilised hen's eggs [Lüpke, 1985].

The ICCVAM report concluded that sufficient data are available to support the use of the BCOP and ICE test methods, in appropriate circumstances and with certain limitations, as a screening test to identify substances as ocular corrosives and severe irritants, in a tiered-testing strategy, as part of a weight-of-evidence approach. Examples of the 'limitations' are alcohols, ketones and solids for the BCOP, which generate false positives and/or false negatives, whereas the ICE scores below par for alcohols, surfactants and solids [ICCVAM, 2006]. In 2007, ESAC unanimously endorsed these statements [ESAC, 2007a].

The HET-CAM and IRE procedure, on the other hand, were reported to require additional optimisation before they could be used in an ocular irritation assessment strategy [ICCVAM, 2006]. This statement was equally endorsed by ESAC in 2007, which added the comment that European Authorities have stated that, although all four tests were not yet validated, positive outcomes from these tests could be used for classification and labelling substances as severe eye irritants (R41[7]) [ESAC, 2007a]. In case of negative results, however, the animal study would still be required for confirmation. Screening for ocular corrosives and severe irritants is for cosmetic ingredients and finished products of limited value, but it is useful in the case of production or manufacturing errors.

b) Eye Irritation Data in SCC(NF)P Opinions
As was the case for skin irritation, the availability of the alternative methods involving gradual reduction and refinement of the original Draize method [EU, 1984b], were impossible to check in SCC(NF)P reports.

On the 164 individual substances evaluated by the SCC(NF)P, 109 contained in vivo eye irritation data. Out of these, 93% were considered acceptable.

The test substance was either used undiluted (in 54% of the cases) or diluted at concentrations ranging from 0.1 to 40%.

The 101 in vivo eye irritation data packages that were considered acceptable by the SCC(NF)P, may be considered candidates for further in vivo/in vitro comparison (e.g. when BCOP and HET-CAM should require further validation in the cosmetic

---

7   R41: Risk of serious damage to eyes.

Table 3. Summary of results from in vivo eye irritation studies considered acceptable by the SCC(NF)P (2002–2006)

Classification by the SCC(NF)P	Data sets	Problems encountered in the in vivo study
Non-irritating	40	8 cases[1] of eye discolouration
Slightly/mildly irritating	22	4 cases[1] of eye discolouration
(Moderately) irritating	22	2 cases[1] of eye discolouration
Severely irritating/risk of serious damage to the eyes	17	3 cases[1] of eye discolouration
None	8	data were not scientifically acceptable; in 1 case[1], discolouration of the animal's skin made readings impossible

[1] All hair dye substances.

field). They can be subdivided in four different categories with regard to their irritating potential (table 3).

In a restricted number of dossiers, in vitro eye irritation data were presented. These not only comprised the BCOP and HET-CAM assays, but equally the NRU [Brantom et al., 1997] and the RBC [Pape et al., 1987] assay (table 4), both cytotoxicity assays.

In two instances, the HET-CAM assay appears to be used as a stand-alone test. In the first case, the test substance had already been shown to be a severe irritant to the rabbit skin, wherefore instillation in the eye was excluded from an ethical point of view [SCCP, 2004c].

In the second case, the HET-CAM assay was combined with the in vitro NRU assay in human keratinocytes. Although the SCCNFP pointed towards the limitations and the non-validation of the performed tests in its final conclusion, no additional testing was required and the substance was declared safe for use based upon both alternative assays [SCCNFP, 2004d].

6.3.4. Skin Sensitisation

a) Background

For more than 35 years, two guinea pig assays have been routinely performed for the evaluation of the sensitising potential of test substances:

1 The Magnusson-Kligman GPMT [Magnusson and Kligman, 1969], which is an adjuvant-type test, meaning that the allergic response to the test substance is

Table 4. Occurrence of BCOP and HET-CAM assays in dossiers studied by the SCC(NF)P (2002–2006)

Method used	Year of alternative assay	Year of in vivo Draize test for the same substance	Reference
BCOP	1999	1995	SCCNFP, 2002
	2003	1996	SCCNFP, 2004f
HET-CAM	1992	1992	SCCNFP, 2003b
	1998	none	SCCP, 2004c
	2001	1989	SCCP, 2005h
	2002	1971	SCCNFP, 2004c
	2002	1971	SCCNFP, 2004e
	2002	none	SCCNFP, 2004d
NRU	2001	1989	SCCP, 2005h
	2002	1971	SCCNFP, 2004c
	2002	none	SCCNFP, 2004d
	2003	1996	SCCNFP, 2004f
RBC	2001	1989	SCCP, 2005h

Table 5. Types of sensitisation data present in dossiers studied by the SCC(NF)P (2002–2006)

Test(s) performed	Data sets
Only non-LLNA	65
Both non-LLNA and LLNA	23
Only LLNA	25

potentiated by intradermal injection of a specific adjuvant mixture. The test mimics the 'real-life' development of an allergic reaction through a repeated application of a slightly irritating concentration of the test material to the animals' skin (induction phase), followed by a rest period and the subsequent application of the highest non-irritating concentration (challenge phase).

2 The Buehler test [Buehler, 1965, 1994], which is a non-adjuvant technique that involves topical application only. The sensitivity of the method is considered to be low compared to the GPMT.

An alternative method, called the murine LLNA, was endorsed by ESAC in 2000 [ESAC, 2000], more than 10 years after the publication on the results of its initial validation study [Kimber and Weisenberger, 1989]. The LLNA is a reduction and refinement animal test which uses mice instead of guinea pigs and which is based on the extent of stimulation of proliferation of lymphocytes in regional lymph nodes draining the site of application of the test substance [EU, 2004f]. The major refinement resides in the fact that the challenge phase of the sensitisation process is not reached in the experimental animal. The LLNA is advised to be the preferred method, but in some instances, and for scientific reasons, the conventional methods still can be used [ESAC, 2000].

Recently, a rLLNA has been approved by ESAC [ESAC, 2007b]. In this assay, only the negative control group and the equivalent of the high-dose group from the full LLNA are used as a screening test to distinguish between sensitisers and non-sensitisers [Kimber et al., 2006]. Since the rLLNA does not allow the determination of the potency of a sensitising chemical, the SCCP does not consider it adequate for risk assessment of cosmetic ingredients [SCCP, 2007a].

In a currently ongoing European project called Sens-it-iv[8], novel testing strategies for in vitro assessment of allergens are investigated. The ultimate deliverables from Sens-it-iv would be in vitro tests ready for formal validation according to international standards and subsequent international regulatory acceptance. The final results of the project will be available after 2010.

b) Skin Sensitisation Data in SCC(NF)P Opinions

For 119 of the 164 studied substances, in vivo skin sensitisation data were available. Out of these, 76% were considered acceptable. The tests were either performed in the guinea pig with an average of 48 animals per tested cosmetic ingredient or in the mouse with an average of 49 animals per test substance. Of all hair dye substances with acceptable sensitisation data packages, 50% were found to be sensitizing.

The non-LLNA assays were, for all but one substance, reported to be performed before 2002. From 2002 onwards, a replacement by the LLNA is observed. For one specific substance where as well a Buehler as a Magnusson Kligman assay is available, the year of test is reported to be 2003, meaning that the tests would have been performed 'illegally'. However, it must be stated that usually the date of test report is mentioned in the SCC(NF)P dossier, thus the actual test may have been performed a couple of months earlier.

Taking the above into consideration, it can be concluded that the LLNA has gradually found its way into the dossiers submitted to the SCC(NF)P.

In a next step, it appeared interesting to check the similarity between results obtained through the LLNA and the non-LLNA studies. As suggested by experts in the field, post-validation data on alternative methods should keep on being published, since they are important for enhancing trust in the methods [Basketter, 2007]. Therefore, the results of the 23 substances for which both types of tests were available, are compared (table 6).

---

8   EU Framework Programme 6 Integrated Project (contract No. LSHB-CT-2005-018681, 2006–2010), more information through: http://www.sens-it-iv.eu (consulted December 2007).

Table 6. Comparison between results for the same substance in the LLNA and non-LLNA assays

Test performed	Result guinea pig study	Result LLNA	Reference (ingredient type)
MKGPMT	negative[1]	positive	SCCNFP, 2003c (oxidative HD)
MKGPMT	positive	negative	SCCNFP, 2004a (oxidative HD)
MKGPMT	negative	negative	SCCNFP, 2004b (semi-perm HD)
MKGPMT Buehler	positive negative	positive	SCCNFP, 2004f (preservative)
MKGPMT	negative	negative	SCCP, 2004a (semi-perm HD)
MKGPMT	equivocal	positive	SCCP, 2004b (fragrance)
Buehler	positive	positive	SCCP, 2005b (fragrance)
MKGPMT Buehler	positive negative[2]	positive	SCCP, 2005c (oxidative HD)
MKGPMT	negative[2]	negative	SCCP, 2005d (semi-perm HD)
MKGPMT Buehler	positive positive	positive	SCCP, 2005e (other)
MKGPMT	negative	positive[1]	SCCP, 2005f (oxidative HD)
MKGPMT	positive	positive	SCCP, 2005g (oxidative HD)
Buehler	negative	negative	SCCP, 2005i (oxidative HD)
MKGPMT	negative	negative	SCCP, 2006b (oxidative HD)
MKGPMT	positive	positive	SCCP, 2006c (fragrance)
MKGPMT Buehler	positive positive	positive	SCCP, 2006d (oxidative HD)
MKGPMT	negative[2]	positive[1]	SCCP, 2006e (semi-perm HD)
Buehler	negative	positive[1]	SCCP, 2006i (oxidative HD)
MKGPMT	positive	positive	SCCP, 2006j (semi-perm HD)
Guinea pig study	positive	positive	SCCP, 2006k (oxidative HD)
MKGPMT	positive	positive	SCCP, 2006m (oxidative HD)
MKGPMT	negative[2]	positive[1]	SCCP, 2006o (oxidative HD)
MKGPMT	negative	negative	SCCP, 2006s (UV filter)

HD = Hair dye, semi-perm = semi-permanent.
[1]Final conclusion of the SCC(NF)P.
[2]Staining of the skin made readings difficult in the guinea pig test.

For 6 of the 23 substances (26%) for which both types of tests were presented, diverging results were obtained. The final decision of the SCC(NF)P was in those instances based upon a case by case judgment:

- For one ingredient, the negative result of the guinea pig study was considered of more value than the positive outcome of the performed LLNA without further detail [SCCNFP, 2003c].
- For a second substance, the overall conclusion was designated as 'equivocal', giving equal weight to the negative LLNA and the positive guinea pig test [SCCNFP, 2004a].
- In four cases, confidence in the guinea pig studies was lowered due to some short-comings. The latter mainly consisted of skin staining by hair dye substances, thus hampering the scoring. Therefore the results from the LLNA were used for the final conclusion [SCCP, 2005f, 2006i, 2006e, 2006o].

As was the case for skin irritation, staining of the skin was on several occasions (for 16 hair dye substances in total) reported to disturb the measurements in the guinea pig studies. In the LLNA, hair dyes have not been reported to cause specific problems.

The rLLNA has only been recently developed and therefore is not detected in the SCC(NF)P opinions between 2002 and 2006.

6.3.5. Repeated Dose Toxicity Testing

a) Background

The outcome of the repeated dose toxicity study is a critical value in risk characterisation, since it allows the determination of a so-called 'safety' or 'uncertainty' factor by comparing the obtained NOA(E)L or LO(A)EL value to the expected daily exposure for the worker/consumer (see section 2.2.4).

In the case of cosmetic ingredients, a MoS is calculated by dividing the NO(A)EL value of the ingredient under study by its expected systemic exposure dosage [SCCP, 2006n]. The SCCP considers the evaluation of the systemic risk via repeated dose toxicity testing a key element in evaluating the safety of new and existing cosmetic ingredients [SCCP, 2007a].

Unfortunately, no alternative methods to fully replace in vivo repeated dose toxicity testing have been developed to date. Efforts in the field include the EU project Predictomics[9], which aimed at predicting liver and kidney chronic toxicity elicited by drugs and xenobiotics. By making use of cellular models that at best represent the human liver and kidney in vivo, and novel technologies ('omics'), Predictomics intended to develop tools for an early prediction of chronic liver and kidney damage. Although successful to some extent (in the field of steatotic compounds), this newly

---

9   EU Framework Programme 6 Specific Targeted Research Project (contract No. LSHB-CT-2004-504761, 2004–2007), more information through: http://www.predictomics.com (consulted February 2008).

Table 7. Occurrence of individual repeated dose toxicity studies in individual substance data packages discussed by the SCC(NF)P

Repeated dose toxicity test	Ingredients	Animals tested
28-day oral toxicity [OECD, 1995a; EU, 1996]	50	rats
90-day oral toxicity [OECD, 1998; EU, 2001]	98	rats and mice
28-day dermal toxicity [OECD, 1981b; EU, 1992d]	18	rats, mice, rabbits and guinea pigs
90-day dermal toxicity [OECD, 1981c; EU, 1988h]	18	rats and rabbits
Chronic toxicity [OECD, 1981e; EU, 1988i]	15	rats, mice and dogs

developed technology only addresses a limited aspect of repeated dose toxicity. Furthermore, the tool developed is only suitable for screening purposes and still needs pre-validation followed by full validation.

Other diffuse efforts are made, but no replacement alternatives are in the pipeline for the moment. Moving to other concepts, such as the TTC [Kroes et al., 2000], may in a limited number of cases enable to reduce the number of animals tested (e.g. in the case of impurity testing).

Nevertheless, the concerns expressed by different parties with regard to the pressure on the use of alternative methods without proper validation [CSTEE, 2004; SCC-NFP, 2004g; Rogiers and Pauwels, 2005; ICCG, 2006; Greim et al., 2006; Greim, 2007], clearly remain of primary importance.

b) Repeated Dose Toxicity Studies in SCC(NF)P Reports
As shown in earlier studies (section 3.2), the majority of full ad hoc reports contain repeated dose toxicity data. In total, 113 substances were tested in one or more repeated dose toxicity assays. The occurrence of individual studies is given in table 7.

For 50 substances, the 90-day oral toxicity study was used as a stand-alone assay for the endpoint of repeated dose toxicity. This is only rarely the case (4 substances) for 28-day studies, which are more considered dose-range finding studies for longer term assays than reliable NO(A)EL-generating studies. Therefore, the reported [SCCP, 2007a] combined ECVAM/NICEATM initiative, exploring the possibility to use in vitro assays for the prediction of starting doses, may induce a reduction in the number of animals.

A final observation is that the majority of repeated dose toxicity studies involved oral administration. This may be an indicator of the fact that they were not performed for cosmetic purposes only, since in that case, the dermal route is expected to be more relevant.

6.3.6. Toxicokinetics (Including Dermal Absorption)

As far as toxicokinetic studies are concerned, mainly dermal absorption data are presented in SCC(NF)P opinions. They are needed for the route-to-route extrapolation from the orally performed repeated dose toxicity studies to the dermal application as intended for the finished cosmetic product.

As discussed in detail in section 3.3.3, an in vitro replacement DA test is available and frequently used.

Other toxicokinetic aspects, such as metabolism, distribution and elimination are not considered as standard information in the safety evaluation of cosmetic ingredients by the SCC(NF)P. However, toxicokinetics are sometimes used as important argumentation in risk assessment procedures, e.g.

– In a specific industry submission to the SCCP, the classic calculation of the MoS was replaced by a 'toxicokinetic-based MoS'. Herein the interspecies factor of the generally accepted MoS of 100 was proposed to be reduced from 10 (subdivided in 2.5 for toxicodynamics and 4 for toxicokinetics) to 1, since (i) the substance's metabolism and toxicokinetics were considered to be very similar between rats and humans and (ii) the rat was considered more susceptible to the observed effects than humans [SCCP, 2006r].

– Some substances are metabolised in human skin. This skin metabolism may significantly differ from the metabolism in the liver. Therefore, the relevance of using results from the classic oral studies in the safety assessment of those types of substances intended to be applied dermally, can be questioned [Nohynek, 2005].

An EU project called LIINTOP[10] currently aims at optimizing in vitro models of the liver and intestines for pharmacokinetic and pharmacodynamic studies, so also in this area efforts to develop alternatives are being carried out. The project, however, only covers a small part of the complex field of toxicokinetics and results are expected after 2009.

6.3.7. Reproductive Toxicity

a) Background

The term 'reproductive toxicity' is used to describe the adverse effects induced (by a substance) on any aspect of mammalian reproduction. It covers all phases of the reproductive cycle, including impairment of male or female reproductive function or capacity and the induction of non-heritable adverse effects in the progeny such as death, growth retardation, structural and functional effects [ECB, 2003]. Mostly performed animal studies in this field are the two-generation reproduction toxicity test

---

10 EU Framework Programme 6 Specific Targeted Research Project (contract No. LSHB-CT-2006-037499, 2007–2009), more information through: http://www.liintop.cnr.it (consulted February 2008).

Rogiers · Pauwels

[EU, 2004e; OECD, 2001b], the teratogenicity assay [EU, 2004d; OECD, 2001a] and the combined reproduction/developmental toxicity screening test [OECD, 1995b].

To date, three alternative methods have been developed:

1 The Whole Embryo Culture Test
2 The MicroMass Test
3 The Embryotoxic Stem Cell Test

These alternatives are restricted to embryotoxicity, thus represent only a limited part of the reproductive cycle [SCCP, 2007a]. In 2001, ESAC endorsed their validity to distinguish between non-embryotoxic, weakly embryotoxic and strong embryotoxic substances, with the exception of the micromass test, for which the predictivity for non-embryotoxic test chemicals and the precision for weakly embryotoxic test chemicals were insufficient [ESAC, 2001].

The SCCP considers alternatives for embryotoxicity testing to be useful in the CMR strategy for screening out embryotoxic substances [SCCP, 2006n], but did not take up tests mentioned in its general strategy (Notes of Guidance) because of doubts of specificity and limited number of results. The committee equally questions their use in the general risk assessment procedures for cosmetic ingredients [SCCP, 2007a].

In the context of REACH, there are efforts to validate an extended in vivo one-generation study to replace the traditional in vivo two-generation study [SCCP, 2007a]. A retrospective analysis of reproduction toxicity reports accessible to the Dutch RIVM showed that the data from the second generation in the two generation study affected neither the overall NOAEL value nor the critical effects observed. Therefore, the authors supported the proposal to replace the study by a one-generation study with a more extensive set of parameters to be measured in the first-generation animals [Janer et al., 2007]. Nonetheless, it was acknowledged that the retrospective study was solely based upon data introduced to the Dutch competent authorities, meaning that there still may be compounds for which effects seen only in the second generation have precluded marketing, and for which data have not been submitted to regulators. This is advised to be taken into consideration before definitively omitting the second generation in the testing strategy [Piersma, 2007].

Finally, a European project called ReProTect[11] aims at developing a novel approach in hazard and risk assessment of reproductive toxicity, by a combination and application of in vitro, tissue and sensor technologies. Results are to be expected after 2009.

b) Reproductive Toxicity Studies in SCC(NF)P Reports
For 104 substances, reproductive toxicity data were presented. Teratogenicity studies occurred in all those data packages and were mainly performed with the rat (94%). For 19 substances, two-generation studies supplemented the presented teratogenicity results.

---

11 EU Framework Programme 6 Integrated Project (contract No. LSHB-CT-2004-503257, 2004–2009), more information through: http://www.reprotect.eu/ (consulted February 2008).

Alternative methods such as the WEC, EST and MM, have not found their practical use in the safety assessment of cosmetic ingredients at the EU level. The classic teratogenicity study still remains the preferred study to examine potential effects on embryonic and foetal development.

6.3.8. Mutagenicity/Genotoxicity and Carcinogenicity

a) Background

In vitro mutagenicity/genotoxicity testing has already been discussed in section 3.3.4. Standard in vitro assays to evaluate potential mutagenic/genotoxic effects of chemical substances have been available for more than 25 years.

The basic principle is that, in case of a positive in vitro result, an in vivo follow-up study is performed. However, experience has learnt that on many occasions, those follow-up studies showed to be negative. The issue of the frequent occurrence of 'false positives' and the low accuracy of a battery combining too many in vitro tests, has been extensively described [Kirkland et al., 2005, 2007].

It is acknowledged that the currently used in vitro testing protocols need to be improved with regard to their specificity and predictivity [Kirkland et al., 2007; Kirsch-Volders and Lombaert, 2008]. With the animal testing ban for cosmetic ingredients, in vivo mutagenicity/genotoxicity follow-up studies will not be allowed in Europe after 11 March 2009 [EU, 2003]. With the high rate of 'false positive' results in the in vitro testing battery, this will pose a serious problem.

Carcinogenicity is still assessed in vivo [EU, 1988j; OECD, 1981d], though does not form part of many SCC(NF)P dossiers (see section 3.2.5.*a*). Recently an EU project called Carcinogenomics[12] started with the aim of developing lung, liver and kidney in vitro methods assessing the carcinogenic potential of test substances. Use will be made of novel assays based on transcriptomics and metabonomics. The overall aim is to speed up the identification of carcinogenic substances, thus reducing animal tests.

Again, this project only covers a minor part of the area of carcinogenicity and results are not expected before 2012.

b) Mutagenicity/Genotoxicity Studies in SCC(NF)P Reports

As already mentioned in section 3.3.4, mutagenicity/genotoxicity data are available for 115 substances. The availability, acceptance and the results of the encountered in vivo assays are displayed in table 8, in a similar manner as was done for the in vitro studies in table 11 of section 3.3.4.b.

---

12 EU Framework Programme 6 Integrated Project (contract No. LSHB-CT-2006-037712, 2006–2011), more information through: http://www.carcinogenomics.eu/ (consulted February 2008).

Table 8. Presence and outcome of the performed in vivo mutagenicity/genotoxicity studies as reported by the SCC(NF)P (2002–2006)

Test	Data sets	Data accepted	Result negative[1]	Result positive[2]	Result equivocal[3]
In vivo mammalian bone marrow chromosome aberration test [OECD, 1997d; EU, 2000b]	10	9	7	1	1
In vivo mammalian erythrocyte micronucleus test [OECD, 1997c; EU, 2000c]	90	61	55	2	4
In vivo UDS with mammalian cells [OECD, 1997f; EU, 2000f]	42	39	39	0	0
In vivo rodent dominant lethal test [OECD, 1984b; EU, 1988g]	2	1	1	0	0
In vivo *Drosophila melanogaster* assay [OECD; 1984a; EU, 1988e]	7	5	3	1	1

[1]Substance failed to induce mutagenic/genotoxic effect under employed test conditions.
[2]Substance induced mutagenic/genotoxic effect under employed test conditions.
[3]No final conclusion (positive or negative) could be drawn based upon the test results.

In order to assess the potential impact of the prohibition to perform in vivo follow-up studies for cosmetic ingredients after the deadline in 2009, the database was searched for compounds for which both in vitro and in vivo data were available.

There appeared to be 27. Of particular interest are the compounds for which the in vitro tests showed a positive result, whereas their in vivo 'counterparts' resulted in the opposite conclusion.

In the 6 cases where the in vitro assay generated either a negative or an equivocal result, the in vivo follow-up study was negative.

The 21 positive in vitro results, however, were only confirmed in vivo in 3 cases (one equivocal and two positive in vivo results).

Without going into detail in complex problems related to mutagenicity/genotoxicity issues, this finding shows that at least 19 compounds would have been prematurely abandoned without in vivo assays.

6.3.9. Photo-Induced Toxicity

a) Background
Photo-induced toxicity encompasses adverse reactions caused by the combination of application of a specific substance and UV or visible radiation. Three types of

Table 9. Outcome of in vitro/in vivo mutagenicity/genotoxicity studies of 27 substances for which both types of studies were presented

Test	Result negative[1]	Result positive[2]	Result equivocal
In vitro mammalian chromosome aberration test [EU, 2000a; OECD, 1997b]	1	6	0
In vivo mammalian chromosome aberration test [OECD, 1997d; EU, 2000b]	4	2	1
In vitro micronucleus test [OECD, 2007]	3	12	1
In vivo micronucleus test [OECD, 1997c; EU, 2000c]	16	0	0
In vitro UDS [EU, 1988c; OECD, 1986d]	1	3	0
In vivo UDS [OECD, 1997f; EU, 2000f]	4	0	0

[1]Substance failed to induce mutagenic/genotoxic effect under employed test conditions.
[2]Substance induced mutagenic/genotoxic effect under employed test conditions.

photo-induced toxicity are commonly discussed, namely photo-irritation, photo-allergy and photo-genotoxicity [Liebsch et al., 2005].

Photo-irritation (also referred to as phototoxicity) is currently assessed through the 3T3 NRU PT, an in vitro method that was developed more than 10 years ago [Spielmann, 1994a, b] and that has meanwhile been taken up in the official guidelines [EU, 2000h; OECD, 2004c].

In order to overcome some limitations of the assay, 3-D skin model phototoxicity assays and the RBC phototoxicity test are commonly performed, more specifically to obtain more specific information on the mechanism of phototoxicity and on the bioavailability of the test substance in human skin [Liebsch et al., 2005; Lelièvre et al., 2007]. Thus, for phototoxicity no in vivo assays are expected to be performed for chemicals and cosmetic ingredients (especially of relevance for UV filters).

Experience with the 3T3 NRU PT test in pharmaceutical industry, however, showed that the method generated a number of positive results that were not confirmed in follow-up in vivo studies. Some technical aspects of the assay, such as the specifications of the light source used, the maximum concentration to be tested, the bioavailability of the compound, the problems with insoluble compounds, were mentioned to require further standardisation, validation and global harmonisation [De Smedt, 2007].

In the field of photoallergy (often referred to as photosensitisation), no replacement alternative methods are available to date. There even is no standard in vivo protocol available for this particular endpoint. Typically, the classic guinea pig assays are supplemented with an additional step of UV-VIS irradiation. There are efforts in the development of a photo-LLNA combined with a photo-MEST and models which

Rogiers · Pauwels

would be able to predict the covalent binding capacities of a light-activated chemical to serum albumin [Liebsch et al., 2005].

As far as photogenotoxicity is concerned, the SCCP Notes of Guidance contain a referenced list of assays for the detection of photochemical clastogenicity/mutagenicity, nearly all consisting of the existing assays, but supplemented with a combined treatment of the chemicals with UV-VIS irradiation light [SCCP, 2006n]. None of these photogenotoxicity assays have been formally validated [Liebsch et al., 2005].

b) Photo-Induced Toxicity Studies in SCC(NF)P Reports
Phototoxicity assays were found for 18 substances in total. For half of them, a 3T3 NRU PT assay was provided. Only in 3 instances, it appeared to be used as a stand-alone assay. In vivo phototoxicity data were found for 14 substances in total and were mainly performed on guinea pigs and mice (on one occasion, solely on human volunteers). A surprising finding is that 4 animal phototoxicity assays are reported with testing dates after 2000, suggesting they were carried out when not legally permitted anymore.

Photosensitisation is only given for 5 substances and mainly in humans and guinea pigs, whereas photogenotoxicity can be found for 7 substances and only includes one case of in vivo testing.

6.4 Cosmetic Animal Numbers Placed into Perspective

6.4.1. Animal Numbers and Timeframe for Cosmetic Ingredients' Testing

Out of the VUB database, a total animal count for the SCC(NF)P opinions between 2002 and 2006 of 103,683 animals (rats, mice, guinea pigs, rabbits, hamsters and dogs) could be extracted. The distribution over the different toxicological endpoints (table 10) shows that repeated dose toxicity, carcinogenicity and reproductive toxicity are the most animal-consuming endpoints. In vivo mutagenicity/genotoxicity accounts for 9.5%, indicating that, although an extended in vitro testing battery is available, the in vivo confirmation assays still are commonly performed.

An important remark here is that in the submitted dossiers it was not specified that the in vivo studies were specifically performed for the approval of the substance as a cosmetic ingredient in the EU. As explained in detail in section 1.3, other European legislations have their own data-generating requirements. Moreover, not only intra- but also extra-EU requirements may have been at the basis of data generation. Therefore, it would not be correct to state that 103,683 animals were used to fulfil the SCC(NF)P requirements for the dossiers discussed by the Committee between 2002 and 2006. The figure is a clear overestimation and this should be clearly taken up in

Table 10. Animal use per toxicological endpoint as reported in SCC(NF)P opinions issued 2002–2006

Type of test	Animal count						
	All species	rat	mouse	guinea pig	rabbit	hamster	dog
Overall sum	103,683	64,105	28,597	5,640	3,823	1,262	256
Acute toxicity	5,987 (5.8%)	4,104	1,327	50	453		53
Local toxicity	1,792 (1.7%)	150	192	135	1,315		
Sensitisation	6,922 (6.7%)		2,424	4,498			
Repeated dose	23,448 (22.6%)	19,848	2,313	312	714	100	161
Toxicokinetics	2,865 (2.8%)	2,620	179	14	50		2
Reproductive toxicity	24,620 (23.7%)	22,334	725		1,271	290	
Mutagenicity/genotoxicity	9,816 (9.5%)	2,896	6,848			72	
Carcinogenicity	27,158 (26.2%)	12,073	14,225		20	800	40
Additional studies[1]	1,075 (1.0%)	80	364	631			

further discussions. In addition, the described studies have been performed over a period of about 25 years (fig. 1).

Table 10 and figure 1 represent animal data for the cosmetic ingredients to be taken up in the Annexes to the Cosmetic Products Directive only, thus they do not represent the overall animal use for all cosmetic ingredients evaluated by a safety assessor in a TIF of finished cosmetic products.

Exact numbers on the overall animal use in the cosmetic area may be difficult to obtain, but the following can be taken into consideration:

– For those substances taken up in the Annexes of the Cosmetic Products Directive, the above figures provide a good idea of the number of animals that were needed to prove their safety, irrespective of the original framework under which the data were generated.

– For the cosmetic ingredients not related to the Annexes of the Cosmetic Products Directive, no specific data requirements are mentioned in the legislation. This means that additional testing for the cosmetic field alone is quite unlikely. Therefore, many raw material suppliers will only present toxicity studies that were generated through the requirements of other vertical EU and/or extra-EU legislations.

According to the latest Commission report on the statistics on the number of animals used for experimental and other scientific purposes in the Member States of the EU, about 1 million animals were used for safety testing in the year 2005. Of these, 4,840 animals (0.5%) belonged to the category of 'Products/substances used or intended to be used mainly as cosmetics or toiletries'.

The total number of 103,683 animals extracted from the VUB database for the 2002–2006 evaluation period leads to a rudimentary figure of about 21,000 animals

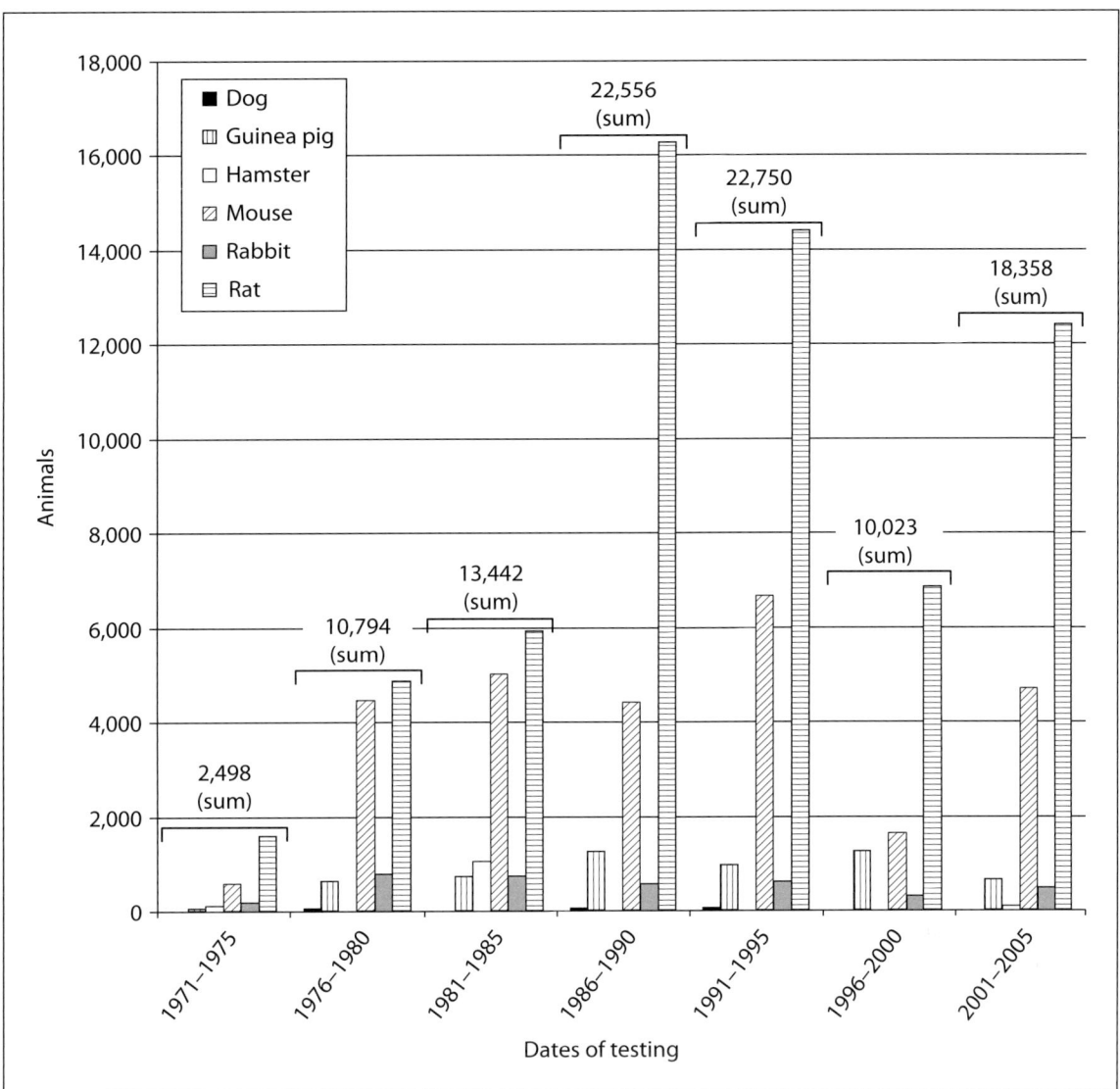

Fig. 1. Timeline of animal testing described in SCC(NF)P opinions 2002–2006. The numbers indicated as the sum represent the total numbers of animals per time period of 5 years.

per year. The fact that the reported number for 2005 is so low can either be caused by the non-reporting of animal testing for cosmetics or by the fact that the testing was performed in a non-cosmetic and/or extra-EU context and thus reported under a different heading or not required to be reported, respectively.

From 2009 on, the value for toxicity studies performed in Europe on cosmetic ingredients will drop to 0, since animal testing will be prohibited [EU, 2003]. Therefore, a huge pressure resides on the development and validation of replacement alternatives. Table 11 summarises the projects for the near future in that area.

Table 11. Prospects for the immediate future of replacement methods useful for safety testing of cosmetic ingredients according to the current methodological status (based on SCCP [2006n] and SCCP [2007a])

Endpoint	Potential replacement test and best case timing
• Acute toxicity:	
– acute oral toxicity	☺ ≥2010: replacement alternative expected through Acute-Tox[1]
– acute dermal and inhalation toxicity	☹ no replacement test foreseen
• Skin corrosivity	☺ TER, EPISKIN™, EPIDERM®, CORROSITEX® available
• Skin irritation	☺ EPISKIN approved by ESAC, awaiting SCCP approval ≤2010
• Eye irritation	☺ HET-CAM, BCOP, ICE, IRE, RBC, NRU form (screening methods which need further elaboration ≤2010)
• Skin sensitisation	☺ >2010: replacement alternative expected through Sens-it-iv[2] >2010
• Dermal absorption	☺ in vitro dermal absorption study available
• Repeated dose toxicity (28-day, 90-day, chronic toxicity)	☹ no replacement test foreseen (some results expected through Predictomics[3] >2009)
• Mutagenicity/genotoxicity	☺ several in vitro studies available
• Carcinogenicity	☺ no replacement test foreseen (some results expected through Carcinogenomics[4] >2012)
• Reproductive toxicity:	☹ no replacement test foreseen
– teratogenicity	☺ WEC, MM, EST: only embryotoxicity (some screening results expected through ReproTect[5] >2009)
– Two-generation reproduction toxicity	☹ no replacement test foreseen
• Toxicokinetics	☹ no replacement test foreseen (some results expected through LIINTOP[6] >2011)
• Photo-induced toxicity	☺ 3T3 NRU-PT available

[1]EU Framework Programme 6 Integrated Project (contract No. LSHB-CT-2004-512051, 2005–2009), more information through: http://www.acutetox.org (consulted December 2007).

[2]EU Framework Programme 6 Integrated Project (contract No. LSHB-CT-2005-018681, 2006–2010), more information through: http://www.sens-it-iv.eu (consulted December 2007).

[3]EU Framework Programme 6 Specific Targeted Research Project (contract No. LSHB-CT-2004-504761), 2004–2007, more information through: http://www.predictomics.com (consulted February 2008)

[4]EU Framework Programme 6 Integrated Project (contract No. LSHB-CT-2006-037712, 2006–2011), more information through: http://www.carcinogenomics.eu/ (consulted February 2008).

[5]EU Framework Programme 6 Integrated Project (contract No. LSHB-CT-2004-503257, 2004–2009), more information through: http://www.reprotect.eu/ (consulted February 2008).

[6]EU Framework Programme 6 Specific Targeted Research Project (contract No. LSHB-CT-2006-037499, 2007–2009), more information through: http://www.liintop.cnr.it (consulted February 2008).

Rogiers · Pauwels

As described under the different points of section 6.3, many efforts have been done over the years with regard to refinement and reduction of existing animal studies. However, replacement appears to be much further away than required in the case of cosmetics. The results of the different EU projects mentioned are expected after 2009 and at best constitute sets of methods that will be at the stage of pre-validation. Taking into account the time necessary for official validation, the deadline of 2013 will not be met.

6.4.2. Projected Animal Numbers and Timeframe under REACH

Whereas in the cosmetic field animal testing will be prohibited from March 2013 on, the introduction of REACH imposes additional animal testing, since it requests toxicological data on about 29,342 existing chemical substances [Pedersen et al., 2003]. Diverging estimates of the animal toll REACH would involve have been formulated. They range from 1.2 to 42 millions of animals [IEH, 2001a, b; van der Jagt et al., 2004; Höfer et al., 2004; JRC, 2006], and largely depend on various assumptions made:

– Whether the pups in the second-generation study are counted or not in the estimated animal number. This makes a significant difference, since the parent animal group at the start of the study consists of 80 males and 80 females, whereas the number of pups after two generations sums up to 1920.
– The estimation of the level of data availability for existing substances, which is not equal for all substances. Such estimates were published by the European Commission in 2003 [Pedersen et al., 2003], based upon comprehensive data from different chemical programmes, including extra-EU initiatives.
– The projected level at which animal numbers can be reduced by exposure-based waiving of certain tests, by the availability of alternative methods and/or by making use of QSAR grouping and read-across techniques [Pedersen et al., 2003].

Under the aegis of a European project called CONAM[13], the *ecopa* investigated the future use of experimental animals and the implementation of alternative methods under REACH. An important part of the work consisted of the design of the *ecopa calculator*[14], a software tool calculating realistic numbers of experimental animals to be used under REACH [Rogiers et al., 2007].

The *ecopa calculator* works with 2 different scenarios, namely:
(i) the available data scenario: reflecting the actual availability of data as estimated by the European Commission [Pedersen et al., 2003],
(ii) the reduced data need scenario: reflecting acceptance of waiving, QSAR grouping and read-across techniques.

---

13 EU Framework Programme 6 Specific Support Action (contract No. LSSB-CT-2004-504776, 2005–2007), more information through: http://cordis.europa.eu/fetch?CALLER = PROJ_EN&ACTION = D&DOC = 13&CAT = PROJ&QUERY = 1203133402445&RCN = 75331 (consulted February 2008).
14 Available through http://www.ecopa.eu/download.php?file = Animaluse_REACH_calculator.xls (consulted November 2007).

Table 12. Contributions of the individual human toxicological endpoints with regard to animal testing under the available data (AD) and the reduced data need (RDN) scenario (based on figures computed with the *ecopa calculator*)

Type of test	Animals (AD)		Animals (RDN)	
	n	%	n	%
Acute toxicity	541,009	2.1	86,993	1.5
Local toxicity	16,460	0.1	7,330	0.1
Sensitisation (LLNA)	584,814	2.2	260,104	4.4
Repeated dose	1,438,777	5.5	143,715	2.4
Toxicokinetics	0	0.0	0	0.0
Reproductive toxicity	21,663,398	82.6	5,110,855	85.5
Mutagenicity/genotoxicity	1,370,845	5.2	325,386	5.4
Carcinogenicity	605,696	2.3	43,264	0.7
Additional studies	0	0.0	0	0.0
Total	26,220,999		5,977,647	

When calculating the contributions of the individual human toxicological endpoints to the overall animal number, it becomes clear that reproductive toxicity is expected to account for the vast majority of the animal use under REACH (table 12). The two-generation reproduction study accounts for 18,964,150 and 4,448,766 animals in the available data and the reduced data need scenario, respectively.

With regard to the timeline of additional animal testing under REACH, the testing of the higher tonnage bands (most elaborated data requirements) comes first [EU, 2006]. This implies that, in the optimistic reduced data need scenario, 69% of all animal testing would be performed in the first 5.5-year testing window under REACH (fig. 2), involving about 4.1 million of animals over that period.

Compared to the 4,840 animals reported for cosmetic purposes for the year 2005 [EU, 2007] and the worst case calculated 21,000 animals used per year for the testing of cosmetics during the past 25 years, the REACH figures are quite high. Observing the expected evolution of animal testing over the years to come, it is clear that with regard to development of alternative methods, REACH deserves great attention.

6.5 Discussion and Conclusions

Considering the upcoming animal testing ban for cosmetic ingredients, it appeared useful to consult our database on the occurrence and application of existing 3R alternative methods, next to their in vivo 'classical' counterparts. This was performed for

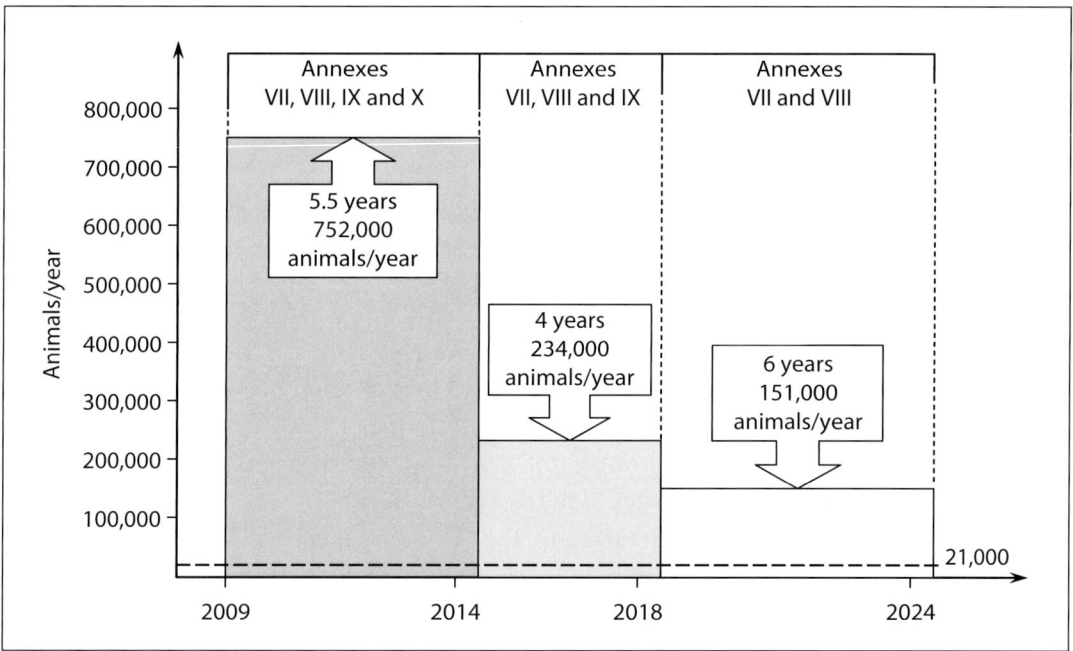

Fig. 2. Projected yearly animal numbers for human toxicity testing under the reduced data need scenario (best case), compared to the worst case level of 21,000 calculated for testing of cosmetic ingredients relevant for the Annexes to Dir. 76/768/EEC. Annex VII: standard information requirements for substances manufactured or imported in quantities of 1 tonne or more. Annex VIII: standard information requirements for substances manufactured or imported in quantities of 10 tonnes or more. Annex IX: standard information requirements for substances manufactured or imported in quantities of 100 tonnes or more. Annex X: standard information requirements for substances manufactured or imported in quantities of 1,000 tonnes or more. Adapted from Rogiers et al. [2007].

every relevant endpoint in order to supplement the prospects for the near future with regard to the development of alternative methods.

As far as acute oral toxicity is concerned, it is observed that at least one of the three officially recognised refinement and reduction tests has gradually been incorporated in submissions to the SCC(NF)P, albeit in a restricted number of dossiers. The reason why the occurrence is limited to 7% of all substances tested, most probably is the availability of an earlier classic LD_{50} assay, making additional testing superfluous.

Concomitant positive news comes from the A-Cute Tox project, which may be successful in providing pre-validated tests for the screening of acute oral toxicity in 2009. However, this timing implies that the formal validation phase still carries the availability of an in vitro testing strategy for acute oral toxicity beyond the cut-off date of 11 March 2009 and that for dermal and inhalation acute toxicity, tests are not available at all.

For skin and eye irritation, the existing in vivo protocols were refined over the years in view of animal protection, whereas for the endpoint of skin corrosion, an official alternative method has been available since 2000. In vitro assays for skin and eye irritation were developed and found practical use in screening strategies. Recently, the Episkin™ method has even received ESAC approval for skin irritation testing, although the SCCP requires additional information to prove the assay's applicability to all cosmetic ingredient types and to dye substances in particular.

The analysis of skin and eye irritation via our database shows a limited occurrence of in vitro assays in SCC(NF)P submissions. This was expected viewing the lack of validation of these methods at the time the presented studies were performed. The compiled in vivo results allow the extraction of lists of reference compounds for further validation (in vivo/in vitro comparison) activities in the field of cosmetics. The results also learn that in vivo testing of hair dyes was repeatedly hampered too by colouration effects which masked skin (or eye) readings.

For the endpoint of skin sensitisation, the LLNA has been available as a refinement alternative since 2002. Our database learns that its introduction into the SCC(NF)P submissions is a fact and that since 2002, with the exception of one case, only LLNA assays have been reported for the endpoint of skin sensitisation. Since an allergic response does not occur after a single contact with a substance and at least a second exposure is necessary, the SCCP considers that the LLNA is a 'repeated dose toxicity test' [SCCP, 2007a], meaning that its performance is still allowed until March 2013 (after 2009 outside Europe). Meanwhile, results are expected from the EU-funded project Sens-it-iv, which at best is expected to deliver a pre-validated alternative after 2010. Considering that full validation needs to follow, it is unlikely that the March 2013 deadline will be met.

The major concerns with regard to the non-availability of replacement alternatives have been expressed for the endpoint of repeated dose toxicity. The EU-funded project Predictomics results in a useful liver tool to perform preliminary screenings of test substances for steatosis, but it still only covers a minor part of the multiple and complex aspects related to in vivo repeated dose toxicity and moreover still requires pre-validation and full validation. Therefore, the availability of replacement tests before March 2013 is excluded. Moving towards new concepts such as the TTC approach or the so-called evidence-based toxicology may help to avoid additional testing, but still is based upon existing information from in vivo studies. For those approaches, the repeated dose toxicity data contained in our database, mainly details and results from 90-day studies, could be a source of useful input data.

In case a newly developed innovative molecule needs to be assessed for its safety, however, the lack of repeated dose toxicity data may induce a true challenge for the risk assessor.

As far as toxicokinetics are concerned, this book mainly focuses on the area of dermal absorption, since the latter is used to perform the route to route extrapolation from results obtained through oral animal toxicity studies to the intended dermal application of a cosmetic product. Although affected by a number of serious problems, an in vitro dermal absorption test is available and commonly used for cosmetic ingredients. Nevertheless, other aspects such as distribution, metabolism and excretion, may also be of importance. For these, no replacement alternatives are envisaged. The EU project LIINTOP may deliver some optimised in vitro liver and intestine models for pharmacokinetic and pharmacodynamic studies after 2009, but certainly does not cover the whole complex field of toxicokinetics.

In the area of reproductive toxicology, research into alternatives has led to the development of three embryotoxicity assays, of which one still is an animal study. However, embryotoxicity covers only a minor part of the whole reproductive cycle. Analysis of our database shows that the in vitro embryotoxicity methods are not commonly encountered in submissions to the SCC(NF)P. The classic in vivo teratogenicity study, however, occurred in all reproductive toxicity data packages. With regard to future developments in the field, it can be stated that the EU project RePro Tect enters its last year, but probably an extension will be necessary in order to deliver a part of the novel approach in reproductive toxicity assessment, as originally planned for 2009. Again, replacement is not foreseeable in the years to come.

Finally, the area of mutagenicity/genotoxicity reveals a major issue related to replacement alternatives, namely the importance of post-validation studies and optimisation of existing validated alternatives. As was also described for the LLNA, post-validation studies are indispensable to increase trust in an alternative method. The in vitro mutagenicity/genotoxicity testing battery has been used extensively for 25 years and experts in the field now declare that the methods need some revision and refinement, especially in case in vivo confirmation would not be possible.

Analysis of the mutagenicity/genotoxicity data included in our database shows that 19 compounds would have been prematurely abandoned due to positive in vitro results which were contradicted in vivo.

The above shows that the scientific world is not able to timely deliver validated replacement alternatives fulfilling the current customary data requirements for the hazard assessment of a cosmetic ingredient by the SCC(NF)P. All the advances on 3R alternatives obtained through individual, European and/or industry initiatives may constitute valuable input for the development of the 'suitable' methods required for the 30,000 chemicals that are expected to be tested under REACH, but only few of them will be relevant for cosmetic ingredients. Even for REACH, which imposes that the highest tonnage levels need to be tested first in time, alternatives will come too late.

Finally, when comparing the projected animal numbers under REACH with the worst case calculated animal numbers for cosmetic ingredients, it becomes clear that the abolition of animal testing for cosmetics may slightly reduce overall animal testing, but only induces a very limited reduction. Looking at the REACH numbers and at the EU 2005 figures of the numbers of animals used during safety assessment of pharmaceutical products, plant protection products and food products, these industries, as recognised by the *epaa*, also require attention.

6.6 **References**

Basketter D: Case study 1: Local Lymph Node Assay (LLNA); in Report on Workshop on 'Dissemination Strategies: How Do They Influence the Uptake of New 3Rs Methods across Laboratories/Boundaries?'. Produced by Working Group 3 of epaa, 2007. Available through http://ec.europa.eu/enterprise/epaa/wg3_ws20071001_report.pdf (consulted February 2008).

Brantom PG, Brunner LH, Chamberlain M, de Silva O, Dupuis J, Earl LK, Lovell DP, Pape WJW, Uttley M, Bagley DM, Baker, FW, Bracher M, Courtellemont P, Declercq L, Freeman S, Steiling W, Walker AP, Carr GJ, Dami N, Thomas G, Harbell J, Jones PA, Pfannenbecker U, Southee JA, Tcheng M, Argembeaux H, Castelli D, Clothier R, Esdaile DJ, Itigaki H, Jung K, Kasai Y, Kojima H, Kristen U, Larnicol M, Lewis RW, Marenus K, Moreno O, Peterson A, Rasmussen ES, Robles C, Stern M: A summary of the COLIPA International Validation Study on alternatives to the Draize Rabbit Eye Irritation Test. Toxicol In Vitro 1997;11:141–179.

Bruner LH, Parker RD, Bruce RD: Reducing the number of rabbits in the low-volume eye test. Fundam Appl Toxicol 1992;19:330–335.

Buehler EV: Delayed contact hypersensitivity in the guinea pig. Arch Dermatol 1965;91:171–177.

Buehler EV: Occlusive patch method for skin sensitization in guinea pigs: the Buehler method. Food Chem Toxicol 1994;32:97–101.

CSTEE: Opinion of the Scientific Committee on Toxicity, Ecotoxicity and the Environment (CSTEE) on the BUAV-ECEAE report on 'The way forward – action to end animal toxicity testing'. Doc. C7/VR/csteeop/anat/08014 D(04), European Commission, 2004.

De Smedt A: In vitro 3T3 NRU Phototoxicity test. Oral communication during the Annual Conference 2007 of the European Partnership for Alternative Approaches to Animal Testing: 'Regulatory Acceptance', Brussels, November 2007, electronically available through http://ec.europa.eu/enterprise/epaa/conf_2007.htm (consulted February 2008).

Draize JH, Woodard G, Calvery HO: Methods for the study of irritation and toxicity of substances applied topically to the skin and mucous membranes. J Pharmacol Exp Ther 1944;83:377–390.

ECB: European Chemicals Bureau. Technical Guidance Document on Risk Assessment in support of Commission Directive 93/67/EEC on Risk Assessment for new notified substances, Commission Regulation (EC) No 1488/94 on Risk Assessment for existing substances and Directive 98/8/EC of the European Parliament and of the Council concerning the placing of biocidal products on the market. Doc. EUR 20418 EN/1, European Commission, 2003.

ESAC: ESAC statement on the validity of the local lymph node assay for skin sensitisation testing, adopted by the ECVAM Scientific Advisory Committee (ESAC) at its 14th Meeting of 14–15 March 2000 at ECVAM, Ispra, Italy.

ESAC: ESAC statement on the use of scientifically-validated in vitro tests for embryotoxicity, adopted by the ECVAM Scientific Advisory Committee (ESAC) at its 17th Meeting of 16–17 October 2001 at ECVAM, Ispra, Italy.

ESAC (2007a): ESAC statement on the conclusions of the ICCVAM retrospective study on organotypic in vitro assays as screening tests to identify potential ocular corrosives and severe irritants as determined by the US EPA, EU(R41) and UN GHS classifications in a tiered testing strategy, as part of a weight of evidence approach, adopted by the ECVAM Scientific Advisory Committee (ESAC) at its 26th Meeting of 26–27 April 2007 at ECVAM, Ispra, Italy.

ESAC (2007b): ESAC Statement on the Reduced Local Lymph Node Assay (rLLNA), adopted by the ECVAM Scientific Advisory Committee (ESAC) at its 26th Meeting of 26–27 April 2007 at ECVAM, Ispra, Italy.

ESAC (2007c): ESAC Statement on the Validity of In Vitro Tests for Skin Irritation, adopted by the ECVAM Scientific Advisory Committee (ESAC) at its 26th Meeting of 26–27 April 2007 at ECVAM, Ispra, Italy.

EU: B.4. Acute toxicity skin irritation. Commission Directive 84/449/EEC of 25 April 1984 adapting to technical progress for the sixth time Council Directive 67/548/EEC on the approximation of laws, regulations and administrative provisions relating to the classification, packaging and labelling of dangerous substances. Off J 1984a;L251:124–126.

EU: B.5. Acute toxicity eye irritation. Commission Directive 84/449/EEC of 25 April 1984 adapting to technical progress for the sixth time Council Directive 67/548/EEC on the approximation of laws, regulations and administrative provisions relating to the classification, packaging and labelling of dangerous substances. Off J 1984b;L251:127–130.

Rogiers · Pauwels

EU: B.15. Mutagenicity testing and screening for carcinogenicity. Gene mutation – *Saccharomyces cerevisiae*. Commission Directive 88/302/EEC of 18 November 1987 adapting to technical progress for the ninth time Council Directive 67/548/EEC on the approximation of laws, regulations and administrative provisions relating to the classification, packaging and labelling of dangerous substances. Off J 1988a;L133:55–57.

EU: B.16. Mitotic recombination – *Saccharomyces cerevisiae*. Commission Directive 88/302/EEC of 18 November 1987 adapting to technical progress for the ninth time Council Directive 67/548/EEC on the approximation of laws, regulations and administrative provisions relating to the classification, packaging and labelling of dangerous substances. Off J 1988b;L133:58–60.

EU: B.18. DNA damage and repair – Unscheduled DNA Synthesis – mammalian cells in vitro. Commission Directive 88/302/EEC of 18 November 1987 adapting to technical progress for the ninth time Council Directive 67/548/EEC on the approximation of laws, regulations and administrative provisions relating to the classification, packaging and labelling of dangerous substances. Off J 1988c;L133:64–67.

EU: B.19. Sister Chromatid Exchange assay in vitro. Commission Directive 88/302/EEC of 18 November 1987 adapting to technical progress for the ninth time Council Directive 67/548/EEC on the approximation of laws, regulations and administrative provisions relating to the classification, packaging and labelling of dangerous substances. Off J 1988d;L133: 68–70.

EU: B.20. Sex-linked recessive lethal test in *Drosophila melanogaster*. Commission Directive 88/302/EEC of 18 November 1987 adapting to technical progress for the ninth time Council Directive 67/548/EEC on the approximation of laws, regulations and administrative provisions relating to the classification, packaging and labelling of dangerous substances. Off J 1988e;L133:71–72.

EU: B.21. In vitro mammalian cell transformation tests. Commission Directive 88/302/EEC of 18 November 1987 adapting to technical progress for the ninth time Council Directive 67/548/EEC on the approximation of laws, regulations and administrative provisions relating to the classification, packaging and labelling of dangerous substances. Off J 1988f;L133:73–75.

EU: B.22. Rodent dominant lethal test. Commission Directive 88/302/EEC of 18 November 1987 adapting to technical progress for the ninth time Council Directive 67/548/EEC on the approximation of laws, regulations and administrative provisions relating to the classification, packaging and labelling of dangerous substances. Off J 1988g;L133:76–78.

EU: B.28. Sub-chronic inhalation toxicity study: 90-day repeated dermal dose study using rodent species. Commission Directive 88/302/EEC of 18 November 1987 adapting to technical progress for the ninth time Council Directive 67/548/EEC on the approximation of laws, regulations and administrative provisions relating to the classification, packaging and labelling of dangerous substances. Off J 1988h;L133: 8–11.

EU: B.30. Chronic toxicity test. Commission Directive 88/302/EEC of 18 November 1987 adapting to technical progress for the ninth time Council Directive 67/548/EEC on the approximation of laws, regulations and administrative provisions relating to the classification, packaging and labelling of dangerous substances. Off J 1988i;L133:27–31.

EU: B.32. Carcinogenicity test. Commission Directive 88/302/EEC of 18 November 1987 adapting to technical progress for the ninth time Council Directive 67/548/EEC on the approximation of laws, regulations and administrative provisions relating to the classification, packaging and labelling of dangerous substances. Off J 1988j;L133:32–36.

EU: B.1. Acute toxicity (oral). Commission Directive 92/69/EEC of 31 July 1992 adapting to technical progress for the seventeenth time Council Directive 67/548/EEC on the approximation of laws, regulations and administrative provisions relating to the classification, packaging and labelling of dangerous substances. Off J 1992a;L383A:110–115.

EU: B.4. Acute toxicity (skin irritation). Commission Directive 92/69/EEC of 31 July 1992 adapting to technical progress for the seventeenth time Council Directive 67/548/EEC on the approximation of laws, regulations and administrative provisions relating to the classification, packaging and labelling of dangerous substances. Off J 1992b;L383:113–116.

EU: B.5. Acute toxicity (eye irritation). Commission Directive 92/69/EEC of 31 July 1992 adapting to technical progress for the seventeenth time Council Directive 67/548/EEC on the approximation of laws, regulations and administrative provisions relating to the classification, packaging and labelling of dangerous substances. Off J 1992c;L383:117–120.

EU: B.9. Repeated dose (28 days) toxicity (dermal). Commission Directive 92/69/EEC of 31 July 1992 adapting to technical progress for the seventeenth time Council Directive 67/548/EEC on the approximation of laws, regulations and administrative provisions relating to the classification, packaging and labelling of dangerous substances. Off J 1992d;L383A:144–147.

EU: Council Directive 93/35/EEC of 14 June 1993 amending for the sixth time Directive 76/768/EEC on the approximation of the laws of the Member States relating to cosmetic products. Off J 1993; L151:32–37.

EU: B.7. Repeated dose (28 days) toxicity (oral). Commission Directive 96/54/EC of 30 July 1996 adapting to technical progress for the twenty-second time Council Directive 67/548/EEC on the approximation of the laws, regulations and administrative provisions relating to the classification, packaging and labelling of dangerous substances. Off J 1996;L248: 1–5, Annex IVD.

EU: B.10. Mutagenicity – in vitro mammalian chromosome aberration test. Commission Directive 2000/32/EC of 19 May 2000 adapting to technical progress for the 26th time Council Directive 67/548/EEC on the approximation of the laws, regulations and administrative provisions relating to the classification, packaging and labelling of dangerous substances. Off J 2000a;L136:35–42.

EU: B.11. Mutagenicity – in vivo mammalian bone marrow chromosome aberration test. Commission Directive 2000/32/EC of 19 May 2000 adapting to technical progress for the 26th time Council Directive 67/548/EEC on the approximation of the laws, regulations and administrative provisions relating to the classification, packaging and labelling of dangerous substances. Off J 2000b;L136:43–49.

EU: B.12. Mutagenicity – in vivo mammalian erythrocyte micronucleus test. Commission Directive 2000/32/EC of 19 May 2000 adapting to technical progress for the 26th time Council Directive 67/548/EEC on the approximation of the laws, regulations and administrative provisions relating to the classification, packaging and labelling of dangerous substances. Off J 2000c;L136:50–56.

EU: B.13/14. Mutagenicity – reverse mutation test bacteria. Commission Directive 2000/32/EC of 19 May 2000 adapting to technical progress for the 26th time Council Directive 67/548/EEC on the approximation of the laws, regulations and administrative provisions relating to the classification, packaging and labelling of dangerous substances. Off J 2000d;L136: 57–64.

EU: B.17. Mutagenicity – in vitro mammalian cell gene mutation test. Commission Directive 2000/32/EC of 19 May 2000 adapting to technical progress for the 26th time Council Directive 67/548/EEC on the approximation of the laws, regulations and administrative provisions relating to the classification, packaging and labelling of dangerous substances. Off J 2000e;L136:65–72.

EU: B.39. Mutagenicity – Unscheduled DNA synthesis (UDS) test with mammalian liver cells in vivo. Commission Directive 2000/32/EC of 19 May 2000 adapting to technical progress for the 26th time Council Directive 67/548/EEC on the approximation of the laws, regulations and administrative provisions relating to the classification, packaging and labelling of dangerous substances. Off J 2000f;L136:80–85.

EU: B.40. Skin corrosion (rat skin transcutaneous electrical resistance assay and human skin model assay). Commission Directive 2000/33/EC of 25 April 2000 adapting to technical progress for the 27th time Council Directive 67/548/EEC on the approximation of laws, regulations and administrative provisions relating to the classification, packaging and labelling of dangerous substances. Off J 2000g; L136:91–97.

EU: B.41. Phototoxicity – in vitro 3T3 NRU phototoxicity test. Commission Directive 2000/33/EC of 25 April 2000 adapting to technical progress for the 27th time Council Directive 67/548/EEC on the approximation of laws, regulations and administrative provisions relating to the classification, packaging and labelling of dangerous substances. Off J 2000h;L136:98–107.

EU: B.26. Sub-chronic oral toxicity test: repeated dose 90-day oral toxicity study in rodents. Commission Directive 2001/59/EC of 6 August 2001 adapting to technical progress for the 28th time Council Directive 67/548/EEC on the approximation of the laws, regulations and administrative provisions relating to the classification, packaging and labelling of dangerous substances. Off J 2001;L225:150–156.

EU: Directive 2003/15/EC of the European Parliament and of the Council of 27 February 2003 amending Council Directive 76/768/EEC on the approximation of the laws of the Member States relating to cosmetic products. Off J 2003;L066:26–35.

EU: B.1.bis. Acute toxicity (oral) – Fixed Dose Method. Commission Directive 2004/73/EC of 29 April 2004 adapting to technical progress for the 29th time Council Directive 67/548/EEC on the approximation of the laws, regulations and administrative provisions relating to the classification, packaging and labelling of dangerous substances. Off J 2004a;L152:156–168 & Corrigendum: Off J 2004a;L216:177–189.

EU: B.1.tris. Acute toxicity (oral) – Acute toxic class method. Commission Directive 2004/73/EC of 29 April 2004 adapting to technical progress for the 29th time Council Directive 67/548/EEC on the approximation of the laws, regulations and administrative provisions relating to the classification, packaging and labelling of dangerous substances. Off J 2004b;L152:170–186 & Corrigendum: Off J 2004b;L216:190–205.

EU: B.4. Acute toxicity – Dermal irritation/skin corrosion. Commission Directive 2004/73/EC of 29 April 2004 adapting to technical progress for the 29th time Council Directive 67/548/EEC on the approximation of the laws, regulations and administrative provisions relating to the classification, packaging and labelling of dangerous substances. Off J 2004c;L152: 188–199 & Corrigendum: Off J 2004c;L216:206–215.

EU: B.31. Teratogenicity study – rodent and non-rodent. Commission Directive 2004/73/EC of 29 April 2004 adapting to technical progress for the 29th time Council Directive 67/548/EEC on the approximation of the laws, regulations and administrative provisions relating to the classification, packaging and labelling of dangerous substances. Off J 2004d;L152:214–225 & Corrigendum: Off J 2004d;L216:227–235.

EU: B.35. Two-generation reproduction toxicity test. Commission Directive 2004/73/EC of 29 April 2004 adapting to technical progress for the 29th time Council Directive 67/548/EEC on the approximation of the laws, regulations and administrative provisions relating to the classification, packaging and labelling of dangerous substances. Off J 2004e;L152:227–241 & Corrigendum: Off J 2004e;L216:236–246.

EU: B.42. Skin sensitisation: Local Lymph Node Assay. Commission Directive 2004/73/EC of 29 April 2004 adapting to technical progress for the 29th time Council Directive 67/548/EEC on the approximation of the laws, regulations and administrative provisions relating to the classification, packaging and labelling of dangerous substances. Off J 2004f;L152:243–248 & Corrigendum: Off J 2004f;L216:247–252.

EU: Regulation (EC) No 1907/2006 of the European Parliament and of the Council of 18 December 2006 concerning the Registration, Evaluation, Authorisation and Restriction of Chemicals (REACH), establishing a European Chemicals Agency, amending Directive 1999/45/EC and repealing Council Regulation (EEC) No 793/93 and Commission Regulation (EC) No 1488/94 as well as Council Directive 76/769/EEC and Commission Directives 91/155/EEC, 93/67/EEC, 93/105/EC and 2000/21/EC. Off J 2006;L396:1–849. Corrigendum in Off J 2006;L136:3–280.

EU (2007): Report from the Commission to the Council and the European Parliament. Fifth Report on the Statistics on the Number of Animals used for Experimental and other Scientific Purposes in the Member States of the European Union {SEC (2007)1455}, Brussels, 5 November 2007, COM (2007) 675 final.

Gautheron P, Dukic M, Alix D, Sina JF: Bovine corneal opacity and permeability test: an in vitro assay of ocular irritancy. Fundam Appl Toxicol 1992;18:442–449.

Greim H, Arand M, Autrup H, Bolt HM, Bridges J, Dybing E, Glomot R, Foa V, Schulte-Hermann R: Toxicological comments to the discussion about REACH. Arch Toxicol 2006;80:121–124.

Greim H: Toxicological comments to the discussion about REACH (Greim H, Arand M, Autrup H, Bolt HM, Bridges J, Dybing E, Glomot R, Foa V, Schulte-Hermann R, Arch Toxicol 2006;80:121–124). Reply to the letter to the editor: the need for a new toxicity testing and risk analysis paradigm to implement REACH or any other large scale testing initiative, by Blaauboer BJ, Andersen, ME (Arch Toxicol 2007;81:385–387). Arch Toxicol 2007;81:895–896.

Höfer T, Gerner I, Gundert-Remy U, Liebsch M, Schulte A, Spielmann H, Vogel R, Wettig K: Animal testing and alternative approaches for the human health risk assessment under the proposed new European chemicals regulation. Arch Toxicol 2004;78:549–564.

ICCG: ICCG/1/06 (2006): Inter Committee Coordination Group of Scientific Committees (ICCG) Position Statement 'Alternatives to animal tests'. Adopted by the ICCG during the ICCG meeting of 3 July 2006 after consultation of each of the non-food Scientific Committees.

ICCVAM (2006): ICCVAM test method evaluation report: In vitro ocular toxicity test methods for identifying severe irritants and corrosives. Interagency Coordinating Committee on the Validation of Alternative Methods (ICCVAM), National Toxicology Program (NTP) and Interagency Center for the Evaluation of Alternative Toxicological Methods (NICEATM). NIH Publication No: 07–4517, November 2006. Available electronically at http://iccvam.niehs.nih.gov/methods/ocudocs/ocu_brd.htm#ICCSev (consulted Feb 2008).

IEH (2001a): Institute of Environment and Health. Testing Requirements for Proposals under the EC White Paper 'Strategy for a Future Chemicals Policy' (Web Report W6), IEH, Leicester, UK, July 2001, available through http://www.silsoe.cranfield.ac.uk/ieh/pdf/w6.pdf (consulted Feb 2008)

IEH (2001b): Institute of Environment and Health. Assessment of the feasibility of replacing current regulatory in vivo toxicity tests with in vitro tests within the framework specified in the EC White Paper 'Strategy for an EU Chemicals Policy' (Web Report 10), IEH, Leicester, UK, December 2001, available through http://www.silsoe.cranfield.ac.uk/ieh/pdf/w10.pdf (consulted Feb 2008).

Janer G, Hakkert BC, Slob W, Vermeire T, Piersma AH: A retrospective analysis of the two-generation study: what is the added value of the second generation? Reprod Toxicol 2007;24:97–102.

6

JRC (2006): Joint Research Centre. Briefing note on number of animals expected to be used under REACH summary of re-assessment performed by the JRC, October 2006, European Commission Directorate General JRC, Institute for Health and Consumer Protection, available through http://ihcp. jrc.ec.europa.eu/docs/ecb/REACHanimalfigures.pdf (consulted Feb 2008).

Kimber I, Weisenberger C: A murine local lymph node assay for the identification of contact allergens. Assay development and results of an initial validation study. Arch Toxicol 1989;63:274–282.

Kimber I, Dearman RJ, Betts CJ, Gerberick GF, Ryan CA, Kern PS, Patlewicz GY, Basketter DA: The local lymph node assay and skin sensitization: a cut-down screen to reduce animal requirements? Contact Dermat 2006;54:181–185.

Kirkland DJ, Aardema M, Hendersen L, Müller L: Evaluation of the ability of a battery of three in vitro genotoxicity tests to discriminate rodent carcinogens and non-carcinogens I. Sensitivity, specificity and relative predictivity. Mutat Res 2005;584:1–256.

Kirkland D, Pfuhler S, Tweats D, Aardema M, Corvi R, Darroudi F, Elhajouji A, Glatt H, Hastwell P, Hayashi M, Kasper P, Kirchner S, Lynch A, Marzin D, Maurici D, Meunier JR, Müller L, Nohynek G, Parry J, Parry E, Thybaud V, Tice R, van Benthem J, Vanparys P, White P: How to reduce false positive results when undertaking in vitro genotoxicity testing and thus avoid unnecessary follow-up animal tests: Report of an ECVAM Workshop. Mutat Res 2007;628:31–55.

Kirsch-Volders M, Lombaert N: In vitro genotoxicity/mutagenicity-requirements, strategies and problems; in Rogiers V, Pauwels M (eds): Proceedings of Safety Assessment of Cosmetics in the EU – Follow-up Course, 4–6 February 2008. Brussels, Belgium, 2008, p 387.

Kroes R, Galli C, Munro I, Schilter B, Tran L, Walker R, Wurtzen G: Threshold of toxicological concern for chemical substances present in the diet: a practical tool for assessing the need for toxicity testing. Food Chem Toxicol 2000;38:255–312.

Lelièvre D, Justine P, Christiaens F, Bonaventure N, Coutet J, Marrot L, Cotovio J: The episkin phototoxicity assay (EPA): Development of an in vitro tiered strategy using 17 reference chemicals to predict phototoxic potency. Toxicol In Vitro 2007;21:977–995.

Liebsch M, Spielmann H, Pape W, Krul C, Deguercy A, Eskes C: UV-induced effects. Altern Lab Anim 2005;33(suppl 1):131–146.

Lüpke NP: Hen's egg chorio-allantoic membrane test for irritation potential. Food Chem Toxicol 1985;23:287–291.

Magnusson B, Kligman AM: The identification of contact allergens by animal assay. The guinea pig maximization test. J Invest Dermatol 1969;52:268–276.

Nohynek GJ, Duche D, Garrigues A, Meunier PA, Toutain H, Leclaire J: Under the skin: Biotransformation of para-aminophenol and para-phenylenediamine in reconstructed human epidermis and human hepatocytes. Toxicol Lett 2005;158:196–212.

OECD: OECD Guideline for testing of chemicals – Guideline 401 (1981a): Acute Oral Toxicity. Organization for Economic Cooperation and Development, Paris, adopted 12 May 1981, deleted 20 December 2002.

OECD: OECD Guideline for testing of chemicals – Guideline 410 (1981b): Repeated Dose Dermal Toxicity: 21/28-Day Study. Organization for Economic Cooperation and Development, Paris, adopted 12 May 1981.

OECD: OECD Guideline for testing of chemicals – Guideline 411 (1981c): Subchronic Dermal Toxicity: 90-Day Study. Organization for Economic Cooperation and Development, Paris, adopted 12 May 1981.

OECD: OECD Guideline for testing of chemicals – Guideline 451 (1981d): Carcinogenicity Studies. Organization for Economic Cooperation and Development, Paris, adopted 12 May 1981.

OECD: OECD Guideline for testing of chemicals – Guideline 452 (1981e): Chronic Toxicity Studies. Organization for Economic Cooperation and Development, Paris, adopted 12 May 1981.

OECD: OECD Guideline for testing of chemicals – Guideline 477 (1984a): Genetic Toxicology: Sex-Linked Recessive Lethal Test in Drosophila melanogaster. Organization for Economic Cooperation and Development, Paris, updated guideline adopted 4 April 1984.

OECD: OECD Guideline for testing of chemicals – Guideline 478 (1984b): OECD Guideline for testing of chemicals – Guideline 477:Genetic Toxicology: Rodent Dominant Lethal Test. Organization for Economic Cooperation and Development, Paris, updated guideline adopted 4 April 1984.

OECD: OECD Guideline for testing of chemicals – Guideline 479 (1986a): Genetic Toxicology: In vitro Sister Chromatid Exchange Assay in Mammalian Cells. Organization for Economic Cooperation and Development, Paris, original guideline adopted 23 October 1986.

OECD: OECD Guideline for testing of chemicals – Guideline 480 (1986b): Saccharomyces cerevisiae, Gene Mutation Assay. Organization for Economic Cooperation and Development, Paris, original guideline adopted 23 October 1986.

OECD: OECD Guideline for testing of chemicals – Guideline 481 (1986c): Genetic Toxicology: Saccharomyces cerevisiae, Mitotic Recombination Assay. Organization for Economic Cooperation and Development, Paris, original guideline adopted 23 October 1986.

OECD: OECD Guideline for testing of chemicals – Guideline 482 (1986d): Genetic Toxicology: DNA Damage and Repair, Unscheduled DNA Synthesis in Mammalian Cells in vitro. Organization for Economic Cooperation and Development, Paris, original guideline adopted 23 October 1986.

OECD: OECD Guideline for testing of chemicals – Guideline 407 (1995a): Repeated Dose 28-Day Oral Toxicity Study in Rodents. Organization for Economic Cooperation and Development, Paris, adopted 12 May 1981, last updated 27 July 1995.

OECD: OECD Guideline for testing of chemicals – Guideline 421 (1995b): Reproduction / Developmental Toxicity Screening Test. Organization for Economic Cooperation and Development, Paris, original Guideline, adopted 27 July 1995.

OECD: OECD Guideline for testing of chemicals – Guideline 471 (1997a): Bacterial Reverse Mutation Test. Organization for Economic Cooperation and Development, Paris, adopted 26 May 1983, last updated 21 July 1997.

OECD: OECD Guideline for testing of chemicals – Guideline 473 (1997b): In vitro Mammalian Chromosomal Aberration Test. Organization for Economic Cooperation and Development, Paris, updated 21 July 1997.

OECD: OECD Guideline for testing of chemicals – Guideline 474 (1997c): Mammalian Erythrocyte Micronucleus Test. Organization for Economic Cooperation and Development, Paris, adopted 21 July 1997.

OECD: OECD Guideline for testing of chemicals – Guideline 475 (1997d): Mammalian Bone Marrow Chromosomal Aberration Test. Organization for Economic Cooperation and Development, Paris, adopted 21 July 1997.

OECD: OECD Guideline for testing of chemicals – Guideline 476 (1997e): In vitro Mammalian Cell Gene Mutation Test. Organization for Economic Cooperation and Development, Paris, adopted 4 April 1984, last updated 21 July 1997.

OECD: OECD Guideline for testing of chemicals – Guideline 486 (1997f): Unscheduled DNA Synthesis (UDS) Test with Mammalian Liver Cells in vivo. Organization for Economic Cooperation and Development, Paris, adopted 21 July 1997.

OECD: OECD Guideline for testing of chemicals – Guideline 408 (1998): Repeated Dose 90-Day Oral Toxicity Study in Rodents. Organization for Economic Cooperation and Development, Paris, adopted 12 May 1981, last updated 21 September 1998.

OECD: OECD Guideline for testing of chemicals – Guideline 414 (2001a): Prenatal Developmental Toxicity Study. Organization for Economic Cooperation and Development, Paris, adopted 12 May 1981, last updated 22 January 2001.

OECD: OECD Guideline for testing of chemicals – Guideline 416 (2001b): Two-Generation Reproduction Toxicity Study. Organization for Economic Cooperation and Development, Paris, adopted 26 May 1983, last updated 22 January 2001.

OECD: OECD Guideline for testing of chemicals – Guideline 420 (2001c): Acute Oral Toxicity – Fixed Dose Method. Organization for Economic Cooperation and Development, Paris, adopted 17 July 1992, last updated 17 December 2001.

OECD: OECD Guideline for testing of chemicals – Guideline 423 (2001d): Acute Oral toxicity – Acute Toxic Class Method. Organization for Economic Cooperation and Development, Paris, adopted 22 March 1996, last updated 17 December 2001.

OECD: OECD Guideline for testing of chemicals – Guideline 425 (2001e): Acute Oral Toxicity: Up-and-Down Procedure. Organization for Economic Cooperation and Development, Paris, adopted 21 September 1998, last updated 17 December 2001.

OECD: OECD Guideline for testing of chemicals – Guideline 430 (2004a): In Vitro Skin Corrosion: Transcutaneous Electrical Resistance Test (TER). Organization for Economic Cooperation and Development, Paris, original guideline adopted April 2004.

OECD: OECD Guideline for testing of chemicals – Guideline 431 (2004b): In Vitro Skin Corrosion: Human Skin Model Test. Organization for Economic Cooperation and Development, Paris, original guideline adopted April 2004.

OECD: OECD Guideline for testing of chemicals – Guideline 432 (2004c): In vitro 3T3 NRU phototoxicity test. Organization for Economic Cooperation and Development, Paris, adopted 13 April 2004.

OECD: OECD Guideline for testing of chemicals – Guideline 433 (2004d): Acute Inhalation Toxicity – Fixed Concentration Procedure (2nd version). Organization for Economic Cooperation and Development, Paris, draft guideline approved June 2004.

OECD: OECD Guideline for testing of chemicals – Guideline 434 (2004e): Acute Dermal Toxicity – Fixed Dose Procedure (1st version). Organization for Economic Cooperation and Development, Paris, draft guideline approved May 2004.

OECD: OECD Guideline for testing of chemicals – Guideline 436 (2004f): Acute Inhalation Toxicity – Acute Toxic Class (ATC) Method (1st version). Organization for Economic Cooperation and Development, Paris, draft guideline approved December 2004.

OECD: OECD Guideline for testing of chemicals – Draft Guideline 487 (2007): In Vitro Mammalian Cell Micronucleus Test (MNvit). Organization for Economic Cooperation and Development, Paris, draft (3rd version) approved 13 December 2007.

Pape WJW, Pfannenbecker U, Hoppe U: Validation of the red blood cell test system as in vitro assay for the rapid screening of irritation potential of surfactants. Mol Toxicol 1987;1:525–526.

Pedersen F, de Bruijn J, Munn S, van Leeuwen K (2003): Assessment of additional testing needs under REACH – effects of (Q)SARs, risk based testing and voluntary industry initiatives. JRC Report EUR 20863 EN, available through http://ecb.jrc.it/documents/ REACH/publications/ (consulted Feb 2008).

Piersma AH: The regulatory view. Oral presentation given during the 8th Annual *ecopa* Workshop: 'Potential improvement in the development of alternative methods: Needs in risk assessment of new technologies and their products vs. use of alternatives', held 24–25 November 2007. Brussels, Belgium, 2007.

Prinsen MK, Koëter HB: Justification of the enucleated eye test with eyes of slaughterhouse animals as an alternative to the Draize eye irritation test with rabbits. Food Chem Toxicol 1993;31:69–76.

Prinsen MK: The chicken enucleated eye test (CEET): a practical (pre)screen for the assessment of eye irritation/corrosion potential of test materials. Food Chem Toxicol 1996;34:291–296.

Rogiers V, Pauwels M: Good science must be the key factor in the development and use of alternative methods for safety assessment of cosmetics; in: Proceedings of the 5th World Congress to Animal Experimentation. ALTEX 23 2005;(special issue):346–352.

Rogiers V, Garthoff B, Webb S, Pauwels M, Müller K, Devolder T, Spielmann H (2007): The Impact of REACH, The report of the CONAM / ecopa Chemical Policy Working Group, March 2007, available through the *ecopa* Website http://www.ecopa.eu/ (consulted April 2007).

SCCNFP: SCCNFP/0522/01 (2002): Opinion on Salicylic Acid, adopted by the SCCNFP during the 20th plenary meeting of 04 June 2002.

SCCNFP: SCCNFP/0650/03 (2003a): Opinion concerning Benzoic Acid, 2-[4-(Diethylamino)-2-Hydroxybenzoyl]-, Hexylester, adopted by the SCCNFP during the 24th plenary meeting of 24–25 June 2003.

SCCNFP: SCCNFP/0682/03 (2003b): Opinion concerning 6-Nitro-O-Toluidine (Colipa n° B56), adopted by the SCCNFP during the 24th plenary meeting of 24–25 June 2003.

SCCNFP: SCCNFP/0736/03 (2003c): Opinion concerning Basic Orange 31, adopted by the SCCNFP during the 25th plenary meeting of 20 October 2003.

SCCNFP: SCCNFP/0783/04 (2004a): Opinion concerning Acid Yellow 1 (Colipa n° B1), adopted by the SCCNFP on 23 April 2004 by means of the written procedure.

SCCNFP: SCCNFP/0785/04 (2004b): Opinion concerning Acid Orange 7 (Colipa n° C15), adopted by the SCCNFP on 23 April 2004 by means of the written procedure.

SCCNFP: SCCNFP/0787/04 (2004c): Opinion concerning Acid Blue 9 (Colipa n° C40), adopted by the SCCNFP on 23 April 2004 by means of the written procedure.

SCCNFP: SCCNFP/0792/04 (2004d): Opinion concerning Acid Red 18 (Colipa n° C175), adopted by the SCCNFP on 23 April 2004 by means of the written procedure.

SCCNFP: SCCNFP/0795/04 (2004e): Opinion concerning Pigment Red 57, adopted by the SCCNFP during the 28th plenary meeting of 25 May 2004.

SCCNFP: SCCNFP/0811/04 (2004f): Opinion concerning Benzisothiazolinone (Colipa n° P96), adopted by the SCCNFP on 1 July 2004 by means of the written procedure.

SCCNFP: SCCNFP/0834/04 (2004g): Opinion concerning 'Report for establishing the timetable for phasing out animal testing for the purpose of the cosmetics directive' issued by ECVAM (30/04/ 2004), adopted by the SCCNFP on 1 July 2004 by means of the written procedure.

SCCP: SCCP/0683/03 (2004a): Opinion on Basic Brown 17 (Colipa n° B7), adopted by the SCCP during the 2nd plenary meeting of 7 December 2004.

SCCP: SCCP/0838/04 (2004b): Opinion on Hydroxyisohexyl 3-cyclohexene Carboxaldehyde (sensitisation only), adopted by the SCCP during the 2nd plenary meeting of 7 December 2004.

SCCP: SCCP/0843/04 (2004c): Opinion on Tea Tree Oil, adopted by the SCCP during the 2nd plenary meeting of 7 December 2004.

SCCP: SCCP/0837/04 (2005a): Opinion on Ethyl Lauroyl Arginate (Colipa n° P95), adopted by the SCCP during the 3rd plenary meeting of 15 March 2005.

SCCP: SCCP/0868/05 (2005b): Opinion on Cresylpropionaldehyde (p-Methyldihydrocinnam-aldehyde) (sensitisation only), adopted by the SCCP during the 3rd plenary meeting of 15 March 2005.

SCCP: SCCP/0876/05 (2005c): Opinion on Isatin (Colipa n° A129), adopted by the SCCP during the 3rd plenary meeting of 15 March 2005.

SCCP: SCCP/0878/05 (2005d): Opinion on Acid Blue 62 (Colipa n° C67), adopted by the SCCP during the 4th plenary meeting of 21 June 2005.

SCCP: SCCP/0883/05 (2005e): Opinion on 2-Mercaptobenzothiazole (MBT) (sensitisation only), adopted by the SCCP during the 4th plenary of 21 June 2005.

SCCP: SCCP/0898/05 (2005f): Opinion on 4-Amino-m-cresol (Colipa n° A74), adopted by the SCCP during the 5th plenary meeting of 20 September 2005.

SCCP: SCCP/0908/05 (2005g): Opinion on 2,6-Dimethoxy-3,5-pyridinediamine HCl (Colipa n° A101), adopted by the SCCP during the 5th plenary meeting of 20 September 2005.

SCCP: SCCP/0918/05 (2005h): Opinion on Climbazole (Colipa n° P64), adopted by the SCCP during the 5th plenary meeting of 20 September 2005.

SCCP: SCCP/0923/05 (2005i): Opinion on Quinolinium, 4-formyl-1-methyl-, salt with 4-methylbenzenesulfonic acid (1:1) (Colipa n° A157), adopted by the SCCP during the 6th plenary meeting of 13 December 2005.

SCCP: SCCP/0917/05 (2006a): Opinion on Alkyl (C$_{16}$, C$_{18}$, C$_{22}$) trimethylammonium chloride for other uses than as a preservative, adopted by the SCCP on 17 March 2006 by means of the written procedure.

SCCP: SCCP/0924/05 (2006b): Opinion on Hydroxyethyl-2-nitro-p-toluidine (Colipa n° B75), adopted by the SCCP on 17 March 2006 by means of the written procedure.

SCCP: SCCP/0935/05 (2006c): Opinion on Coumarin (sensitisation only), adopted by the SCCP during the 8th plenary meeting of 20 June 2006.

SCCP: SCCP/0947/05 (2006d): Opinion on 6-Hydroxyindole (Colipa n° A128), adopted by the SCCP during the 7th plenary meeting of 28 March 2006.

SCCP: SCCP/0952/05 (2006e): Opinion on Dihydroxyindole (Colipa n° A111), adopted by the SCCP during the 7th plenary meeting of 28 March 2006.

SCCP: SCCP/0957/05 (2006f): Opinion on 2-Methyl-5-hydroxyethylaminophenol COLIPA No. A31, adopted by the SCCP during the 7th plenary meeting of 28 March 2006.

SCCP: SCCP/0963/05 (2006g): Opinion on p-Methylaminophenol Sulphate (Colipa n° A22), adopted by the SCCP during the 7th plenary meeting of 28 March 2006.

SCCP: SCCP/0978/06 (2006h): Opinion on m-Aminophenol (Colipa n° A15), adopted by the SCCP during the 10th plenary meeting of 19 December 2006.

SCCP: SCCP/0979/06 (2006i): Opinion on 2,4-Diaminophenoxyethanol and its salts (Colipa n° A42), adopted by the SCCP during the 7th plenary meeting of 28 March 2006.

SCCP: SCCP/0981/06 (2006j): Opinion on HC Red no 1 (Colipa n° B48), adopted by the SCCP during the 9th plenary meeting of 10 October 2006.

SCCP: SCCP/0983/06 (2006k): Opinion on N,N-bis(2-hydroxyethyl)-p-phenylenediamine sulfate (Colipa n° A50), adopted by the SCCP during the 8th plenary meeting of 20 June 2006.

SCCP: SCCP/0989/06 (2006l): Opinion on p-Phenylenediamine (Colipa n° A7), adopted by the SCCP during the 9th plenary meeting of 10 October 2006.

SCCP: SCCP/1001/06 (2006m): Opinion on 4-Amino-2-hydroxytoluene (Colipa n° A27), adopted by the SCCP during the 9th plenary meeting of 10 October 2006.

SCCP: SCCP/1005/06 (2006n): The SCCP's Notes of Guidance for the Testing of Cosmetic Ingredients and their Safety Evaluation, adopted by the SCCP during the 10th plenary meeting of 19 December 2006.

SCCP: SCCP/1025/06 (2006o): Opinion on HC Violet n° 1 (Colipa n° B66), adopted by the SCCP during the 8th plenary meeting of 20 June 2006.

SCCP: SCCP/1035/06 (2006p): Opinion on HC Blue N° 2 (Colipa n° B37), adopted by the SCCP during the 10th plenary meeting of 19 December 2006.

SCCP: SCCP/1036/06 (2006q): Opinion on 3-nitro-p-hydroethylaminophenol (Colipa n° B54), adopted by the SCCP during the 10th plenary meeting of 19 December 2006.

SCCP: SCCP/1042/06 (2006r): Opinion on 4-Methyl-benzylidene Camphor (Colipa n° S60), adopted by the SCCP during the 9th plenary meeting of 10 October 2006.

SCCP: SCCP/1069/06 (2006s): Opinion on Benzophenone-3 (Colipa n° S38), adopted by the SCCP during the 10th plenary meeting of 19 December 2006.

SCCP: SCCP/1111/07 (2007a): Memorandum on actual status of alternative methods on the use of experimental animals in the safety assessment of cosmetic ingredients in the European Union, adopted by the SCCP during the 12th plenary meeting of 19 June 2007.

SCCP: SCCP/1145/07 (2007b): Memorandum on the in vitro test Episkin™ for skin irritation testing, adopted by the SCCP during the 14th plenary meeting of 18 December 2007.

Spielmann H, Balls M, Brand M, Döring B, Holzhütter HG, Kalweit S, Klecak G, L'Epattenier H, Liebsch M, Lovell WW, Maurer T, Moldenhauer F, Moore L, Pape WJW, Pfannenbecker U, Potthast J, De Silva O, Steiling W, Willshaw A: EC/COLIPA project on in vitro phototoxicity testing: first results obtained with the Balb/c 3T3 cell phototoxicity assay. Toxicol In Vitro 1994a;8:793–796.

Spielmann H, Lovell WW, Hölzle E, Johnson BE, Maurer T, Miranda M, Pape WJW, Sapora O, Sladowski D: In vitro phototoxicity testing. The report and recommendations of ECVAM Workshop 2. Altern Lab Anim 1994b;22:314–348.

van der Jagt K, Munn S, Tørsløv J, de Bruijn J (2004): Alternative approaches can reduce the use of test animals under REACH. JRC Report EUR 21405 EN, available through http://ecb.jrc.it/documents/REACH/publications (consulted Feb 2008).

6

7 Headlines of Safety Assessment of Cosmetics in Europe and Future Perspectives

Rogiers V, Pauwels M (eds): Safety Assessment of Cosmetics in Europe.
Curr Probl Dermatol. Basel, Karger, 2008, vol 36, pp 166–182

Headlines of Safety Assessment of Cosmetics in Europe

The safety assessment of cosmetics in the EU is a complex undertaking, requiring insight in a number of EU legislative documents and knowledge on basic toxicology and the general risk assessment paradigm. Above all, it requires experience in the field.

This book is subdivided in several chapters, each covering a separate aspect of cosmetic safety assessment. The following points recapture the major results obtained as well as the content of the individual sub-discussions held at the end of each experimental chapter.

The Current EU Cosmetic Regulatory Framework for Cosmetics (Chapter 1)

Although many cosmetic safety assessors are scientists trained in the fields of medicine, pharmacy, chemistry, biology and/or (regulatory) toxicology, finding their way in the complex cosmetic-related EU regulatory framework is not always evident. Therefore, chapter 1 contains an overview of the relevant features of the Cosmetic Products Directive and a practical overview of some other legal texts that may have an impact on cosmetic safety evaluation. These are either called 'vertical legislations', meaning that they regulate a specific category of compounds or mixtures of which some may also act as cosmetic ingredients, or 'horizontal legislations', implying that they regulate a broad range of product types, including cosmetic products. The vertical legislations include the ones on dangerous substances, dangerous preparations, biocides, detergents, food additives, etc. The horizontal legislations are the ones on the protection of experimental animals, on general product safety, on prepackaged products, nominal quantities and aerosols. Chapter 1 is conceived as a useful guide to make the scientific safety assessor more familiar with this complex web of cosmetic-related EU legislations.

Challenges Related to Cosmetic Safety Assessment in the EU (Chapter 2)

The Cosmetic Products Directive unambiguously states that a cosmetic product *must not cause damage to human health when applied under reasonably foreseeable conditions of use.* Whereas for the European risk assessment process of pharmaceuticals, biocides, plant protection products and dangerous substances, comprehensive guidance documents have been published, the cosmetic counterpart never followed. This forms a first challenge for the qualified safety assessor who, by signing the safety report, takes responsibility for the safety of that particular finished cosmetic product. Considering that many cosmetics are extensively and frequently used by the general public, their safety assessment needs to be based on solid scientific grounds. Consequently, the safety assessor needs appropriate training in the field to be able to assemble the required information and to formulate a well-reasoned scientific statement on the safe use of the product under study. In this process, the need for appropriate exposure data for all cosmetic product types is a lasting problem point.

The major challenge in the safety assessment of cosmetic products, however, emerged in 2003 with the publication of the seventh amendment to the Cosmetic Products Directive, which placed the cosmetic industry and many concerned parties in a deadlock. On the one hand, the EU legislator considers that cosmetic products need to be inherently safe for the consumer, whereas on the other hand, animal testing on these products and their ingredients is considered unacceptable from an ethical point of view, resulting in a testing and marketing ban with clear and irrevocable deadlines. Since the cosmetic testing ban comes into force in 2009, time has run short and a solution to overcome the deadlock is urgently needed, but not evident.

Safety Assessment of Cosmetic Ingredients Performed at the European Level (Chapter 3)

At the European level, the SCC(NF)P deals with the safety assessment of a restricted number of cosmetic ingredients, namely those that are related to the Annexes of the Cosmetic Products Directive, and for which health concerns could exist. The related data requirements are quite elaborated and include acute and local toxicity, dermal absorption, mutagenicity/genotoxicity and several long-term toxicity studies. In order to objectively depict the safety assessment paradigm used for those ingredients and to identify potential problem points, the multitude of information and the scientific experience gathered through the discussions of the SCC(NF)P between 2000 and 2006 (publicly available through the committees' websites[1, 2]) were assembled under a structured form in a carefully designed database. A first aim when constituting this electronic tool was to investigate which studies were usually performed (data availability) and which ones were frequently considered of inferior scientific quality (data acceptance).

---

1   http://ec.europa.eu/health/ph_risk/committees/sccp/sccp_opinions_en.htm (consulted February 2008).
2   http://ec.europa.eu/health/ph_risk/committees/04_sccp/sccp_opinions_en.htm (consulted February 2008).

Our results show that, irrespective of the fact whether the final SCC(NF)P report has a positive or a negative outcome, the list of available tests is quite constant for the vast majority of industry submissions. It consists of identification of the compounds under study and their physicochemical properties, acute oral toxicity, skin and eye irritation, skin sensitisation, in vitro dermal absorption, 90-day oral toxicity, mutagenicity/genotoxicity and reproductive toxicity. Only in vitro dermal absorption studies appear to be more available in submissions resulting in a positive opinion. This is a clear indication that data availability alone is no guarantee for success. Indeed, the main determining factor shows to be the acceptance by the SCC(NF)P of the individual studies present in the dossier.

To this respect, three domains are identified as problem areas, namely identity/physicochemistry of the compounds under study, in vitro dermal absorption and mutagenicity/genotoxicity. The concerned studies were often of inferior quality and consequently were the mostly requested additional data by the SCC(NF)P after full evaluation of the dossier.

In-depth analysis of the identity/physicochemical data packages reveals inadequate identification of test substances and their impurities and the deduction/calculation instead of actual measurement of physicochemical parameters. Therefore, these data packages can quite easily be remediated by using officially recognised methods and by presenting measured instead of calculated values and/or data retrieved from the literature. To this respect, the SCCP Notes of Guidance give some clear instructions with reference to officially accepted methodologies [SCCP, 2006].

As far as the in vitro dermal absorption study is concerned, the situation is more complex. The output of our database reveals that the observed problems are mainly related to the in vitro methodology. The main issues are situated in the use of a sample concentration deviating from in-use conditions, problems related to the receptor fluid (solubility of test substance unknown or inappropriate choice of type of receptor fluid), failure to separate skin compartments for individual measurements, excess amounts of substance applied, insufficient number of skin samples tested, and inappropriate statistics or high variability rates. This great number of deviations can partly be attributed to the fact that the study suffers from a plenitude of available official protocols and guidance documents with slightly differing requirements. Therefore, a first step forward could be a harmonisation of the existing guidelines, compiling them into one document containing some common provisions, followed by the specific requirements per sector. It is our belief that this could significantly help performing laboratories to deliver more adequate results and to improve the overall acceptance level of the study.

However, the high variability rates encountered during testing still cast doubt on the scientific value of the results when included in quantitative calculations. For substances that are so innocuous that the MoS calculation with 100% dermal absorption leads to a value superior to 100, there is no problem, since these ingredients are safe. For substances generating MoS values in the order of 10–100, application of conservative values as used for plant protection products seems to be rather attractive. They allow the assumption of a DA value of 10% provided the molecular weight and the Log P_{ow} of the substance under study fall within pre-defined ranges [DG SANCO, 2004]. Application of this methodology is one of the actual questions of Colipa, representing the European cosmetic industry, to the SCCP. It is on the agenda for discussion in the near future. Today, however, it is not yet recognised by the SCCP as a valid methodology. For a large number of cosmetic ingredients, DA remains a problem area, as alternatives to the in vitro DA study, namely QSARs and mathematical models, are not ready for regulatory acceptance [Bouwman et al., 2006; van de Sandt et al., 2007] and in vivo methods are not an option after March 2009, viewing the testing ban that comes into force.

For the endpoint of mutagenicity/genotoxicity, it is observed that, although some test-specific remarks reoccur in a number of SCC(NF)P opinions, the main problem seems to be the incompleteness of the submitted data sets. A combination of the complexity of the mechanisms involved (case-by-case expert judgment required) and frequently changing SCC(NF)P data requirements, probably contributes to the uncertainties and the debate in this particular field. In addition, now that a retrospective analysis of the past 25 years of use is possible, the scientific community acknowledges that the existing in vitro assays require thorough review and optimisation [Kirkland et al., 2007; Kirsch-Volders and Lombaert, 2008]. This is quite alarming since after the cut-off date of 11 March 2009, positive in vitro mutagenicity/genotoxicity results obtained for a new cosmetic ingredient cannot be followed anymore by an in vivo assay and will therefore imply the loss of the compound.

A further outcome of our study is the observation that an evolution took place in the SCC(NF)P strategy in the past couple of years. Currently, the Committee expresses on a regular basis temporary positive opinions awaiting the delivery of requested additional data, whereas, in earlier years, a minor lack of data automatically caused the refusal of a compound. The SCC(NF)P also invested efforts in reducing the time period between industry submission and publication of the final report and in improving transparency in its decision-making process. From industry side, efforts were done to improve submission quality and efficiency. Observation of the interesting discussions between the SCC(NF)P and the cosmetic industry and personal communications with senior scientists from both sides have led to the formulation of the following points of thought:

– The importance and impact of the wording of scientific opinions should not be underestimated. The phrasing 'The information submitted is inadequate to assess the safe use of the substance' is most commonly used to indicate that insufficient data are presented to formulate either a positive or a negative opinion. However, it could be interpreted as 'The compound is most likely unsafe'. Although it is acknowledged that risk perception is not the first concern of the SCCP, it has importance for the cosmetic industry, especially when a message from the committee unintentionally could be misunderstood by the media and consumer organisations.

– When additional data are requested, it is not always clear what is exactly meant or asked for. General statements as '... according to the requirements of the Notes of Guidance...' induce uncertainty in the exact list of tests to be performed. It is acknowledged that the performance of certain assays could depend on the outcome of other tests and as such a final list can not always be pre-defined. On the other hand, when a detailed enumeration of requested additional data is provided, it could easily be interpreted as the final list, which, upon delivery of the corresponding results, would automatically lead to a positive opinion.

– Regularly adapting the SCCP data requirements is indispensable to keep up with the most recent advances in scientific knowledge and with newly reported adverse effects related to cosmetics. However, it appears difficult to accept by industry that dossiers would be rejected due to lacking information that was not yet requested at the time of submission. Therefore, we believe that, with the exception of cases of serious health concerns, the process would be improved by taking into consideration the data requirements of the date of initial submission.

– The possibility to organise industry hearings exists. The number and extent, however, are based upon a delicate balance between the time management of the scientific committee, the relevance of the interventions and the importance of the subject/substance under study. Industry hearings may indeed quickly clarify some problem points and are in certain cases considered to be very useful and timesaving, but it is crucial that the delegates bring scientific and to the point information. The SCCP could envisage drawing up the necessary criteria for organising industry hearings, including for example the time span given, requested qualifications of delegates and specific questions/topics to be addressed. In addition, hearings on certain topics could be publicly announced on the SCCP website so that concerned parties have the possibility to add useful input to the discussion before the hearing takes place. This allows the scientific committee to discuss all the available information in one meeting, instead of repeatedly re-opening discussions based upon newly provided information.

Safety Assessment of Cosmetic Ingredients Present in Technical Information Files of Finished Products (Chapter 4)

Since the safety assessment of a finished product is legally required to be based upon the intrinsic properties of its individual ingredients and their level of exposure, a first step in the overall process will be the collection of physicochemical and toxicological information on the individual ingredients contained in the finished product under study.

As the majority of cosmetic ingredients do not go through the safety evaluation performed by the SCC(NF)P, their available data packages usually are much less extended than the ones described in chapter 3. They will mainly be triggered by the data requirements of other data-generating European legislations the ingredients under study have to comply with. Of most relevance to this respect is the legislation on dangerous substances and, more specifically, the new road taken with REACH, the newly published regulation on chemicals, imposing harmonised data requirements for all dangerous substances depending on their tonnage levels. Monitoring the implementation and practical realisation of REACH is key in maintaining a realistic view on safety data availability for a large number of cosmetic ingredients. Spending some time to get familiar with the European legislation into force not only leads to a realistic picture of data expectations, but equally supports negotiations for obtaining (non-)confidential data from manufacturers and suppliers.

Indeed, in the process of data collection, the raw material supplier should be the first source of information for the specific cosmetic ingredients purchased, with their particular specifications such as the purity/impurities profiles. In order to confirm or supplement those data, however, it is often necessary to collect safety data through the open literature and physicochemical/toxicological databases.

Therefore chapter 4 provides assistance in performing a database search for a cosmetic ingredient. It focuses on the adequate identification of the compound under study, on the choice of a useful set of data sources and finally, on the evaluation of the reliability and relevance of the retrieved data. The provided list of databases and Internet links is based upon our years of experience and is therefore not exhaustive. It is, nevertheless, intended to constitute a good starting point for someone who is inexperienced in toxicological database searching.

Once all available data on the ingredients of the finished cosmetic product have been collected, the competent safety assessor is equipped to further investigate their safe use in the finished product. Since no official guidance for this complex process is available, chapter 4 assembles some additional factors to be considered, such as the envisaged use of the cosmetic product and its presentation, the outcome of the functional complaint system and available results from human skin compatibility testing with the finished product. In the end, however, the qualified safety assessor needs to rely on personal experience and scientific skills to formulate the required assumptions and make the final statement on the safe use of the cosmetic product. As it is already difficult to base a judgment upon animal data that are commonly used for risk assessment, it will undoubtedly become an even greater challenge to correctly interpret and use results from replacement alternatives alone or from a mixture of in vivo and in vitro data on the same compound in view of assessing the safety of that particular cosmetic ingredient.

The Cosmetic Technical Information File in Practice (Chapter 5)

The safety assessor's report is only one of the eight points that need to be addressed in the European TIF or PIR of a finished cosmetic product. As the cosmetic legislation is very concise on the general content and the form of such a TIF, chapter 5 provides a set of recommendations on the different legally required items. For example, details are provided on the representation of the product's composition, physicochemical and microbiological properties, manufacturing method and stability, safety assessment, effects claimed and animal testing. A structured framework, in particular of relevance for small and medium-sized enterprises, is taken up in appendix 3. This framework is subdivided in an administrative part, an ingredients dossier and a finished product part.

It gives indirect guidance to the safety assessor, but is also inspection friendly as the administrative part contains all items that are commonly checked by inspectors.

Chapter 5 is mainly based upon years of personal experience in compiling TIFs for cosmetic companies and upon contacts with regulators and industrial toxicologists.

The recommendations and the framework were presented during international meetings and were welcomed by many parties, including European and extra-European Competent Authorities. More specifically, the Canadian authorities and those of several Asian countries have expressed their interest in the way the TIF framework is presented here.

The Use of Alternative Methods in the Safety Assessment of Cosmetic Ingredients (Chapter 6)

The SCCP safety assessment of cosmetic ingredients to be placed on the Annexes or of concern to human health, and the qualified safety assessor's evaluation of all ingredients of a finished product to be taken up in a TIF, will be affected by the introduction of the gradual animal testing and marketing bans imposed by the current EU legislation. The lack of replacement alternatives for the most important endpoints in the current risk assessment paradigm, namely repeated dose toxicity, carcinogenicity and reproduction toxicity testing, is of great concern for many academics and scientific committee members [Seibert, 2006; Bridges, 2006; Greim et al., 2006]. To objectively investigate the problem, chapter 6 provides an overview of the actual status of the existing (validated) 3R alternatives and the prospects for the near future per toxicological endpoint. Simultaneously, the content and search possibilities of our database are employed to investigate actual animal use and the presence of alternative methods so far in ingredient dossiers studied by the SCC(NF)P.

In the field of acute toxicity testing, the mostly encountered study is the acute oral toxicity test, which initially consisted of the classical LD_{50} test, involving determination of the dose causing lethality in 50% of the experimental animals after one single oral exposure. This protocol was replaced in 2001 by three reduction and refinement alternatives.

Our database reveals that of these three, the fixed dose procedure appears to have found its way into submissions to the SCC(NF)P. Nearly no LD_{50} tests are found with testing dates after 2001. Since the three alternative methods still involve the use of animals, a replacement strategy is highly needed (before 2009). This is taken up by the EU-funded Acute-Tox project, which at best will be successful in providing pre-validated tests for the screening of acute oral toxicity in 2009. For dermal and inhalation acute toxicity, tests are not available.

Nevertheless, replacement testing in the field of acute toxicity does not appear to be the first concern in the cosmetic sector. Although the results may give an indication on the starting dose in repeated dose experiments, they mainly serve for the classification of chemicals at the EU level. This does not apply to cosmetics, but gives a relevant indication of the potential toxic effects involved in case of acute poisoning with a massive dosage. This is not common for cosmetic ingredients, but could happen in case of mistakes in production, serious misuse of products or accidents with bulk products.

As far as local toxicity is concerned, skin corrosion is assessed through validated in vitro methodology available since 2000. Meanwhile, the official in vivo skin and eye irritation protocols were gradually subjected to refinement and reduction measures also taken up in the official guidelines. Although some newly developed in vitro assays for skin and eye irritation exist, their use is restricted to screening strategies and they generally require further development and validation to fully replace the animal assays. One exception is the Episkin™ method for skin irritation testing, which recently received ESAC approval. Its general use in the cosmetic field, however, is delayed, as the SCCP requires additional information to prove the assay's applicability to all cosmetic ingredient types present on the Annexes and to dye substances in particular [SCCP, 2007b]. Indeed, the actual endpoint consists of a colour formation (MTT test), eventually supported by interleukin 1-α production. Until now, it has not been clearly proven that coloured substances or colours formed do not interfere with this endpoint [Faller et al., 2007].

Out of our database, we learn that neither in vivo nor in vitro skin corrosion tests are encountered in the dossiers studied. It must be acknowledged that corrosive substances are seldom deliberately added to cosmetic products. Exceptions are strong acids and bases used to bring cosmetic formulations to pH. Since these are neutralised, they do not pose a health problem. The same goes for corrosive substances that are diluted to sufficiently low concentration levels [Hall, 2007].

The occurrence of the reduction and refinement measures taken up in the official skin and eye irritation protocols, could not be checked via our database as they have been gradually introduced. Instead we analysed the presence of the in vitro screening methods for skin and eye irritation in the SCC(NF)P opinions. It turned out to be very limited. This was expected viewing the lack of validation of these methods at the time the presented studies were performed.

Finally, in view of the request of the SCCP to industry to show that the Episkin method can be used for hair dye substances in particular, all available in vivo skin irritation results were extracted from our database and the cosmetic ingredients involved were ranked according to the different categories of skin irritation they belong to. As such, a pool of potential reference compounds becomes available which could be used in further validation activities (in vivo/in vitro comparison).

For the endpoint of skin sensitisation, the LLNA has been available as a refinement alternative for the original Magnusson-Kligman Guinea Pig Maximisation and Buehler tests since 2002. Because the method consists of an induction phase involving multiple applications over time, the assay is generally considered to be a 'repeated dose toxicity test', meaning that its performance is allowed until March 2013 (outside Europe after 2009). The SCCP also argued in this direction in its last memorandum on alternative methods [SCCP, 2007a].

Our database learns that, from its date of issue onwards, the LLNA has been systematically incorporated in the submissions to the SCC(NF)P. Only one exception was found.

As the LLNA involves the use of mice, however, replacement tests are urgently required for the cosmetic field. The EU-funded project Sens-it-iv at best is expected to deliver a pre-validated in vitro strategy after 2010.

This is quite disturbing, as sensitisation is seen as an important and health damaging endpoint in the safety evaluation of cosmetics. Dermatological departments in Europe, as in the rest of the world, frequently report allergic reactions caused by the use of cosmetic products and ingredients, such as fragrances, hair dyes and preservatives [Nardelli et al., 2008; McFadden, 2008; Jong et al., 2007].

In the area of mutagenicity/genotoxicity, a standard in vitro testing battery has been in use for more than 25 years. As such, one would expect that this type of hazard determination is well covered and does not pose a problem for the near future. The opposite, however, is true. Indeed, it was reported that the in vitro mutagenicity/genotoxicity testing battery suffers from a high level of false-positive results [Kirkland et al., 2005]. As these cannot be overruled anymore by negative in vivo tests from 11 March 2009 onwards, the problem is considered to be quite serious.

Since the majority of industry submissions to the SCC(NF)P contained in vivo and in vitro data in this field, a comparison of the in vitro study results and their in vivo confirmation data was possible. This exercise confirms the occurrence of a large number of positive in vitro results that were not confirmed through subsequent in vivo testing. More specifically, over a period of 6 years, 19 compounds of the Annexes would have been wrongfully abandoned without the possibility of in vivo confirmation.

The remaining endpoints, namely repeated dose toxicity, toxicokinetics, reproductive toxicity and carcinogenicity, are the ones for which the major concerns with regard to the non-availability of replacement alternatives were expressed.

Results from our database indicate that the mostly performed tests with respect to potential systemic toxicity caused by cosmetic ingredients are the 90 day oral toxicity study with the rat and the teratogenicity test with the rat or the rabbit (repeated dose and reproductive toxicity, respectively).

Concerned EU-funded projects in these fields may result in useful cell culture and/or tissue models enabling preliminary screenings of test substances, but each of them only covers a minor part of the multiple aspects related to the complex endpoints under study. Bearing in mind that in the general design of a repeated dose toxicity study the observations and measurements performed involve clinical signs, histopathology, haematology, body weight, food consumption, organ weights, clinical biochemical parameters and urinanalysis, the total number of individual observations and measurements amounts to more than 100 [Rogiers and Pauwels, 2005]. It therefore requires a very complex and well-elaborated in vitro testing strategy to provide the same level of knowledge as obtained in vivo. Therefore, the availability of replacement tests before March 2013 in this field is totally excluded.

In a final step, our database was used to calculate the number of animals that were involved in the data generation for the dossiers submitted to the SCC(NF)P. Bringing these numbers into a broader European perspective was subsequently done by comparing them with figures reported in other sectors. To this respect, the expected animal numbers under REACH appear quite interesting. REACH is the most recent regulation on chemicals requiring that all chemical substances placed on the EU market above 1 tonne/year benefit from a minimal toxicological data package. As such, 30,000 chemicals must be tested under REACH in the years to come. Viewing the high number of animals that would be involved in such an extended testing scheme, ECVAM, together with external experts, gave substantial input on the possible use of alternative methods under REACH [Vogelgesang, 2002; Worth and Balls, 2000]. This resulted in a final version of the regulation foreseeing the use of 'suitable' alternative methods to reduce animal numbers in testing. As such, the aforementioned pre-validated alternative methods may not be ready in time for cosmetics, but still constitute valuable input for the 'suitable' methods that can be used under REACH. Nonetheless, considering that the main testing window of REACH is estimated to come between 2009 and 2014, alternatives may also come too late for this sector [Garthoff, 2007].

With regard to the order of magnitude of animal testing under the Cosmetic Products Directive and under REACH, animal data extracted from our database are compared to estimated animal numbers under REACH, all calculated by making use of the *ecopa calculator*[3]. The comparison reveals that the abolition of animal testing for cosmetics may slightly reduce overall animal use, but only to a very limited extent. More specifically, in a worst case calculation, 21,000 animals are estimated to be used per year for the safety assessment of cosmetic ingredients by the SCC(NF)P, whereas REACH is projected to induce the use of 752,000 animals per year during the first 5.5 years. However, it must be emphasized that these figures can only be seen as best estimates.

---

3   Available through http://www.ecopa.eu/download.php?file = Animaluse_REACH_calculator.xls (consulted November 2007).

The figure of 21,000 animals/year for cosmetic ingredients is on the one hand an overestimation, since many of the tests taken into consideration were most probably performed for other than cosmetic purposes or to meet extra-EU requirements. On the other hand, it may be considered an underestimation as only those substances studied by the SCC(NF)P are taken into account. Nevertheless, ingredients not studied by the SCC(NF)P will not likely be subjected to additional testing for cosmetic purposes, as there is no legal requirement in that direction.

The figure of 752,000 animals/year for REACH is based on a number of estimations too. It takes into consideration the potential availability of 'suitable' alternative methods and waiving of tests [Rogiers, 2007]. This is done according to a transparent scheme, but after all remains an estimate.

A reoccurring finding in both schemes is that repeated dose toxicity and reproductive toxicity are the most animal-consuming endpoints. Unfortunately these form part of the areas without replacement alternatives.

Future Perspectives

This book contains guidance for the European cosmetic safety assessor on the potential relevance of existing EU legislations, on the efficient search for safety data on cosmetic ingredients, on the performance of a scientifically based risk assessment and on the compilation of a TIF for a finished cosmetic product. Taking into account the continuous changes in European legislation and the scientific advances in the fields of toxicology and alternative methods, this guidance will be frequently updated and shared with interested parties during international congresses and meetings.

Our database will, in the near future, be brought to a higher level by transcribing the information into more powerful software and by regularly updating the content (starting with the introduction of the available 2007 and 2008 SCCP data). As such, it can remain to be of use in the general investigation of the problem areas in the safety assessment of cosmetic ingredients, in the investigation of consistency in decision-making, and in the study of the incorporation of alternatives in SCCP opinions. It could also be envisaged to become a valuable addition to the newly created European Commission database on cosmetic ingredients (CosmIng). Since the latter is only in a preliminary stage, however, a tangible proposal can not yet be formulated.

Since our database makes use of objective, scientifically based data, we believe that its assistance in the validation and post-validation process of alternative methods can be of sustainable nature. Should, for example, a specific in vitro mutagenicity/genotoxicity assay be optimised or replaced by a new one, the database can generate a list of reference compounds for which scientifically accepted in vivo results are available. As such, it can assist in in vitro/in vivo comparison exercises. The pool of potential reference compounds will become more extended with every update.

The key question for the future, however, remains how the European authorities, cosmetic industry and all other concerned parties will overcome the deadlock of the currently imposed animal testing ban. A lot of uncertainty exists. For example, it is not known whether the European Court of Justice will withdraw a cosmetic product from the market because it contains an ingredient that has undergone mandatory animal testing after 2013 under the provisions of REACH or through extra-EU requirements.

This will mainly depend upon the legal interpretation of the phrasing 'in order to meet the requirements of this Directive' which refers to the prohibited animal testing. Although a variety of speculations on this subject exist, it is quite impossible to foresee how the legal framework in the EU will evolve during the next couple of years. The current wording of the European cosmetic legislation and the proposed recast make it quite clear that the testing and marketing bans are irrevocable, irrespective of the fact whether the scientific world will be able to come up with the necessary replacement alternatives to guarantee human safety.

Phrases like 'It will gradually become possible to ensure the safety of ingredients used in cosmetic products by using non-animal alternative methods...' in the preamble of the Seventh Amendment to the Cosmetic Products Directive, indicate that the European legislator expects the scientific world to find timely solutions. However, viewing the advances in the development of alternative methods, it is crystal clear that the current customary data requirements for hazard assessment of cosmetic ingredients by the SCCP and safety assessors in general, are not ready to be met by replacement alternatives, certainly not before 2013. Original ideas are highly needed, but cannot be bought with financial means. This was proven by the EU Seventh Framework Programme call titled 'Defining a long-term research strategy for the full replacement of animal tests for repeat dose systemic toxicity', which involved a budget of EUR 3.5 million spread over 7 years[4], but for which no one applied. Instead of defining unrealistic goals, the identification of gaps and research priorities deserves first attention.

This is the way followed by the participants of Working Group 2 of the *epaa*[5]. Learning from all previous experiences in the industrial and academic world and from EU-funded projects, and taking up the major problem points identified through listing of data gaps, appears useful. An example in this context is the correct compilation of lists of reference compounds used during in vitro validation studies. Misclassification and not taking actual literature data into sufficient consideration have been observed. Another example is the reoccurring problem of the lack of reliable metabolisation systems present in cell and tissue cultures, delivering in vitro results that are not in correlation with the existing in vivo data.

---

4   ENV.2007.3.3.1.2. Defining a long-term research strategy for the full replacement of animal tests for repeat dose systemic toxicity, presented during the Seventh Framework Programme Info day – Environment Theme, 23 January 2007, Brussels, Belgium.

5   Working Group 2 – Prioritisation, promotion and implementation of future research based on the application of the 3Rs, details through http://ec.europa.eu/enterprise/epaa/wg_2.htm (consulted February 2008).

More than anything, however, it is our belief that clear and scientifically correct messages need to be communicated. Good alternative methods for specific endpoints exist, but have their strengths and limitations. Ignoring the latter gives the wrong impression to the outside world that the perfect alternative is available, whereas the limitations will later become apparent once the method is in use. This initial over-selling of alternatives is detrimental as it undermines the highly needed regulatory trust.

Therefore, this discussion concludes with a brief overview of the endpoints that need to be covered by replacement alternatives before 2009 and 2013 for the testing of cosmetic ingredients. Where relevant, the validated methods are accompanied by some already encountered post-validation problems.

A first set of replacement tests, expected to be ready before 11 March 2009, includes the endpoints of acute oral, dermal and inhalation toxicity, skin corrosion, skin and eye irritation, phototoxicity and mutagenicity/genotoxicity.

As explained in chapter 6, this deadline appears to be achievable for skin corrosion, skin irritation, phototoxicity and mutagenicity/genotoxicity. However, looking objectively at some scientific facts, we need to acknowledge the following:

– The Episkin method for skin irritation still requires approval by the SCCP. There are doubts on its applicability to hair dyes substances [SCCP, 2007b], as in the field of phototoxicity, the concerned MTT colourimetric method was reported to cause problems with the testing of dyes [Lelièvre et al., 2007]. The method therefore has great potential, but may not be suitable for all substance types.

– The validated in vitro phototoxicity assay is widely used, but has also been reported to generate a number of positive results that were not confirmed in vivo. Some technical aspects of the assay, such as the specifications of the light source used, the maximum concentration to be tested, the bioavailability of the compound, problems with insoluble compounds and mixtures, appear to require further standardisation, validation and global harmonisation [De Smedt, 2007]. A potential solution, that actually is used by the industry, could be the additional use of 3-D skin models when the 3T3 NRU PT is positive [Liebsch, 1995; Lelièvre, 2007]. This strategy may be valid, but is not yet validated for this purpose.

– The in vitro mutagenicity/genotoxicity testing battery suffers from its high rate of 'false positive' results (by preference referred to as 'low predictivity'), implying that the existing protocols need further optimisation [Kirkland et al., 2007; Kirsch-Volders and Lombaert, 2008]. Our own restricted study of 27 compounds with scientifically acceptable in vitro and in vivo data sets, identifies 19 substances that would be lost without the possibility of performing in vivo studies and thus confirms this problem.

A second set of required replacement tests, including skin sensitisation, repeated dose toxicity, toxicokinetics, reproductive toxicity and carcinogenicity, is linked to the marketing cut-off date of 11 March 2013. The developments of alternatives in this field are unfortunately only at the research level:

- In the field of skin sensitisation, the LLNA is a refinement alternative that has been in use since 2004. Our own restricted 'post-validation' exercise on 23 substances, comparing results obtained through the LLNA with the outcome of the original guinea pig assays, shows that in 26% of the cases diverging conclusions were drawn. This confirms the concerns of scientists in the field who stress the importance of follow-up and reporting of post-validation results of the LLNA [Basketter, 2007]. Irrespective of this post-validation exercise, however, the assay will not be allowed after 2013 for cosmetic ingredients. The EU project Sens-it-iv may deliver a pre-validated alternative after 2010, but chances that its full validation will be achieved before 2013, are small.
- For repeated dose toxicity, the scientific world is at the level of developing cell culture and tissue models for a number of organs, but the goal of full replacement is still out of reach. At this point, the critical question may arise whether the European legislator is not trying to achieve the impossible. If all the intensive efforts to date have not even generated a first perspective for the area of repeated dose toxicity, it can be questioned whether additional money and logistics alone will enable delivery of the hoped-for replacement strategy. The fact that no scientific partner seems to be willing to accept EUR 3.5 million (EU-funded project) bringing ideas together on full replacement of repeated dose toxicity studies, is a sign on the wall.
- The same lack of full replacement perspectives is observed in the field of reproduction toxicity testing. Three alternatives are proposed (WEC, EST, MM), but are restricted to embryotoxicity, meaning that they only represent a limited part of the reproductive cycle. In 2001, ESAC endorsed the validity of the WEC and the EST to distinguish between non-embryotoxic, weakly embryotoxic and strong embryotoxic substances. Nevertheless, doubt exists about the predictivity of the EST and the test is rather seen as a screening tool than as a quantitative assay [Rogiers, 2007]. Also the SCCP questioned the use of the alternative embryotoxicity assays in the general risk assessment procedures for cosmetic ingredients [SCCP, 2007a].
- In the field of carcinogenicity, no alternative methods are foreseen. The Carcinogenomics project has started and encountered an important problem of in vitro/in vivo comparison studies, namely the correct categorisation of compounds tested in vivo. Too often this is mistaken with the classification of dangerous substances in the EU. However, the latter is not always based on scientific criteria alone. Out of precaution, certain chemicals may be placed in a higher category than the one they belong to. Therefore it is crucial that, at the start of in vivo/in vitro comparison studies, the literature on the in vivo data is carefully reviewed and that every chemical is classified according to a set of scientific criteria specifically designed for the purpose [Vinken et al., 2008].

As a final note, we would like to emphasize that the additional time to go through the full validation process (necessary in the field of cosmetics) [Spielmann and Liebsch, 2001] cannot be neglected when discussing promising in vitro methods present in the pipeline.

We have come into an era where a number of alternative methods are being used by industry as screening methods, meaning that results are available and that in vitro/in vivo comparison becomes possible. Showing that this correlation is sufficiently high is a way of building trust in alternative methods. Although in vivo studies also have their limitations, it must be recognised that they managed to induce a certain level of trust to ensure human safety over time. In order to bring any newly developed alternative method to the same and preferably to an even higher level, the efforts in their development, validation and not to forget post-validation, need to be continued.

References

Basketter D: Case study 1: Local Lymph Node Assay (LLNA); in Report on Workshop on 'Dissemination Strategies: How do they influence the uptake of new 3Rs methods across laboratories/boundaries?'. Working Group 3 of *epaa*, 2007. Available through http://ec.europa.eu/enterprise/epaa/wg3_ws20071001_report.pdf (consulted February 2008).

Bouwman T, Cronin MTD, Bessems JGM, van de Sandt JJM: Evaluation of published QSARs for percutaneous absorption. Toxicol Lett 2006;164:S322.

Bridges J: REACH – Outcome and implementation aspects (oral presentation); *ecopa* Workshop 'REAlity CHeck: Proposals Amendments and Conclusions from the Alternative Point of View, February 2006, Brussels.

De Smedt A: In vitro 3T3 NRU Phototoxicity test (oral communication); Annu Conf 2007 Eur Partnership Alternat Approaches Anim Test: Regulatory Acceptance, November 2007, Brussels.

DG SANCO: Sanco/222/2000: Guidance Document on Dermal Absorption. European Commission, Health and Consumer Protection Directorate General, Doc. Sanco/222/2000 revision 7 of 19 March 2004.

Faller C, Aeby P, Goebel C: In vitro assessment of the skin irritation potential of hair dyes using a reconstructed human epidermis (RHE) model (poster); 6th World Congr Alternat Animal Use Life Sci, Theme 8: 'Applying New Science and Technology from Basic Research to the 3Rs', August 2007, Tokyo.

Garthoff B: Potential improvement in the development of alternative methods: needs in risk assessment of new technologies versus use of alternatives (oral presentation); 8th Annu *ecopa* Workshop: Potential Improvement in the Development of Alternative Methods: Needs in Risk Assessment of New Technologies and Their Products vs. Use of Alternatives, November 2007, Brussels.

Greim H, Arand M, Autrup H, Bolt HM, Bridges J, Dybing E, Glomot R, Foa V, Schulte-Hermann R: Toxicological comments to the discussion about REACH. Arch Toxicol 2006;80:121–124.

Hall B: Some practical examples of safety assessment for cosmetic products (oral presentation); Safety Assessment of Cosmetics in the EU – Training Course, April 2007, Brussels.

Jong CT, Statham BN, Green CM, King CM, Gawkrodger DJ, Sansom JE, English JS, Wilkinson SM, Ormerod AD, Chowdhury MM: Contact sensitivity to preservatives in the UK, 2004–2005:results of multicentre study. Contact Dermat 2007;57:165–168.

Kirkland DJ, Aardema M, Hendersen L, Müller L: Evaluation of the ability of a battery of three in vitro genotoxicity tests to discriminate rodent carcinogens and non-carcinogens I. Sensitivity, specificity and relative predictivity. Mutat Res 2005;584:1–256.

Kirkland D, Pfuhler S, Tweats D, Aardema M, Corvi R, Darroudi F, Elhajouji A, Glatt H, Hastwell P, Hayashi M, Kasper P, Kirchner S, Lynch A, Marzin D, Maurici D, Meunier JR, Müller L, Nohynek G, Parry J, Parry E, Thybaud V, Tice R, van Benthem J, Vanparys P, White P: How to reduce false positive results when undertaking in vitro genotoxicity testing and thus avoid unnecessary follow-up animal tests: Report of an ECVAM Workshop. Mutat Res 2007;628:31–55.

Kirsch-Volders M, Lombaert N: In vitro genotoxicity/mutagenicity-requirements, strategies and problems; in Rogiers V, Pauwels M (eds): Proceedings of Safety Assessment of Cosmetics in the EU – Follow-up Course, 46 February 2008. Brussels, Belgium, 2008, p 387.

Lelièvre D, Justine P, Christiaens F, Bonaventure N, Coutet J, Marrot L, Cotovio J: The episkin phototoxicity assay (EPA): Development of an in vitro tiered strategy using 17 reference chemicals to predict phototoxic potency. Toxicol In Vitro 2007;21:977–995.

Liebsch M, Döring B, Donelly TA, Logemann P, Rheins LA, Spielmann H: Application of the human dermal model Skin2 ZK 1350 to phototoxicity and skin corrosivity testing. Toxicol In Vitro 1995;9:557–562.

McFadden JP, White IR, Frosch PJ, Sosted H, Johansen JD, Menne T: Allergy to hair dye. BMJ 2007;334:220.

Nardelli A, Carbonez A, Ottoy W, Drieghe J, Goossens A: Frequency of and trends in fragrance allergy over a 15-year period. Contact Dermat 2008;58:134–141.

Rogiers V: Disappointment or hopes for new methodology. Oral presentation given during the 8th Annual ecopa Workshop: 'Potential improvement in the development of alternative methods: Needs in risk assessment of new technologies and their products vs. use of alternatives', held 24–25 November 2007. Brussels, Belgium, 2007.

Rogiers V, Pauwels M: Good science must be the key factor in the development and use of alternative methods for safety assessment of cosmetics; in: Proceedings of the 5th World Congress to Animal Experimentation. ALTEX 2005;23(special issue):346–352.

SCCP: SCCP/1005/06 (2006): The SCCP's Notes of Guidance for the Testing of Cosmetic Ingredients and their Safety Evaluation, adopted by the SCCP during the 10th plenary meeting of 19 December 2006.

SCCP: SCCP/1111/07 (2007a): Memorandum on the actual status of alternative methods on the use of experimental animals in the safety assessment of cosmetic ingredients in the European Union, adopted by the SCCP during the 12th plenary meeting of 19 June 2007.

SCCP: SCCP/1145/07 (2007b): Memorandum on the in vitro test Episkin™ for skin irritation testing, adopted by the SCCP during the 14th plenary meeting of 18 December 2007.

Seibert H: REACH and epaa: the way to innovate by dual partnership? The view from outside: Academia. Oral presentation given during the 7th Annual ecopa Workshop: 'REACH for help: science backup?', held 25–26 November 2006. Brussels, Belgium, 2006.

Spielmann H, Liebsch M: Lessons learned from validation of in vitro toxicity test: from failure to acceptance into regulatory practice. Toxicol In Vitro 2001; 15:585–590.

van de Sandt JJ, Dellarco M, Van Hemmen JJ: From dermal exposure to internal dose. J Expo Sci Environ Epidem 2007;17:S38–S47.

Vinken M, Doktorova T, Ellinger-Ziegelbauer H, Ahr H-J, Lock E, Carmichael P, Roggen E, van Delft J, Kleinjans J, Castell J, Bort R, Donato T, Ryan M, Corvi R, Keun H, Sansone S-A, Rocca-Serra P, Stierum R, Jennings P, Pfaller W, Gmuender H, Vanhaecke T, Rogiers V: Critical selection of model compounds for the development of omics-based in vitro carcinogenicity screening assays. Mutat Res Rev, submitted February 2008.

Vogelgesang J: The EC White Paper on a strategy for a future chemicals policy. Altern Lab Anim 2002;30(suppl 2):211–212.

Worth AP, Balls M (eds): Alternative (non-animal) methods for chemicals testing: current status and future prospects. A report prepared by ECVAM and the ECVAM Working Group on Chemicals. Altern Lab Anim 2002;30(suppl 1):1–125.

Appendices

A

Rogiers V, Pauwels M (eds): Safety Assessment of Cosmetics in Europe.
Curr Probl Dermatol. Basel, Karger, 2008, vol 36, pp 183–187

Appendix 1: The Transposition of Directive 76/768/EEC into Belgian Law: A Practical Example

Transposing a European directive into national legislation is a complex process. Although the transpositions are mandatory and bound to clear deadlines, every national Competent Authority has a specific administrative path to follow and needs to take into consideration all related existing pieces of national legislation.

As this book was written in Belgium, the transposition of the Cosmetic Products Directive into Belgian legislation is taken as a practical example. The starting point is the Royal Decree No. 98-100 on cosmetics, published in October 1997 and taking up the provisions of Dir. 76/768/EEC and the 6 amendments and 21 adaptations to technical progress[1] existing at that time. The incorporation of the subsequently issued European rules related to cosmetics is summarized in the table on page187. A comparison of the European transposition deadlines with the dates of the corresponding Royal Decrees shows that the majority of deadlines were met. In some cases, however, the Belgian Competent Authorities expressed practical difficulties in implementing the imposed measures, whereas, on other occasions, the time span given was too short to run through the necessary administrative steps.

With regard to the respective contents of the Cosmetic Products Directive and the Royal Decree on cosmetics, some specific national provisions and a number of differences can be observed. The following are considered worth mentioning:

Specific National Provisions
1 Before a cosmetic product, either manufactured in Belgium or imported, can be placed on the Belgian market, it needs to be notified to the national Competent Authority. The specific notification requirements include:
– trade name of the cosmetic product,
– function of the cosmetic product,

---

1 79/661/EEC, 82/147/EEC, 82/368/EEC, 83/191/EEC, 83/341/EEC, 83/496/EEC, 83/574/EEC, 84/415/EEC, 85/391/EEC, 86/179/EEC, 86/199/EEC, 87/137/EEC, 88/233/EEC, 88/667/EEC, 89/174/EEC, 89/679/EEC, 90/121/EEC, 91/184/EEC, 92/8/EEC, 92/86/EEC, 93/35/EEC, 93/47/EEC, 94/32/EC, 95/34/EC, 96/41/EC, 97/1/EC, 97/45/EC.

- name and full address of responsible for placing on the market,
- function of the responsible for placing on the market (manufacturer/importer/supplier),
- address of the premises where the commercial activity takes place,
- address of archiving of product information (TIF),
- name(s) of the responsible person(s) for the safety assessment and quality control of the cosmetic product,
- proof of payment of notification fee.

2 Every cosmetic manufacturing site on Belgian territory is obliged to give yearly notice of its activities to the National Competent Authority, providing:
- name, full address and contact details of manufacturer (legal/natural person),
- address(es) of the promises where the manufacturing takes place,
- name(s) of the responsible person(s) for the safety assessment and quality control of the cosmetic product.

In addition, every manufacturer needs to keep the following readily available:
- trade names and functions of all the cosmetic products manufactured,
- address of archiving of product information (TIF).

3 It is specified in the Belgian cosmetic legislation that the product information (TIF) should be made up in Dutch, French, German or English.

4 Forty-eight hours before a cosmetic product is newly placed on the Belgian market, the national poison control centre needs to be notified. This can either be performed electronically (making use of so-called 'frame formulations') or through paper copies. In the latter case, the full qualitative and quantitative composition needs to be provided[2].

Differences between the Belgian Legislation and the European Directive

1 The Royal Decree requires manufacturing to be in accordance with Good Manufacturing Practices. To that respect, reference to national and international (Council of Europe, Colipa) guidance documents is added to the transposed text of the directive.

2 The Belgian legislation mentions detailed qualification requirements, not only for the safety assessor of cosmetic products, but also for the person responsible for the quality control at the production level. The safety assessor needs to have obtained a university degree in e.g. (medical) sciences and needs at least 3 years of experience in the cosmetic field, unless he/she has followed an appropriate training course. The responsible for quality control at the production level needs to present a (non-) university degree in the field of cosmetology and/or at least 5 years of practical experience in the field.

---

2   More detail (in Dutch) through http://www.poisoncentre.be/article.php?id_article = 354 (consulted April 2008).

3 With regard to the existing data on undesirable effects on human health, the Belgian legislation specifies that a distinction needs to be made between side effects under normal use and side effects related to inappropriate use. This is not mentioned as such in the European legislation.

4 The European CMR provisions (see section 1.2.8.d) are not taken over in the Belgian Royal Decree. Nonetheless, Annex II to the Cosmetic Products Directive is systematically supplemented with all chemicals that have been newly taken up in Annex I to the Dangerous Substances Directive and that are classified CMR Category 1 or 2. Since the Belgian legislation automatically incorporates these changes into its own Annex II, the CMR provisions will find their practical application in Belgium too, irrespective of the fact whether the European text on CMRs is taken over or not.

5 The Belgian legislation states that the address where the product information can be found, not only needs to be clearly indicated on the label, but underlined in case more than one address is displayed. This is a generally accepted measure all over Europe, but it is not literally mentioned in the articles of the Cosmetic Products Directive.

As Belgium is only one of the 27 Member States the EU currently counts, the transposition of a Directive into the different national legislations is a complex process.

Directive	Subject	Deadline for transposition	Belgian Royal Decree No.	Date of Royal Decree
98/16/EC (05/03/1998)	adaptation annex II	01/04/1998	98-3181	16/10/1998
98/62/EEC (03/09/1998)	adaptation annexes III, VI and VII	30/06/1999	2000-432	14/01/2000
2000/6/EC (29/02/2000)	adaptation annexes II, III, VI and VII	01/07/2000	2000-2071	08/06/2000
2000/11/EC (10/03/2000)	adaptation annex II	01/06/2000	2000-2071	08/06/2000
2002/34/EC (15/04/2002)	adaptation annexes II, III and VII	15/04/2003	2003-1463	20/02/2003
2003/1/EC (06/01/2003)	adaptation annex II	15/04/2003		
2003/15/EC (27/02/2003)	articles amended, adaptation annexes II and III, creation annexes VIIIa and IX	11/09/2004	2004-4701	22/12/2004
2003/16/EC (19/02/2003)	adaptation annex II	28/02/2003		
2003/80/EC (05/09/2003)	adaptation annex VIIIa	11/09/2004		
2003/83/EC (24/09/2003)	adaptation annexes II, III and VI	24/09/2004		
2004/88/EC (07/09/2004)	adaptation annex III	01/10/2004		
2004/94/EC (15/09/2004)	adaptation annex IX	21/09/2004		
2004/93/EC (21/09/2004)	adaptation annexes II and III	01/10/2004		
2005/9/EC (28/01/2005)	adaptation annex VII	28/07/2005	2005-1838	15/07/2005
2005/42/EC (20/06/2005)	adaptation annexes II and VI	31/12/2005	2006-119	22/12/2005
2005/52/EC (09/09/2005)	adaptation annex III	01/01/2006		
2005/80/EC (21/11/2005)	adaptation annexes II and III	22/05/2006	2006-2408	10/06/2006
2006/65/EC (19/07/2006)	adaptation annexes II and III	01/09/2006	2006-3750	15/09/2006
2006/78/EC (29/09/2006)	adaptation annex II	30/03/2007	2007-1261	08/02/2007
2007/1/EC (29/01/2007)	adaptation annex II	21/08/2007	2007-2974	07/06/2007
2007/17/EC (22/03/2007)	adaptation annexes III and VI	23/09/2007	2007-4174	28/09/2007
2007/22/EC (17/04/2007)	adaptation annexes IV and VI	18/01/2008		
2007/53/EC (29/08/2007)	adaptation annex III	19/04/2008	2008-1036	12/03/2008
2007/54/EC (29/08/2007)	adaptation annexes II and III	18/03/2008		
2007/67/EC (22/11/2007)	adaptation annex III	31/12/2007	2007-4872	11/12/2007

European Directives available through: http://europa.eu.int/eur-lex/lex/RECH_naturel.do (consulted April 2008). Belgian legislation (in Dutch) available through: http://www.ejustice.just.fgov.be/doc/rech_n.htm (consulted April 2008).

A

Rogiers V, Pauwels M (eds): Safety Assessment of Cosmetics in Europe.
Curr Probl Dermatol. Basel, Karger, 2008, vol 36, pp 188–190

Appendix 2

A. List of studied SCC(NF)P opinions

SCCNFP opinions (n = 109)			SCCP opinions (n = 76)	
SCCNFP/0232/99	SCCNFP/0658/03	SCCNFP/0762/03	SCCP/0852/04	SCCP/0952/05
SCCNFP/0229/99	SCCNFP/0660/03	SCCNFP/0798/04	SCCP/0843/04	SCCP/0947/05
SCCNFP/0234/99	SCCNFP/0665/03	SCCNFP/0783/04	SCCP/0881/05	SCCP/0948/05
SCCNFP/0235/99	SCCNFP/0661/03	SCCNFP/0781/04	SCCP/0883/05	SCCP/0964/05
SCCNFP/0231/99	SCCNFP/0668/03	SCCNFP/0784/04	SCCP/0932/05	SCCP/0984/06
SCCNFP/0215/99	SCCNFP/0663/03	SCCNFP/0785/04	SCCP/0849/04	SCCP/0988/06
SCCNFP/0295/00	SCCNFP/0648/03	SCCNFP/0786/04	SCCP/0873/05	SCCP/0986/06
SCCNFP/0241/99	SCCNFP/0625/02	SCCNFP/0787/04	SCCP/0837/04	SCCP/0935/05
SCCNFP/0340/00	SCCNFP/0710/03	SCCNFP/0788/04	SCCP/0863/05	SCCP/0965/05
SCCNFP/0403/00	SCCNFP/0689/03	SCCNFP/0790/04	SCCP/0851/04	SCCP/0983/06
SCCNFP/0373/00	SCCNFP/0678/03	SCCNFP/0791/04	SCCP/0891/05	SCCP/0990/06
SCCNFP/0372/00	SCCNFP/0677/03	SCCNFP/0792/04	SCCP/0918/05	SCCP/1025/06
SCCNFP/0005/98	SCCNFP/0682/03	SCCNFP/0803/04	SCCP/0666/03	SCCP/1013/06
SCCNFP/0130/99	SCCNFP/0688/03	SCCNFP/0793/04	SCCP/0683/03	SCCP/1008/06
SCCNFP/0385/00	SCCNFP/0681/03	SCCNFP/0806/04	SCCP/0876/05	SCCP/0996/06
SCCNFP/0494/01	SCCNFP/0676/03	SCCNFP/0805/04	SCCP/0875/05	SCCP/0989/06
SCCNFP/0129/99	SCCNFP/0680/03	SCCNFP/0821/04	SCCP/0867/05	SCCP/1001/06
SCCNFP/0503/01	SCCNFP/0675/03	SCCNFP/0789/04	SCCP/0902/05	SCCP/1002/06
SCCNFP/0539/01	SCCNFP/0679/03	SCCNFP/0782/04	SCCP/0879/05	SCCP/0981/06
SCCNFP/0561/02	SCCNFP/0694/03	SCCNFP/0822/04	SCCP/0878/05	SCCP/1040/06
SCCNFP/0504/01	SCCNFP/0670/03	SCCNFP/0817/04	SCCP/0898/05	SCCP/1017/06
SCCNFP/0514/01	SCCNFP/0649/03	SCCNFP/0795/04	SCCP/0908/05	SCCP/1042/06
SCCNFP/0525/01	SCCNFP/0650/03	SCCNFP/0779/04	SCCP/0838/04	SCCP/1029/06
SCCNFP/0532/01	SCCNFP/0671/03	SCCNFP/0794/04	SCCP/0847/04	SCCP/1068/06
SCCNFP/0486/01	SCCNFP/0695/03	SCCNFP/0832/04	SCCP/0868/05	SCCP/1015/06
SCCNFP/0411/00	SCCNFP/0732/03	SCCNFP/0833/04	SCCP/0871/05	SCCP/1056/06
SCCNFP/0585/02	SCCNFP/0697/03	SCCNFP/0826/04	SCCP/0872/05	SCCP/1069/06
SCCNFP/0522/01	SCCNFP/0733/03	SCCNFP/0811/04	SCCP/0869/05	SCCP/1044/06
SCCNFP/0600/02	SCCNFP/0736/03	SCCNFP/0814/04	SCCP/0893/05	SCCP/1043/06
SCCNFP/0601/02	SCCNFP/0735/03		SCCP/0917/05	SCCP/1036/06
SCCNFP/0610/02	SCCNFP/0730/03		SCCP/0985/06	SCCP/1035/06
SCCNFP/0505/01	SCCNFP/0740/03		SCCP/0923/06	SCCP/1051/06
SCCNFP/0583/02	SCCNFP/0734/03		SCCP/0943/05	SCCP/1034/06
SCCNFP/0609/02	SCCNFP/0756/03		SCCP/0924/05	SCCP/1033/06
SCCNFP/0587/02	SCCNFP/0667/03		SCCP/0963/05	SCCP/0978/06
SCCNFP/0604/02	SCCNFP/0672/03		SCCP/0957/05	SCCP/0991/06
SCCNFP/0657/03	SCCNFP/0767/03		SCCP/0962/05	

A. List of studied SCC(NF)P opinions (continued)

SCCNFP opinions (n = 109)		SCCP opinions (n=76)
SCCNFP/0659/03	SCCNFP/0761/03	SCCP/0979/06
SCCNFP/0643/03	SCCNFP/0760/03	SCCP/0958/05
SCCNFP/0669/03	SCCNFP/0743/03	SCCP/0951/05

B. Opinions in which more than one compound is discussed

SCCNFP/SCCP report code	Compounds discussed (INCI names)
SCCNFP/0295/00	Calcium Hydroxide Lithium Hydroxide
SCCNFP/0486/01	Benzoyl Peroxide Hydroquinone Methylether Hydroquinone
SCCNFP/0532/01 and SCCP/0891/05	Benzoic Acid Sodium Benzoate
SCCNFP/0663/03	Ethoxyethanol Ethoxyethanol Acetate Methoxyethanol Methoxyethyl Acetate
SCCNFP/0670/03	Methylchloroisothiazolinone Methylisothiazolinone
SCCNFP/0817/04	Musk Xylene Musk Ketone
SCCP/0847/04	Atranol Chloroatranol
SCCP/0849/04	Methylchloroisothiazolinone Methylisothiazolinone
SCCP/0869/05	*Tagetes Erecta* Flower Extract and Oil *Tagetes Minuta* Flower Extract and Oil *Tagetes Patula* Flower Extract and Oil
SCCP/0873/05 and SCCP/1017/06	Methylparaben Ethylparaben Propylparaben Butylparaben Isopropylparaben Isobutylparaben
SCCP/0917/05	Steartrimonium Chloride Cetrimonium Chloride Behentrimonium Chloride

C. List of ingredients discussed in multiple opinions

Compound discussed (INCI name)	SCCNFP/SCCP report codes
p-Phenylenediamine	SCCNFP/0129/99, SCCP/0989/06
2,6-Dihydroxy-3,4-dimethylpyridine	SCCNFP/0229/99, SCCP/1034/06
m-Aminophenol	SCCNFP/0231/99, SCCP/0978/06
Hydroxypropyl bis(N-hydroxyethyl-p-phenylenediamine) HCl	SCCNFP/0340/00, SCCP/1051/06
Acetyl Hexamethyl Tetralin	SCCNFP/0372/00, SCCNFP/0609/02
Lawsone	SCCNFP/0385/00, SCCNFP/0561/02, SCCNFP/0583/02, SCCNFP/0798/04
Hexahydrohexamethyl Cyclopentabenzopyran	SCCNFP/0403/00, SCCNFP/0610/02
Diethyl Phthalate	SCCNFP/0411/01, SCCNFP/0767/03
Lawsonia Inermis Extract	SCCNFP/0505/01, SCCP/0943/05
Benzoic Acid	SCCNFP/0532/01, SCCP/0891/05
Sodium Benzoate	SCCNFP/0532/01, SCCP/0891/05
Benzethonium Chloride	SCCNFP/0539/01, SCCNFP/0762/03
Methyldibromoglutaronitrile	SCCNFP/0585/02, SCCNFP/0806/04, SCCP/0863/05, SCCP/1013/06
Triclosan	SCCNFP/0600/02, SCCP/1040/06
Methylisothiazolinone/Methylchloroisothiazolinone	SCCNFP/0625/02, SCCNFP/0670/03, SCCNFP/0805/04, SCCP/0849/04
Zinc Oxide	SCCNFP/0649/03, SCCP/0932/05
Dimethylamino Hydroxybenzoyl Hexyl Benzoate	SCCNFP/0650/03, SCCNFP/0756/03, SCCP/0996/06
Dihydroxyindole	SCCNFP/0657/03, SCCP/0952/05
6-Hydroxyindole	SCCNFP/0667/03, SCCP/0947/05
Hydroxyisohexyl 3-Cyclohexene Carboxaldehyde	SCCNFP/0743/03, SCCP/0838/04
4-Methylbenzylidene Camphor	SCCNFP/0779/04, SCCP/1042/06
Acid Blue 62/CI 62045	SCCNFP/0782/04, SCCP/0878/05
Methyl-, Ethyl-, Propyl-, Butyl-, Isopropyl, Isobutylparaben	SCCP/0873/05, SCCP/1017/06

Rogiers V, Pauwels M (eds): Safety Assessment of Cosmetics in Europe.
Curr Probl Dermatol. Basel, Karger, 2008, vol 36, pp 191–207

Appendix 3: Proposed Framework for a Cosmetic Technical Information File

Administrative Dossier

1.   Trade name of the product and responsible company

Trade name:
Responsible company: Name:
                       Address:

Reference number/code:

2.   Product category (according to Dir. 93/35/EEC)

3.   Integral composition of the product

Internal code	Supplier	Trade name	INCI name	Function	Concentration (% w/w)
1.					
2.					
3.					
4.					
5.					
6.					
7.					
8.					
9.					
…					

4. Persons with ultimate responsibility

Product responsible:
Name:
Post held:
Qualifications:
Address:
Telephone: Fax:
E-Mail:

File coordinator:
Name:
Post held:
Qualifications:
Address:
Telephone: Fax:
E-Mail:

Manufacturing of the product:
Name:
Post held:
Qualifications:
Address:
Telephone: Fax:
E-Mail:

Packaging of the product:
Name:
Post held:
Qualifications:
Address:
Telephone: Fax:
E-Mail:

Safety assessor:
Name:
Post held:
Qualifications:
Address:
Telephone: Fax:
E-Mail:
CV in addendum

Ingredients Dossier

1. Identit(y)(ies), supplier(s) and composition(s) of the ingredient

Trade name	Supplier	Internal code	Components		Concentration % (w/w)
1.	A.	…	I.	INCI name: Chemical name: Other names[1]: CAS No.: Origin[2]: Function:	
			II.	INCI name: Chemical name: Other names[1]: CAS No.: Origin[2]: Function:	
			III.	INCI name: Chemical name: Other names[1]: CAS No.: Origin[2]: Function:	
			…		
2.	B.	…	I.	INCI name: Chemical name: Other names[1]: CAS No.: Origin[2]: Function:	
			II.	INCI name: Chemical name: Other names[1]: CAS No.: Origin[2]: Function:	
			III.	INCI name: Chemical name: Other names[1]: CAS No.: Origin[2]: Function:	
			…		
…	…	…	…		

[1]If relevant: Pharmacopeia, linnean name, CI number, …
[2]For example plant, animal, synthetic, fermentation product, …

2. Details on manufacturer and supplier of the ingredient

Trade name	Internal code	Supplier	Manufacturer
1.		Name: Address: Contact:	Name: Address:
2.		Name: Address: Contact:	Name: Address:
…		…	…

3. Physicochemistry and microbiology

3.1. Physicochemical properties

General: Physical state (solid/liquid/gas):
Colour:
Odour:
Solubility (in …, at …°C):
Log P_{ow} (at …°C):
Flash point:
…

Liquids: Boiling point:
Density (at …°C):
pH (at …°C):
Viscosity (at …°C):
Vapour pressure (at …°C):
…

Solids: General appearance (crystal form, amorphous, …):
Melting point:
pH (% in …, at …°C):
…

Gases: Density (at …°C):
Ignition point:
…

3.2. Physicochemical inspections

Parameter	Method	Frequency of inspection	Expected result (or range)	Archiving No./code
1.				
2.				
3.				
…				

Storage of samples of the different batches: …

3.3. Microbiological inspections

Parameter	Method	Frequency of inspection	Expected result (or range)	Archiving No./code
1.				
2.				
3.				
…				

Storage of samples of the different batches: …

4. Toxicity data

4.1. Acute oral toxicity
LD_{50}-oral-rat =   mg/kg
Other acute oral toxicity data:
Reference(s):

4.2. Acute dermal toxicity
LD_{50}-dermal-rat =   mg/kg
Other acute dermal toxicity data:
Reference(s):

4.3. Acute inhalation toxicity
LC_{50}-inhalation-rat =   mg/l/xh
Other acute inhalation toxicity data:
Reference(s):

4.4.   Skin irritation
non-irritating/irritating/causes burns/causes severe burns

A. In vivo test(s)
Method:
Date of test:
Performing laboratory:
Species:
Dose:
Number of animals/subjects:
Time of exposure:
Occlusive/semi-occlusive:
Relevant scores:
Conclusion:
Reference(s):

B. In vitro test(s)
Method:
Date of test:
Performing laboratory:
Short description:
Results:
Conclusion:
Reference(s):

4.5.   Eye irritation
non-irritating/irritating/danger of serious eye damage

A. In vivo test(s)
Method:
Date of test:
Performing laboratory:
Species:
Number of animals/subjects:
Dose:
Time of exposure:
Relevant scores:
Conclusion:
Reference(s):

B. In vitro test(s)
Method:
Date of test:
Performing laboratory:
Short description:
Results:
Conclusion:
Reference(s):

4.6.   Skin sensitisation
non-sensitising/sensitising

A. In vivo test(s)
Method:
Date of test:
Performing laboratory:
Species:
Number of animals/subjects:
Doses:
Relevant scores:
Conclusion:
Reference(s):

B. In vitro test(s)
Method:
Date of test:
Performing laboratory:
Short description:
Results:
Conclusion:
Reference(s):

4.7.   Long-term toxicity data
Type of test:
Date of test:
Performing laboratory:
Short description:
Result(s):
Reference(s):

4.8.   Additional relevant toxicological data
Type of test:
Date of test:
Performing laboratory:
Short description:
Result(s):
Reference(s):

4.9.   Available ecotoxicological data
Type of test:
Date of test:
Performing laboratory:
Short description:
Result(s):
Reference(s):

5.   First aid measures

After ingestion:
After skin contact:
After eye contact:
After inhalation:
Reference(s):

6.   Risk and safety instructions

*6.1.   EU labelling according to Dir. 67/548/EEC and amendments (Dangerous
        Substances)*
A. EU-labelling of the raw material
B. Symbols and R-phrases
C. S-phrases

*6.2.   Specific labelling and/or restrictions according to Dir. 76/768/EEC and amendments
        (Cosmetic Products) or national legislation(s)*
A. Preconditions for use
B. Warnings
C. . . .

Finished Product Dossier

1. Fabrication of the product

1.1. Place(s) of manufacturing
Name:
Address:
Telephone: Fax:

1.2. Manufacturing method

1.3. Person responsible for manufacture
Name:
Post held:
Qualifications:
Address:
Telephone: Fax:
E-Mail:

2. Stability of the product

2.1. Physical stability

2.2. Microbiological stability

3. Physicochemical properties and microbiological data on the product

3.1. Physicochemical properties

Parameter	Method	Frequency of inspection	Expected result (or range)	Archiving No./code
1.				
2.				
3.				
...				

Storage of samples of the different batches: …

3.2. Microbiological examinations

Parameter	Method	Frequency of inspection	Expected result (or range)	Archiving No./code
1.				
2.				
3.				
…				

Storage of samples of the different batches: …

4. Safety data concerning the finished product

4.1. Overview of the toxicological data of the ingredients

INCI name	Concentration (w/w)	Function(s)	Toxicological data
Ingredient 1			
Ingredient 2			
Ingredient 3			
…			

4.2. Communication of the necessary data to the National competent authorities and/or poison control centres (according to National legislations)

Member State	Official Instance	Transmission date	Reception date
1.	A.		
	B.		
	…		
2.	A.		
	B.		
	…		
…	…		

4.3. Toxicological animal testing performed on the finished product

Test 1	Type of test	
	Date of test	
	Performing laboratory	
	Contact address	
	Results	
	Reference(s)	
Test 2	Type of test	
	Date of test	
	Performing laboratory	
	Contact address	
	Results	
	Reference(s)	
…	…	

4.4. Toxicological tests using alternative methods

Test 1	Type of test	
	Date of test	
	Performing laboratory	
	Contact address	
	Results	
	Reference(s)	
Test 2	Type of test	
	Date of test	
	Performing laboratory	
	Contact address	
	Results	
	Reference(s)	
…	…	

A

4.5.   Human tests performed on the finished product (patch tests, in-use tests, …)

4.6.   Undesirable effects on human health reported during use of the product
A. Short description of the complaint system in place

B. Reported undesirable effects on human health

Date	Complaints (normal use)	Follow-up
	1.	
	2.	
	3.	
	…	
Date	Complaints (improper use)	Follow-up
	1.	
	2.	
	3.	
	…	

4.7.   Safety assessor
Name:
Post held:
Qualifications:
Address:
Telephone: Fax:
E-Mail:

The safety assessor writes a detailed report, taking into account all the relevant data concerning the ingredients (chemical, physicochemical and toxicological properties in Ingredients Dossier), the data or argumentation concerning the finished product (Finished Product Dossier, section 4.1–4.6), the envisaged exposure of the user to the product and the preconditions for use and warnings which must mandatorily be transferred to the labelling.

Different types of conclusions are possible, such as:

1) The safety assessor can estimate that, given the present level of knowledge, the product does not show any foreseeable risk to human health under conditions of normal use.

2) The safety assessor can define certain conditions and/or restrictions before granting his/her final consent (e.g. modification of labelling, modification of conditions of use, restrictions on certain concentration levels, …).

3) The safety assessor can conclude that the use of the product could lead to incontestable negative consequences for the user (based on ingredient/finished product data, reports of side effects, …). Therefore the safety of the product cannot be ensured.

--   --

Signature   Date

5. Efficiency of the finished product

5.1. Claims made

Claim 1:

Claim 2:

…

5.2. Executed efficacy tests

Tests performed to substantiate claim 1:

Test 1	Type of test	
	Results	
	Reference(s)	
Test 2	Type of test	
	Results	
	Reference(s)	
…	…	

Tests performed to substantiate claim 2:

Test 1	Type of test	
	Results	
	Reference(s)	
Test 2	Type of test	
	Results	
	Reference(s)	
...	...	

...

5.3.   Additional information or argumentation

6.   Packaging and labelling

6.1.   Overview of data on ingredients concerning packaging and labelling

6.2.   Labelling of the finished product
A. Mandatory obligations
B. Additional labelling

6.3.   Packaging materials and weight/volume

6.4.   Packaging procedure

6.5.   Identification of the batch number

6.6.   Check on the end product
A. Weight check

Archiving No.	Aspect	Weighing	Frequency
1)			
2)			
3)			
...			

B. Other checks

6.7. Person responsible for packaging
Name:
Post held:
Qualifications:
Address:
Telephone:
E-Mail:

A

Rogiers V, Pauwels M (eds): Safety Assessment of Cosmetics in Europe.
Curr Probl Dermatol. Basel, Karger, 2008, vol 36, pp 208–209

Appendix 4: Data Input Forms: General Information

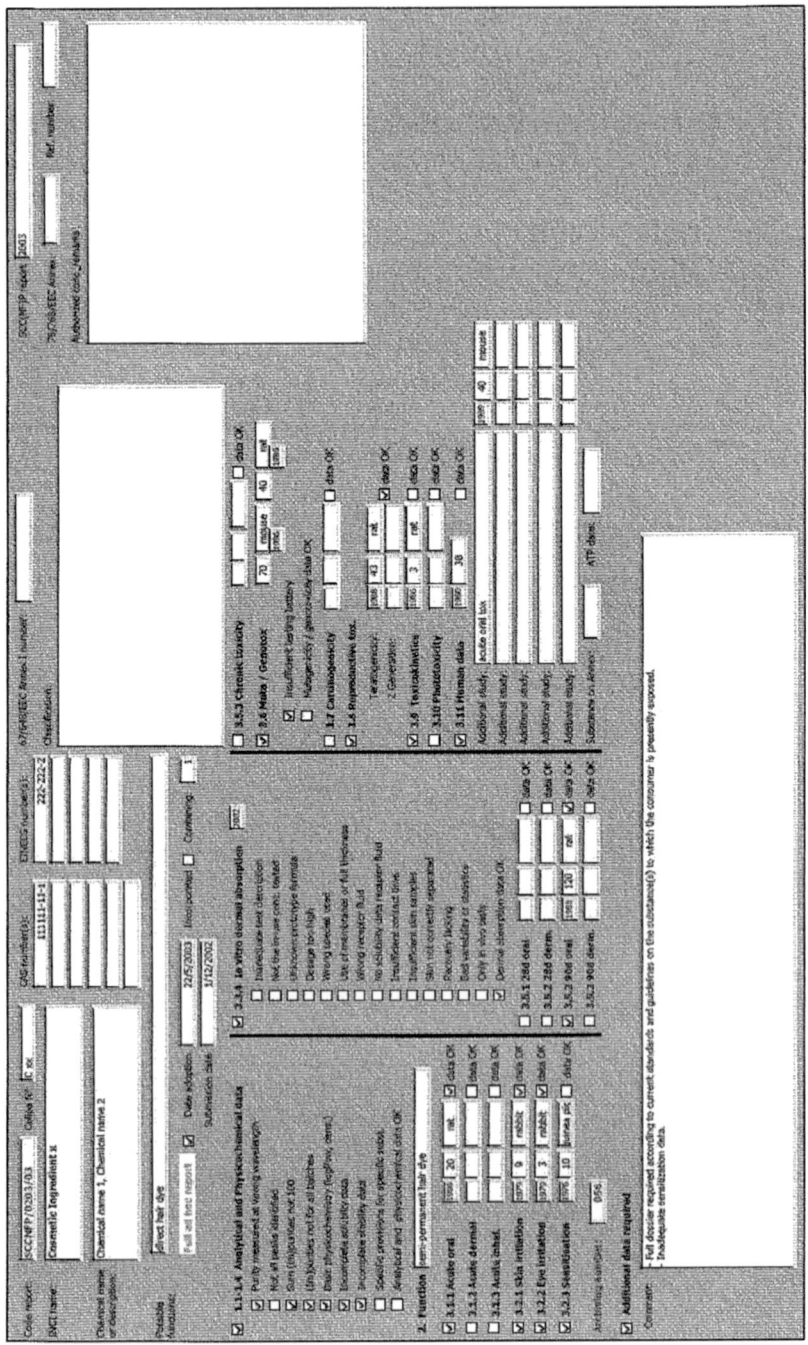

Code report: SCCNFP/0203/03 **Cosp.N°** C xx **EINECS number(s):** 222-222-2 **CAS number(s):** 11111-11-1 **Archiving number:** 056 **2. function:** semi-permanent hair dye

INCI name: Cosmetic Ingredient x

Chemical name or description: Chemical name 1, Chemical name 2

Possible functions: direct hair dye

☐ 3.5.3 Chronic toxicity
☐ 3.7 Carcinogenicity

Additional study: acute oral tox ☐ Data OK
Additional study ☐ Data OK
Additional study
Additional study

☑ Full ad hoc report ☑ Data dossier 22/5/2003 Incorporated ☐ Condensing: 1

☑ Insufficient testing policy ☐ Mutagenicity / genotoxicity data OK

☑ 3.6 Muta / Genotox

IN VITRO TESTS

☑ OECD 471/480, EC B13/21/15: (Reverse) mutation test in bacteria (incl. Ames test)
  1 test(s) mentioned, latest date: 1985 Overall result: negative ☑ Data OK

☑ OECD 476, EC B17: In vitro mammalian cell gene mutation test
  1 test(s) mentioned, latest date: 1991 Overall result: equivocal ☐ Data OK

☑ OECD 473, EC B10: In vitro mammalian chromosome aberration test
  1 test(s) mentioned, latest date: 2001 Overall result: negative ☑ Data OK

☑ OECD 487: In vitro micronucleus test
  test(s) mentioned, latest date: Overall result: ☐ Data OK

☑ OECD 482, EC B18: In vitro Unscheduled DNA Synthesis (UDS)
  1 test(s) mentioned, latest date: 1986 Overall result: negative ☐ Data OK

☐ OECD 479, EC B19: In vitro Sister Chromatid Exchange (SCE) assay
  test(s) mentioned, latest date: Overall result: ☐ Data OK

☐ OECD 481, EC B16: Mitotic recombination assay in Saccharomyces cerevisiae
  test(s) mentioned, latest date: Overall result: ☐ Data OK

☐ EC B11: In vitro mammalian cell transformation assay
  test(s) mentioned, latest date: Overall result: ☐ Data OK

IN VIVO TESTS

☑ OECD 474, EC B12: In vivo mammalian erythrocyte micronucleus test
  1 test(s) mentioned, latest date: 1986 Overall result: negative ☑ Data OK

☐ OECD 475, EC B11: In vivo mammalian bone marrow chromosome aberration test
  test(s) mentioned, latest date: Overall result: ☐ Data OK

☑ OECD 486, EC B39: In vivo Unscheduled DNA Synthesis (UDS) with mammalian cells
  1 test(s) mentioned, latest date: 1986 Overall result: equivocal ☐ Data OK

☐ OECD 478, EC B22: In vivo rodent dominant lethal test
  test(s) mentioned, latest date: Overall result: ☐ Data OK

☐ OECD 477, EC B20: In vivo Drosophila Melanogaster assay
  test(s) mentioned, latest date: Overall result: ☐ Data OK

☐ Photomutra/photogenotox

70 mouse 40 rat 1986 sets

☑ **Additional data required**
- Full dossier required according to current standards and guidelines on the substance(s) to which the consumer is presently exposed.
- Inadequate sensitization data.

A

Subject Index